BARRY CROCKER

BARRY CROCKER
Last of the Entertainers

NEW
HOLLAND

In Memory of Doreen (Dene) Crocker
24 January 1936 to 31 January 2023

With Barry Humphries, Bruce Beresford, Phillip Adams and Ron Brown at the premiere of *The Adventures of Barry McKenzie*, Melbourne, 1972.

Contents

Foreword   9

Introduction   10

Chapter 1   The Boy and His Box Brownie   13

Chapter 2   The Sinatra Chronicles   38

Chapter 3   Return of the Don and the Sizzling '70s   52

Chapter 4   King of Moomba   56

Chapter 5   The World's a Stage – Telethons and Carols   69

Chapter 6   From Banjo to Katy   78

Chapter 7   Feet Back on the Ground   104

Chapter 8   Rediscovering Banjo   126

Chapter 9   Family Affairs   135

Chapter 10   Eureka   151

Chapter 11   Fiddler on the Roof   171

Chapter 12   The Bazza Legend Rolls On   186

Epilogue   217

Foreword

You might recall a Monty Python song wherein a chorus of Australians, all called Bruce, sing about other Bruces, thus creating the impression to ignorant pommy bastards that Bruce is the preferred or perhaps compulsory pre-nom for all antipodean males. This shows a lack of thorough research, as far and away our most popular male name is, of course, Barry.

Or Bazza, if you're on consenting adult terms.

Don't stop with the three greatest living Barrys – Crocker, Humphries and McKenzie – even if they do constitute our Holy Trinity of Bazzas. Think back in history and recall Captain Barry Cook discovering the place, or Sir Barry Menzies being our most legendary prime minister, at least until Barry Whitlam, whose ascendency to power was helped by Barry Crocker's notable showbiz mates like Barry Limb, Barry Hannan and Little Barrie in singing the 'It's Time' song.

Barry Bradman remains our greatest batsman, and Barry Jones our all-time quiz champion, while Dame Barry Melba remains unchallenged as our greatest soprano.

Barry Crocker is, as you know, Melba's great-grandson, inheriting her transcendental tonsils and prominent chin. I've known him for 50 years, since he was knee-high to a Jurassic grasshopper. Born six-feet tall in the old money, Barry immediately shot up until he could be seen clearly only on cloudless days.

Barry Humphries believes that Barry Crocker was born only for one purpose. To play Barry McKenzie. His mother was visited in the manger by Three Wise Men bearing a strong similarity to Humphries, Beresford and myself who told her of her unborn babe's destiny. And lo it came to pass in the Year of our Lord 1971 that the Holy Trinity of Barrys went forth unto London and made one of the most sensitive, beautiful nature documentaries since David Attenborough's tender account of the sex life of the Northern Territory termite.

Phillip Adams
October 2011

Introduction

In the late 1950s, a Peter Sellers LP called *Songs for Swinging Sellers* was released in which Peter, as the posh lady interviewer, asks a young rock'n'roll star, apparently based on Tommy Steele and also voiced by Sellers, what his main ambition in show business is.

The young star, after some coaxing from his manipulative manager, finally answers in a firm cockney accent, 'I wanna be an all-round entertainer.' The appropriately named Twit Conway goes on to express an interest in playing old Vic in the Shakespeare Company as well.

Everyone has an interpretation of what the 'all-round entertainer' should be. The term once invoked the image of a singer who could dance a little, tell jokes and hold an audience's attention with anecdotes of his life and career.

In my world, in order to wear this label successfully, the description of the 'all-round entertainer' expands, with the ability to perform not only as an actor in films, television, and on stage, but also to direct, write books and plays, and even pen his own autobiography.

The definition of the 'all-round entertainer' is a generational conundrum. When I became a showbiz professional in 1956, I found myself part of the end of

the age of vaudeville, being lucky enough to learn from those who had been there and done that, and now I am wearing the shoes of those who paved the way for me.

Sadly, most of those contemporaries who shared the same journey have either shuffled off the mortal coil or are in retirement. Now, with the departure of Ernie Sigley, Jimmy Hannan, Graham Kennedy, Stuart Wagstaff, Don Lane, and Bert Newton I find myself left alone now to carry the torch, hence the title of this book.

I feel it is up to me to represent Australia's last-person-standing of a golden era. I firmly believe that this country now turns out some of the best talent in the world, be it in acting, singing, writing, directing, as well as in the more technical fields. I am blessed to have been able to share the ups and downs of my life, and to help in some small way many of those who are still on the road to establishing their own brilliant careers.

Apart from the personal triumphs encountered in the entertainment business, there are of course many pitfalls, disappointments, deceptions, and misconceptions. Although not intentional, some people have been hurt by my sometimes selfish ambition, love, lust and the desire for success. As I grow older, I would hope to heal those wounds.

Through this book, with its words and many photographs, I pass on the story of a wonderful and rewarding more than 60 years of parading my wares around the globe. It hasn't all been smooth sailing, but I'm glad to have been on the voyage.

Barry Hugh Crocker AM, May 2023

EARLY "BOX BROWNIE" PHOTOS

BAZ AND DARCY

BOYS FROM THE BUSH

BAZ, TEDDY WILLIAMS
ALAN PEEL, BOBBY FLEMMING
& ERNIE BOURNE.

PICNIC 1954

MUM AND LOSS

My grandparents' house in Little Ryrie Street, Geelong, where I would discover the box brownie and my passion for photography.

CHAPTER 1

The Boy and His Box Brownie

Boy with a Camera

When I was about 10 years old, I lived with my mum and dad and sister Laurel in Chilwell, an old suburb of Geelong in Victoria. One of my favourite pastimes was stickybeaking in cupboards, drawers or any old boxes I found lying around, either at our own house or in any relative's home we happened to be visiting. My explorations were innocent and pretty much tolerated, as most of our family owned little of any real value, and they knew I'd put everything back in its place. The grown-ups were probably glad to have me out of the lounge room, so adult conversations could be enjoyed without any disruption from this rather overactive, in-need-of-attention, little pain in the arse! In those simpler times, before the modern invasion of email, SMS text messages and Facebook, the casual dropping in of rellies and other visitors was a welcome joy. Face-to-face interaction was the order of the day. These days, to show up on a cousin's doorstep, without some electronic forewarning, is considered most unusual.

While all the mature family chat went on in the lounge room, I'd be scavenging around like a little rag-and-bone man, adding anything I could find to my eclectic repository of bits and pieces ... 'Do you still want this old mug, Uncle Howard?' 'Can I have this bit of wire?' As well as the nooks and crannies of people's homes, the local tip was an absolute treasure trove, and I'd spend countless happy hours discovering fabulous things. My mother would usually demand that I return these treasures to their original locations, but occasionally I struck gold.

On my visits to Grandpa Crocker's house, although I was at first reluctant to explore, I would gird my loins to give me the courage to enter the dark front bedroom. This room was normally off limits, but because my grandfather adored my grandmother, and my grandmother adored me, the old soldier feared her chastising, so he would grit his teeth and turn a blind eye to my meanderings. Like most family men of his generation, Joseph Ernest Crocker was still recovering from the effects of the Great Depression, but he was always meticulously turned out. He had served his King and Country in the South African War in 1901, and the soldier's discipline had stuck to him like the blood and filth of battle on his old khaki uniform. Grandpa Joe was a fastidious man who would smooth down curtains and re-flatten creased doilies. There was a place for everything, and everything had to be in its place, including my small self. The curtains were always drawn in that bedroom, and my eyes would need to become accustomed to the gloom before my search could proceed.

I'd usually make my way to the magnificent dark brown oak wardrobe, a symbol of Grandpa's better days. He had once been a funeral director and restaurateur. When the huge wooden doors creaked open, I would discover, once again, the signs of the more opulent lifestyle that my father's family had enjoyed in an earlier generation. It was on one such day that gold was found. Grandpa's many suits were held by their polished wooden hangers, like troops lined up on the parade ground, waiting to be assigned a duty. On one special hanger in the corner, as if overseeing his other clothes, were the robes, hat and sashes of his Freemason outfit. Grandpa obviously held some rank with this then-prestigious organisation, but I never learned, or much cared about the Masons. My curiosity lay in the bottom of the cupboard. There, contained inside a large black leather case, surrounded by other goodies, were Grandpa's highly polished bowling balls. I'd wince at their weight and wonder what was the point of keeping them so shiny when they were only good for throwing around a lawn? After rolling them around the floor, I would replace them, rubbing them gently with my hankie to make sure no fingerprints remained. In other compartments were velvet-lined boxes containing rows of campaign ribbons and medals. I would study these at great length, admiring their workmanship, and imagine what bravery my grandfather must have displayed to have them in his possession. There were several hats and canes, all neatly lined up.

On each of my visits, I would go through more or less the same ritual, lifting out, inspecting, and replacing, but on this particular day I came across something I had never noticed before. On the left-hand side of the wardrobe floor, half hidden under some clothing, was a compact, leather-covered metal box. The black fabric had seen better days, but I noticed that this mystery object had a rectangular magnifying glass on top, and when I looked into it, I could see tiny, miniaturised images of the objects in the room. I had seen cameras before, but never one like this. I had stumbled upon what was to become an obsession that would be with me for the rest of my days! I had met the new love of my life, the Kodak Brownie box camera.

During several more visits, my apprehension grew as I slowly built up the courage to confess my cheekiness at straying so deep into my grandfather's cupboard full of memories. In the end I blurted it out. I was sorry, but I had discovered the camera. Instead of the expected admonishment, he said, 'God, that old thing, it hasn't been used in ages!'

'Can I have it, Grandpa?' I pleaded.

'Of course he can have it,' Grandma declared. 'Joe, you haven't taken a picture in years.'

They allowed me to walk away with the much-treasured gift, but it would be some time before I could afford to run some 120-sized black-and-white film around the sprockets. Unlike today, when it seems as if every child from the age of five owns a full-colour digital phone camera, such basic photography was expensive. Times were tough in the 1940s, and film and print were luxuries, especially for small boys with limited financial means. I still have some of the black-and-white snaps I took all those years ago. What pleases me greatly is that, when digitally reproduced, the quality of the images shows that damn good camera lenses were made back then.

I am bitterly sorry that I never got to ask my grandfather about his medals and other parts of his life. Not long after I received the camera, as I was approaching my twelfth birthday, my grandmother Mary died of cancer at the age of 61, and Joseph Ernest Crocker, pining for his wife, followed her only six months later.

My memories of the man are represented by his own miniature Bible, a gift to me from my cousin Ruth. The Bible was originally given to Joseph by his mother to guide him on his travails in the Boer War. He and his dashing younger brother, Albert Hugh, served with the 5th Victorian Mounted Rifles, where they were forced to endure the infamous ambush at Wilmansrust, in which many of their mates were slaughtered.

Following that brutal experience, both of the brothers were slightly wounded and they were soon shipped back to Victoria. The little Bible must have worked for my grandfather, and it is interesting to see the various psalms he underlined, in order to strengthen his belief that he would survive the horrors of war.

Previously, in The Adventures of Barry Crocker ...

After 412 pages of my 2003 memoir *The Adventures of Barry Crocker: Bazza*, my publisher felt I should take a rest. After reaching page 403, I was only coming towards the end of the sizzling '70s. There was much more to tell, for I had managed to persist, fight and survive the next 30-something years. The need to bare my soul still needed to be recognised, to help clean the slate ... and besides, my radiologist had told me the X-rays showed that, yes, there was another book in there.

So here it is. This penny dreadful will be an amalgamation of my strengths and weaknesses, coupled with my absolute love of the camera that captures those moments when we are totally unaware and vulnerable, or maybe even downright dishonest. Every picture tells, sells, a story. If you didn't catch up with *The Adventures*, here is a synopsis of my first 40-odd years of life ... oh, and by the way, if you don't already own a copy of my first book, you can find it in every library in Australia, at all the best garage sales, not to mention most of the nation's op shops.

What Goes Around, Comes Around

I was born on 4 November 1935 in Victoria's Geelong Hospital, a healthy eight-pound-plus bundle of joy to my parents Hugh and Jean (nee Houston) Crocker.

My dad was a hard-working honest man, and he supported my dreams during both the good and the bad times, even when others were suggesting that I should get a proper job. He loved my mum, and I believe he never strayed in the marriage, but I also believe my mother took advantage of his dedication in order for her to dominate the household. Dad would rather run a mile than be involved in a marital stoush, so she ruled the roost. As a young man, I took exception to my father's quest for peace and quiet, so I would take on my mother at her own game. We played the parts of battling banshees, but she absolutely adored me, and I drove her to distraction by being and doing everything contrary to her desires. I supposed in my adolescent mind that I was getting even for Dad. Times were tough financially, not much to sing about really. We had come through the Great Depression, so the rubbing of two pennies together at the end of the week not only indicated we'd survived, but their metallic scratching might even be the only musical sounds heard in the house. In the weeks after the bills had been paid, the only rubbing together would be the calloused hands of my father, praying he could hang on to his job at the Ford Motor Company.

My mother with baby Laurel and me, Geelong, 1940.

Dad had started in the wet rub, and after 33 years of devoted service he graduated to become foreman of tractors. On retirement, he received a gold watch. Ford would later reward Hugh's only son for his father's loyalty, paying him a vast amount of money to promote one of their latest models in a huge advertising campaign.

We didn't realise how poor we were. My mother had been raised on a farm, and she could take the most meagre scrapings and present them each night as if they were a totally different feast! Thank God for the potatoes, peas and gravy that helped disguise the lamb roast, lamb fritters, lamb stew, and lamb bubble-and-squeak. And thank God we'd run out of lamb by the time custard was served on Sunday! Mum would make friends with the merchants, and I'd watch her charm her way to a bargain, or ask for that little extra bit that would be thrown away

My box brownie snap of Hugh, Jean and Laurel, leaning on our 1937 Dodge, with dog Bluey, at Barker Street, c. 1951.

anyway. In the early years before school, I would accompany her on these daily excursions, so I was well known to the shopkeepers, and I soon learned that the subtle art of flattery can work miracles. At the butcher shop, you could purchase a sheep's head for two shillings, as long as you were prepared to crack it open yourself to get to the good bits. Mum would press a two-bob piece into my hand with a message for the butcher. (Scene: Five-year-old boy approaches wizened old butcher, hands over coin, and says, 'Mum said, can she please have a sheep's head ... and could you leave the legs on?')

Although this is a joke, we'd quite often find a few little offcuts wrapped up in the butcher's paper. This sort of generosity is lost in today's hustle and bustle. Back then, it seems, people actually had time to ask, 'How are you?' And you'd have the time to tell them.

Although my contemporaries were suffering the same fate, that is, the 'in-constant-need-of-money syndrome', I knew I would have to find a way to elevate my status. I was keen to do any sort of job that could raise my financial means above those of my mates. Even at that tender age, I loved to hear the jingle of coins in my pocket. From the moment I started school, I took on extra activities to help build a nest egg. I'd run errands for neighbours, wash up the returned bottles at the chemist, cut up chips for the Greek fish shop owner, and eventually, at around eight years of age, I sold newspapers on the streets of Geelong. Before I gained my financial independence, Mum held the purse strings and the power. As a way of punishing me for some indiscretion, she would say, 'Sorry, no money for the flickers this weekend.' But once I had my own entrance money, I would find a way to escape my locked room, being prepared to wear the punishment later. The only thing that mattered in my life was the Saturday arvo double-feature, costing only sixpence for my ticket to another universe. Transfixed by the magic of the screen, like most of my theatrical peers in later years, I was unconsciously learning.

We identified with our on-screen heroes and dreamed of being transported from our humdrum, boring lives … no wonder that we were destined to become actors. I've already written about my near-drowning, the fisticuffs, my good, bad and disastrous sexual adventures of discovery, my professional cycling period, falling in and out of love, my experience with amateur theatre, my marriage, parenthood, national service training, the drinking, and the too-many-to-mention career shifts … and I had not yet reached the age of 20.

Doreen (nee Cresswell) and Barry Crocker met at the age of 16 at Geelong's eastern beach. When they were introduced he almost fell off his bike, addled by the attractiveness of this newly arrived ten-pound-pom. He became so besotted and temporarily blinded by her beauty that he would join something called the Geelong Musical Comedy Company merely to breathe the same air as she. Tagging along, not knowing what to expect, and having no conception of what this organisation might be, he would stumble unwittingly into the rest of his life …

Speaking Another Language

The idea of joining the local theatrical society had been as foreign to me as entering the Belmont ladies' croquet tournament. But Doreen inhabited these rehearsal rooms, and I was prepared to do anything to inhabit the same space. In the Geelong Musical Comedy Company (GMCC) I was surrounded by people with whom I never thought I would rub shoulders. I had been around the working classes all of my life, but these people were very different: doctors, lawyers, teachers, and folk of the educated kind compared to this kid who had left school at 14, they almost seemed to be speaking another language. My initial fear was that I had stepped out of my class, and therefore I had no right to be mingling in what I considered to be the upper reaches of society. But I learned something the day I auditioned to join the chorus line.

The auditions were for a Christmas show to be presented at the plaza theatre, now the Ford Centre, and several regular GMCC members were not available for the show. New blood was needed to prop up the chorus numbers, so that day I was not the only fledgling wet behind the ears. The piano player was a nice yet somewhat grumpy old lady, affectionally known as 'Birdie' Pidgeon. At my tryout I sang 'God Save the King', which was the only number that she and I both knew. I had always been self-assured about my singing voice. I had the best paperboy call in town, and they made me a first soprano when I sang for ice creams on the local radio station 3GL's *Happy Hammond's Peter's Pals Show*. Indisputably, I had the best Tarzan call in Chillwell. When I sang, the general hubbub in the audition room lowered, and furtive glances were exchanged between Birdie and some of the obvious regulars. 'Thank you Barry, well done. Welcome to the chorus of the GMCC.'

The moment I stepped onto the plaza stage on the opening night of the Christmas Special, I felt that I'd finally discovered my place in the universe. I am not the only one to have experienced this phenomenon, as most of my stage-struck friends describe having a similar metamorphosis when they first faced an appreciative audience. My theory is simply that you don't choose your career, it chooses you.

Not unexpectedly, my working-class mates believed that any boy who dressed up and sang, or recited poetry, had to be a bit of a sissy. Maybe it appeared a bit odd to my teenage associates when I succumbed to the arts. Some of them thought that maybe I'd 'turned'. To my great surprise, I soon discovered that no-one in my family had ever had anything to do with show business, so it must have come as a shock to my parents when I embraced my new-found interest with such a passion. I couldn't wait to get to rehearsals, held two or three times a week in a church hall, not only to hone my craft, but to try to win Doreen, the girl of my dreams, who wasn't at all enamoured with this still very raw recruit.

First Steps Towards a Professional Career

Yes, I would eventually have my day in the sun! With my pitiful begging and my irresistible humour, I slowly won Doreen over, and we fell madly in love. We also fell pregnant, and so we were married as teenagers, as was expected back then. In three years, I graduated from the GMCC chorus to leading roles, and I began to make a name for myself around town, even being paid for appearances at parties and functions.

Although I had learnt the ticket and sign-writing trade, I found myself bludging on the wharves. The joke then was 'eight quid a week and all you can carry'. After work one night at the wool sheds, I received a life-changing message when I was asked to audition for a professional travelling theatre group called Variety on Parade. The company was touring through town and needed a replacement act. With a friend of mine, sign-writer and guitarist Maurie Blick, we scraped together 15 minutes of

The wedding on 12 March 1955.

GMCC's production of *Katinka* – I'm in the centre and Doreen is third from right.

material and we presented ourselves at 7 pm at the Geelong West Town Hall. Our act leaned towards the merely okay, but a month later I was offered a contract to join the touring company.

At first, I thought the telegram was a cruel hoax perpetrated by my co-workers, who had often been the butt of my own lunch hour pranks, but it wasn't. I would be paid four pounds a week more than my job on the wharves, plus travelling expenses. I rushed home to my parents' house, where Doreen, baby Geraldine and I had been residing since my national service discharge. Naturally, I was elated that a professional company considered me good enough to join it, and I bounced around the room like a kid with two bottles of cordial in him. But then Dad sat Doreen and me down quietly on the bed in our room. In moments like these, he would be the one to bring tangibles and logic to a situation. My mother didn't enter the room for the discussion, as she felt the offer was too ludicrous even to think about.

There were a few factors to consider for a 20-year-old father with a young family. Although the Variety money was good, and I promised to bank it religiously each week, there would be other expenses not covered by the contract that would cut into the overall purse. How secure was my contract? Would I be sacked after the first show? Would I miss Doreen and the baby too much while I was away? I listened to all of these back-and-forth options with the glazed look of a kangaroo caught in the headlights. Doreen was reading me, and at the end of the dissections she asked me, 'If you were not married, Barry, would you take the job?' I nodded quietly in the affirmative. She knew I was hooked, and, wisely or unwisely, she set me free.

I would start my professional career at the Mechanics Institute Hall in Wodonga, on the border with New South Wales, on the morning of 10 February 1956. There was a world of difference between being an amateur and a pro. Following my arrival on the early morning train, I was already expected to pull my weight. On this, my first day, I was given a few hours to learn how to be the straight man for the comedian, which meant memorising the sketches, hosting the show, and doing my own 20-minute solo spot … and, oh, playing the drums for the juggler!

Too Tall for the Chorus Line

For an apprentice, there was no better training ground than working with these seasoned pros. I loved listening to their showbiz stories of the triumphs and the tribulations, of the winners and the losers, how they travelled the world, learning the tricks of the trade, how to make an audience love you, even when they don't. I soon learned that slackness, on stage and off, would not be tolerated. These on-the-road shows were peopled by those whose careers were on the way down, and those on the way up. I will forever be grateful for my own brief part in the closing stages of that ancient tradition called vaudeville.

By the end of 1956, I had travelled all over Victoria, playing in town halls, churches, civic centres and tin sheds. We performed five or six shows a week, depending on demand, or the distance we had to travel. The touring company asked me to stay on for another year, and although Doreen had met up with me on the road occasionally, thanks to my parents taking care of the baby, I felt it was time to move on. My work had improved immensely after entertaining a different audience each night for so long, and much to my pleasure and appreciation, I was being given top billing in the newspaper ads. I felt confident that I would be able to walk straight into J. C. Williamson's, Australia's largest theatre chain, and become a star in that company, much as I had with the GMCC.

I auditioned for Williamson's casting director, Terry Vaughn, at Her Majesty's Theatre, that most magnificent of venues. It was a blisteringly hot summer's day, but his words after my performance not only cooled the auditorium, they chilled my heart. 'No, sorry,' he said. 'Your best chance would be in cabaret.' He pointed out that my height was against me, as my lanky frame would take attention away from whoever was the star of the show. My perceived magnificent theatre career was shattered with one sentence, 'Sorry son, you'll have to be a star or nothing!'

Ironically, it would be almost 50 years before I got to tread the boards of Her Majesty's as one of the stars of the brilliant Australian musical play *Eureka* … 'Hey Terry, I'm back!'

Okay, if I was going to continue in my new career, it would have to be cabaret. I would go where the money was, and cabaret, with all its sleaze and corruption, would become my canvas. I ended up on the European-styled cappuccino circuit, appearing in dimly lit dives that sold not only sly grog, but sex and more sex.

I managed to survive these sordid adventures, but my showbiz angel began to steer me into better work at established venues, like the Chevron Hotel, which was the poshest cabaret room on St Kilda Road.

In the same year, the entertainment revolution called television arrived in Australia, and with incredible chutzpah I became one of the first on-screen band leaders at Melbourne's GTV Channel Nine. The instant fame and work offers were more than I could handle. But the more successful I became, the more miserable Doreen became. There would be a lot of separation, and many trips back and forth to Geelong for me to try to work things out.

Rock and roll burst onto the scene, pushing all other forms of music off the dance floors, and I made sure I was part of the new sensation. Business boomed! We moved into better accommodation, and, for the first time in our lives, we had brand-new furniture, a TV set, a radiogram and a near-new Wolseley 440. All paid for on the 'never-never', of course. Hire purchase was the way to go in the days before credit cards.

My fame spread to Queensland, where I opened the exciting new Southport Hotel. During my season, an acute case of peritonitis brought me close to death in the South Brisbane Hospital. Eight centimetres of gangrenous flesh were removed from my appendix, and, according to the operating surgeon, I should have karked it there and then!

After a month's convalescence, I was allowed to return to Melbourne on the proviso that I recuperate for a further month in my own bed. This was reasonable advice, but the rent was in arrears and aggressive people were demanding payments on the lavish lifestyle that I'd provided for my family. We were evicted from the

Judy Garland and the Kray twins.

Cast and crew of Channel 9's *Open House*. Comperes Jane Edwards (on piano), Jim Woody Wood (with moustache), Barbara Foulds (and teddy bear) and band members, 1957.

apartment and everything we thought we owned was repossessed, including the bed in which I was supposed to be recuperating. Although still weak, with a weeping wound that was yet to heal, I convinced Doreen I needed to return to Queensland to fetch the car.

I fibbed about my true condition to Mr Collier, the owner of the Southport Hotel, and he kindly offered me two weeks of work, including paid air fares, to help me get back on my feet. But my run of bad luck had some way to go. I was driving home at dusk from Queensland to Victoria, accompanied by my good friend, a talented guitarist by the name of William John Healey. I found myself lost on the New England Highway, not far from Tenterfield. The road was poorly lit, and the car skidded into some loose gravel on a curve, followed by the sound of shattering glass and screeching metal. We found ourselves spinning over and over. The crash culminated in the death of my young passenger, who had only been bumming a lift back to Melbourne. When I returned to consciousness at Stanthorpe Hospital, a solemn-looking policeman was standing at the foot of my bed. He informed me that, as I was the driver of a car involved in a fatal accident, I was facing charges. It looked like I was guilty until proven innocent. I spent the next week in a small jail cell at Stanthorpe prison, until my father showed up with some bail money, borrowed of course, from my grandmother, to finance my release. This enormous tragedy had a serious impact on my life.

Crocker and Clark

I foresaw Brisbane as being a good place for the family to get a new start, and my premonition proved correct. My injured body healed steadily in the warm climate, and more offers of work continued to arrive. I teamed up with a young English merchant seaman named David Clark, forming a musical comedy act that appealed straight away to variety-loving audiences. Crocker and Clark, as we called ourselves, became the new taste treat of Australian showbiz. We played the biggest rooms in the country, we dominated the Kings Cross strip, and we guest-starred on the top television variety shows of the day. We reached the zenith of variety theatre, starring in two Tivoli shows In Sydney – The Pleasures of Paris Spectacular with Sabrina, and The Tommy Steele Tour, which was the Tivoli's first foray into rock and roll.

Crocker and Clark performed together for four years, until the creative tank started to run dry. By then, I was the father of five children, and my home life was quite a bit different to bachelor David's lifestyle. David went on to South America, and I returned to my solo career in Melbourne. Doreen was happy in the domesticity of our first house in Fawkner, and I tried to be content with it, but I felt as if I was back on the wharves. Sometimes, I would watch the international flights overhead, wondering where they were heading and what sort of excitement lay in their destinations.

In 1962, after much frustration and family debate, I broke free from the shackles of being merely another variety act working around town. Thinking basically of my own desires, I organised a tour of the potentially profitable South-East Asian circuit. In those days, many Aussie acts toured places like the Philippines, Singapore, Kuala Lumpur, Indonesia, Japan, Hong Kong, India, and even as far north as Israel. Frank Boobla, the Melbourne agent for the Asian tours, submitted my photos, biography, and audio tapes to various booking agents overseas, and while they all agreed that I had something to offer, the answer always came back the same: 'We can't sell him without girls in the show!' The venues for these shows were huge edifices fashioned on images of nightclubs seen in American movies. In the East, as we called it then, the populace believed that these fictional movie settings actually existed. They were Las Vegas before Las Vegas! If I wanted to be in on all of this glamour and excitement, I had to find those girls.

Performing in Asia

Pressed up against the wire fence, Doreen smiled reluctantly as she and the kids waved goodbye to Daddy, climbing aboard his flight to Kuala Lumpur, the capital

city of Malaysia. Accompanying me that day at Melbourne's International Airport were the two girls that I had chosen for the Asian tour. Martine Colette, a blonde dancer and singer, who was useful for many talents, particularly that she spoke several languages, including Chinese, and Cheryl Stroud, a brunette, and a most competent singer. The girls were eager to commit to my own routines and they were both very beautiful.

For two years, we would journey from Bangkok to Bombay, with the three of us making intermittent trips home to Australia. One homeward flight in 1963 I had been strongly advised by a Singaporean palm reader who said, 'You must go home now – very important!' The fortune teller's urgency seemed to be telling me something, so I followed his advice. My mother hadn't been well but I thought she could shake off anything; except, in this case, the aggressive cancer that claimed her at only 54 years of age.

Before touring these foreign countries, I'd had no idea that so many people lived in such poverty and deprivation. I could not have comprehended beforehand that so many so-called religions preached ungodly doctrines and vehement hatred for the non-believer. Once exposed to this poverty, I knew that I had never really been poor. Our payment was in American dollars, and after I converted my wages into Aussie currency, my budget, stretched by my ever-growing family obligations, left little for luxuries. The girls, with no such commitments, had a wonderful time buying cheap fabrics from the local markets. Utilising the seamstress talents of Martine, they built up a collection of exotic show dresses. We were the first act in South-East Asia to exhibit the latest Paris fashion, the fishtail frock. Martine's costumes made our act seem far more spectacular than it would have been otherwise.

My Canon 8 mm movie camera was always whirring away, capturing as much footage as my budget would allow. I wanted to document everything, and now those same movies are invaluable to me, not only for nostalgic reflection, but as reassurance that the passage of time hasn't dulled my perspective. My films may be silent, but I can still hear the sounds and voices of those long-ago experiences in my head.

Performing in Europe

In Israel, at the end of 1964, the members of our trio went off in three separate directions. Martine had fallen for an American film director whom she'd met in the Philippines, and she followed him home to the USA. Cheryl returned to Melbourne, and I decided to travel to London, the undisputed theatre capital of the world. I had made good contacts in Asia, and showbiz agents for the big American army bases in Europe had paid attention to my act. They would take my show without the girls! I explained humbly to Doreen that this opportunity couldn't be

Our trio at Tel Aviv's Sabra Club, Israel, 1963.

ignored, and my resume would display a truly international artist, garnering much bigger bucks when I returned to Australia.

My former partner, David Clark, was in a relationship with Shani Wallis, the sensational singer starring in Lionel Bart's smash hit musical, *Oliver!* in the West End. He resided in a large apartment in Knightsbridge, which had a spare room. That was the good news. The bad news was that he was being managed by the notorious Kray twins, London's most vicious and psychopathic gang lords. Days before my arrival, David told them that he wanted out of his contract. Reggie Kray and his mad, gay brother Ronnie were not happy, especially as Ronnie had his own personal plans for David's future. David explained that it might be better if I found alternative lodgings. Fearing for his very life, David left the country, leaving me with six weeks to spend on my own in London, before my concerts were due to start on the US military bases.

My undoubted charm, or was it luck, enabled me to find free lodgings at the Overseas Visitors Club in Earl's Court. I would perform a concert for patrons every second Friday night, and in return, I would stay gratis in Kangaroo House, located two blocks from the club. My room had once been a hallway, so with a single bed, an old wardrobe, and the inevitable coin-hungry gas meter, I was entombed in a 20-foot by six-foot wide cell with no windows. The only luxury was that hot water would be available between the hours of 10.30 am and noon. But hey, beggars …

Money still had to be sent back to the family in Geelong, hopefully to compensate for my continuing absence. To save cash, I ate barely enough food to stay alive. By the time I left for France and Germany, I was a stone lighter, but I went down a treat with the Yanks on the military bases. In 1964 and 1965, swinging London was the place to be and I loved being there. The excitement generated by the music of The Beatles, The Rolling Stones, The Kinks, Herman's Hermits, The Who, and the wild fashions of Carnaby Street, Biba and Derry & Toms in Kensington was tangible. And yet, my act had only half the impact on English audiences than it had on the American military personnel.

Although I received some very appealing English management offers, I decided to fly home via America, and maybe, just maybe, dip my toes in the really deep water.

In the City that Never Sleeps

A new friend was New York comedian Bernie Travers. Our taste in comedy jelled, and that made him my new best mate! We'd had fun together in Europe and I captured our antics with my movie camera. Not only was Bernie there to meet me at John F. Kennedy Airport in his battered old jalopy, but he provided me with a free room in his modest East 62nd Street apartment. I had planned a two-week mini sightseeing holiday, having previously cajoled Doreen into allowing me this brief stopover on my trip home. Two weeks was not enough for the dipping of the toes. I wore Bernie down, dragging him all over New York City to visit every iconic movie location I'd ever seen. Finally, he begged for a little peace, and we called an armistice on my crusade to capture every possible exciting minute in the Big Apple.

During one of these quieter moments, after enjoying coffee and doughnuts in Greenwich Village, Bernie led me to his own agent Marvin Shnayer, who was a veritable New York institution. Bernie went to him hoping for work, but nothing was available to suit Bernie's talents. Marvin however, appeared more interested in my own story when Bernie raved on about our times on the road, mentioning how well I'd gone over with American audiences in Europe. Over his second blintz and coffee, big Marvin asked me, 'Barry, how would you like to do a gig while you're here on holiday? I could fix it if you want.'

What a fantastic credit to add to my bio: 'Barry Crocker, direct from New York ...'

'Well, whaddya think?' Marvin insisted.

My inner gypsy was saying, 'Sure, if you can really organise it.'

Marvin picked up the phone. 'Get me Mr Horowitz,' he demanded.

I stood up to leave the room, but he motioned for me to sit down. After a huge build-up, and lots of ah-hahs, the conversation ended briskly with, 'He'll be there at seven tonight.'

With a new 'Paul McCartney' hairstyle, New York, 1965 – but possibly looking more like Alec Guinness!

This immediate, unexpected booking caught me by surprise. I would be working at The Village Barn on West 8th Street, but only for that one night. I would do three 20-minute spots at $25 a throw.

'Bernie will show you the ropes,' Marvin almost commanded. 'He can talk you through the routine, okay, Bern?'

On that March spring evening, I appeared in front of an American audience, on American soil, for the first time. Early the next morning, Bernie's phone was ringing. After a slight pause, he looked across at me with a sleepy eye. Marvin Shnayer, sounding bright and chipper, was on the other end. 'Hey kid, you did good last night. Horowitz is offering you the gig for the whole two weeks of your holiday, and he's going to double the money!'

With the Bee Gees on *The Barry Crocker Show*, Channel 10, 1967.

Home in Triumph

Nine months later, at Christmas in 1965, after almost two years away from home, I saw my entire family at Essendon airport, scrunched up once more against the wire fence. I waved from the mobile stairway, but my kids would have to wait a little longer for their cuddles. I was whisked through Customs and into the Qantas lounge for the obligatory television and radio interviews. During my time in the USA, an old friend named Neil Harrold had been supplying stories about my overseas conquests to the Australian press. Neil also scored a lucrative deal for me to headline at The Lido, the most lavish new night club in Melbourne.

Marvin Shnayer had arranged for some *important* people with Sicilian accents, dark suits and seemingly limitless amounts of cash, to look at the possibilities of furthering the Crocker career in the USA. This Melbourne gig could be the perfect opportunity to sort out my family situation and return with the brood for a full-on onslaught of America. During this time, Doreen and I had exchanged a constant stream of letters and phone calls, with me trying to excite her about this once-in-a-lifetime deal. But I was now feeling depressed, distraught and downright uneasy, considering the potential upheaval of my family ... after being apart for so long, would Doreen and I still know each other?

The Lido shows were going gangbusters, and the house was overflowing with happy Christmas punters, seven days a week. Further north in Sydney, the new television station Channel Ten had begun broadcasting. The station was looking for new faces to star in a satirical comedy program to rival Channel Seven's *The Mavis Bramston Show*. Talent scouts were dispatched to Melbourne's Lido to check out the amazing new discovery named Barry Crocker, direct from the USA. Neil Harrold secured me a three-month contract as one of the stars of *66 and All That*.

I now had the opportunity to study the local television industry and consolidate my career in Australia, so I explained to my American contacts that it would be three months before I could join them. As it turned out, another ten years would pass before I performed in the USA again. My television years in the late 1960s brought many fabulous firsts, incredible highs, tears of happiness, pain, and debilitating sadness. There were trophies, prizes, awards, and of course, let us not dismiss the rewards! I worked alongside the best, including Graham Kennedy, Bert Newton, Don Lane, Mike Walsh, and many others. I jousted with Bruce Gyngell and the Packer dynasty from Sir Frank onwards. I wouldn't have missed those experiences for quids.

The 70s and on … Crocker's Alter Ego: Barry McKenzie

In 1966, the well-known comedian Barry Humphries and I, together with a young writer/director named Bruce Beresford, met to talk about a film that Barry and Bruce were hoping to make about a larger-than-life character named Barry McKenzie. Bazza, as he was affectionately known, was a regular comic strip character in Peter Cook's satirical London magazine, *Private Eye*. The adventures of this uncouth Aussie ocker were written by Barry Humphries and illustrated by an observational New Zealander named Nicholas Garland. Oddly enough, Barry McKenzie looked remarkably like Barry Crocker. Now

With Barry Humphries at the Melbourne opening of *The Adventures of Barry McKenzie*, 1972.

they had their star, Humphries and Beresford made noises about raising funds. In 1966, I was already making a name for myself with my television series, *The Barry Crocker Show*. I expected that it would be a while before Barry and Bruce got back to me, if ever, and so I dismissed the meeting from my mind.

Early *Barry McKenzie* publicity shoot, 1972. Note Delvene Delaney grasping Bazza's left leg.

Let the Adventures Begin

Around five years later, in the winter of 1971, the cast and film crew assembled on a chilly day in Bloomsbury, London, for the first day's shoot on *The Adventures of Barry McKenzie*. When I first met Barry Humphries, I had no idea of his problems with the grog. He'd been wandering in and out of the *McKenzie* movie project for years, slowed down regularly by his dependence on booze. Now, with producer Phillip Adams, director Bruce Beresford, cinematographer Don McAlpine, and a completely dried-out Barry Humphries, we hoped to be rewarded eventually for our part in helping to resurrect the very dead Australian film industry, which came to pass, as *The Adventurers of Barry McKenzie* would be the first Australian film to make one million dollars at the box office.

On Saturday 22 April 2023, I would lose another dear friend, and a remarkably gifted entertainer, Barry Humphries (or was it Dame Edna), who had succumbed to complications following a hip replacement at Sydney's St Vincent's hospital. His passing sent me into a deep depression that lasted for several days, and the radio and TV commitments that followed honouring him didn't help my situation. I would find out later that he had been diagnosed with Extramamary Paget disease two years earlier, keeping it a secret from all, except those closest to him; the hip surgery had escalated the inoperable condition, causing his death. I felt that Australia had been robbed of its most daring and controversial pied piper, and in my humble opinion, our greatest comedic genius of the last 100 years. His life would be celebrated in a very small private funeral, just family and close friends, at devoted artist chum Tim Storrier's Southern Highlands Hopewood Estate, in Bowral, NSW. Shortly after the ceremony, his ashes would be flown back to his beloved London, in the safe hands of wife Lizzie Spender.

Although my family had been initially excited about coming to London for the duration of the filming, the change of climate would eventually cause considerable problems for Doreen's physical and mental health. When the filming was completed, I flew back to a glorious Aussie summer for cabaret work, leaving Doreen and the kids to endure another bitterly cold English winter. She longed for the blue Australian skies, becoming increasingly depressed by the chilly grey roof of the London winter. Over the next 18 months, I was back and forth between continents, performing in cabaret, compering and guesting on television shows in England and Europe, and also starring in two Variety specials for the Seven Network in Australia. In order to share some of this new-found happiness with Doreen, I would take her off on the odd little holiday, without the kids. One fabulously romantic week in Paris will remain with us forever.

Even so, when it became clear that the second *McKenzie* movie was to be filmed

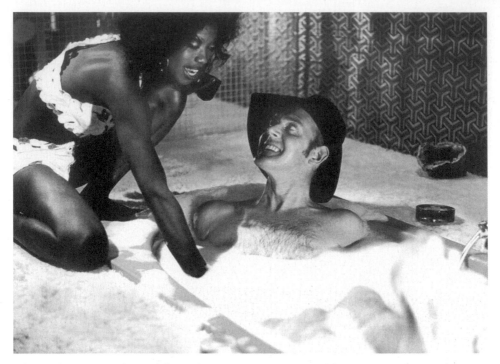

Where's the soap? With Merdelle Jordine in *Barry McKenzie Holds His Own*, 1974.

in England and Europe in the coming year, Doreen's heart told her she couldn't take another London winter and she was determined to return to Australia. To make it up to Doreen, I organised for the family to head home via Los Angeles and Las Vegas, squeezing in as much fun as possible. The kids loved Disneyland, the Hollywood movie lot tours, the genuine American hamburgers and the thick shakes, and I even managed to sneak Doreen off to Las Vegas for a weekend. She made it clear, however, that she wasn't cut out for all this. Imagine travelling around the world with five very active children, dragging luggage in and out of motels and being compressed into easy-to-squabble-with-each-other plane seats. You will understand Doreen's murmuring 'never again' as she stepped off that last international flight.

On 10 October 1973 I found myself alone on the evening of the London premiere of *The Adventures of Barry McKenzie*. On that same night, I became a victim of one of life's most familiar tests, the fool on the refill. Bourbon had mellowed me to the point where complete strangers can chat easily with other complete strangers. I introduced myself to a beautiful girl named Christine Platel. She would come to personify the bittersweet justice duly meted out to me for thinking that I deserved more than my fair share of life's rewards.

On the *Bazza* set with Spike Milligan and Paul Bertram.

34

'Coming to the end of the road' is an often-used cliché, but Doreen and I had hit the cul-de-sac hard. My wife had had enough of showbiz and travel, and, to make matters worse, her demands for us all to live a normal life were falling, as usual, on my deaf ears. We fought hard trying to force our ideals on each other until it reached the point of no return. We would agree to disagree, and the constant yelling at each other to get our point across would cease, much to the delight of our children, who were now growing into their own lives.

After the London film premiere, I found that living a domestic lie was playing havoc with my sensibilities. It was easy enough to slip into work and the family routine, but the comfortable relationship that had always existed between Doreen and me had now become apparent by its weakness. With this new and fateful attraction to Christine, my sharing of the marital bed with my wife felt almost like a form of adultery! I still loved Doreen, but I had also fallen hopelessly in love with someone about whom I knew little, a woman who had shared my lonely London existence for a matter of weeks. I had confessed to Christine, who was only 26 years of age, and thus 11 years my junior, that I was a married man with five children. I explained to her that the marriage was on its last legs; perhaps a little premature, but I couldn't afford to lose Christine.

Torn Between Two Lovers

In Wahroonga, I played the family man, proud dad and loving husband to Doreen. By now, having agreed not to disagree so much, she had taken readily to organising the new building extensions to our house. She enjoyed discussing the trendy, and very expensive, wallpaper designs with their talented creator, a well-known graphic artist named Florence Broadhurst, who came to the house to supervise the hanging. In 1977, poor Florence was bludgeoned to death in her factory, and her murder remains unsolved.

In contrast, when I frequented my other abodes in Europe and America, I lived the lifestyle of a successful single man with a beautiful partner. My mole-like adventures adapted with the seasons. The winter had driven my wife back to Australia, spring had come in the form of Christine, and I enjoyed a glorious five-year-long summer with her. But glorious summers must end, and I was destined to suffer through the worst of winters, justifiably frozen out by the two most important people in my life.

For the next several years, I would lead that double life; in Australia I continued to be the husband and father. While in America I lived the life of a single man, sharing my time with Christine, who happened to be successful and independent with her own apartment. Although now I cringe when thinking of my implausible choices, I found myself in love with two women for totally different reasons, and my

Christine Platel.

heart and mind couldn't find fault with my decision. I wasn't the first man, and I won't be the last, to think he could have it all. By wanting the advantages of a respectable wife and family, as well as a secret lover, I would lose both within the space of a heartbeat.

Amazingly, within weeks, both had decided that enough was enough and I was given my deserved marching orders. In all honesty I had failed them both by not being able to give them what they wanted, simply, my all. There was a big hit song for Mary McGregor in 1976 called 'Torn Between Two Lovers'. In my world, 'ripped asunder' replaced 'torn'!

All my songs sung out of tune,
Can't find the word to rhyme with June,
The silent space that once you filled.
And this heart that loves you still.
– Barry Crocker, from the No Regrets *album*

Throughout the rest of this book, you will read about the two other significant women who would delight and circumvent my life after Doreen and Christine, and they are, in order of appearance, Jenny Main and Katy Manning.

Not in any strict chronological order, I will now immerse myself in the escapades of the boy and his camera. In my pursuit of 'the picture that captures the moment', the one that 'tells the story', I have placed myself in all sorts of precarious positions. Let me list them: opportunist, charlatan, daredevil, philanderer, reckless adventurer, rogue, and sometimes an all-round pain in the arse. On other occasions, I have suffered much derision, not only from complete strangers, but from those closest to me.

CHAPTER 2

The Sinatra Chronicles

Sometimes one's ears are assaulted when encountering an utterance that is not only shattering and unexpected, but totally abhorrent to the one privy enough to

hear the words. This happened to me on Friday 3 March 1989.

Standing at the bottom of the stage's exit steps, my brain disputed what I'd heard.

'I want that fucking nigger off my show.'

Was this really the American idol, Frank Sinatra, screaming a racist order to the huge minder helping him down the stairs? The megastar was leaving in a rage and I could see this was not some throwaway line delivered with his usual good humour. As Mr Sinatra pushed past I wore a frozen half-smile. My teeth were showing, but I really looked as if I'd been kneed in the groin.

The audience at the Sydney Entertainment Centre was yelling for 'More! More!' There would be no encores that night. As Frank's two co-stars dragged themselves away from the ambience of the standing

The Ultimate Event USA program cover, 1988–89.

ovation and made their way to the exit, I could hear his limo, conveniently parked inside the entrance, roar into life and speed away from the centre with its tyres squealing.

The event of a lifetime had been shattered for this boy and his camera.

What could have upset 'The Voice' so much as to make him abandon his adoring public? Could it have been Liza Minnelli? No, that disarming young lady did not fit the profile of someone prepared to undermine Mr Sinatra's stage performance. Frank's vicious tirade that night had been aimed at my childhood inspiration and idol, Sammy Davis Junior.

Francis Albert Sinatra

A lot of the trouble and strife into which I have let myself fall over the years can be attributed to Francis Albert Sinatra. As soon as I found out I could sing like Frank, I wanted to be Frank. To the small-time crooner scraping together a buck or two, Sinatra had it all. The beautiful broads, lots of booze, movie star buddies, and an endless supply of anything his hedonistic heart desired made Frank the epitome of big time success. In those days, the entertainment press was controlled mainly by the Hollywood movie studios, so most of the images and stories emanating from Tinseltown were positive, focusing on the glamour and the glitz, and ignoring any possibility of Mafia financing or drug-fuelled, all-night parties.

A young Frank Sinatra, c. 1935, the year of my birth.

My first brush with the Frank Sinatra legend had been in the form of Ava Gardner, his very glamorous estranged wife. Their brief marriage had been tempestuous, to say the least. Frank had left his first wife, Nancy Barbarto, to shack up with Ava, but at the time he was cooling his heels in Hollywood while Ava had a sojourn in Australia. She was preparing to appear with Gregory Peck and Fred Astaire in Stanley Kramer's epic movie *On the Beach*, which would depict the end of life as we know it. There was a famous quote when Ava endeared herself to the Australian public by proclaiming during the production that 'If you're going to make a movie about the end of the world, you couldn't have picked a better place than Melbourne.'

Melbourne was proposed to be the last refuge for us human beings, before the nuclear clouds finally descended to eradicate us. That was in 1959, when I was working the 'cappuccino circuit' as one half of the double act known as Crocker and Clark. Venues of all shapes and sizes had sprung up in the late 1950s, mainly controlled by Italian and Greek entrepreneurs, who had seen fit to replicate the popular clubs that they once enjoyed in their former countries. One night, David and I heard that Ava Gardner herself would be attending a party in the very same Toorak Street in which we lived.

Ava Gardner, in *Seven Days In May*, 1964.

Fate had stepped in. The possibility of being even that close to the lady made my spine tingle. It was well into the early hours when I turned the car into our street. As we drove along the road, we couldn't help but notice the brightly lit mansion and the loud music pumping into the balmy evening. I brought the car to a halt outside the house. Dave and I sat quietly, soaking in the atmosphere.

'Wouldn't it be great to be invited to that party?' I asked Dave, somewhat rhetorically.

'Yeah ... no way!' he laughed.

I then had one of those rushes of blood to the head that invariably bring me undone.

There had been rumours in the newspapers that Frank Sinatra intended to fly Down Under to patch things up with Ava. I heard myself saying to Dave, 'I'll pretend to be Frank, and maybe they'll take pity on us and invite us in!'

Dave shook his head in a way that implied, 'Don't be so bloody stupid!'

Many of the partygoers were assembled on a large balcony on the first floor. Positioning myself on the footpath underneath the balcony, I went into my best impression of Sinatra: 'When somebody loves you, it's no good unless they love you, all the way ...' I continued crooning, and eventually my vocal gymnastics were noticed by someone up there who apparently alerted the guest of honour.

Abruptly, the party music stopped and the conversation went quiet. People were staring down at me and giving me strange looks. I found myself starting to agree with David's opinion of my ludicrous exercise, and I was soon regretting the foolishness of my impetuous act. When a tall female figure in a sexy white caftan drifted to the front of the balcony, I felt I had no option but to keep on singing. 'Through the good and lean years and through all those in-between years, come what may.'

I may have had some credibility for about half a chorus, but as Ava's eyes became accustomed to the night beyond the balcony, she realised she'd been taken. With a stream of vivid language that would have made my old wharfie mates blush, she ripped into me. Something told me she wasn't practising her lines from *On the Beach*. She must have felt like the female tabby on heat upon discovering that the serenading tom cat was only a possum.

The bottle of expensive champagne she had been holding smashed into pieces at my feet, having narrowly missed my head, and thereby avoiding the chance to knock some sense into it. I felt a tightening of the sphincter as I jumped back into the car and sped off into the night, while David Clark struggled to contain his laughter.

The Perfect Singer

That little setback didn't deter me from catching Frank Sinatra's concerts whenever he came to our shores.

Moving forward to 1984, I recall an occasion when my then lady Jenny Main and I were visiting one of my old stomping grounds in Lake Tahoe, Nevada. I had worked at the Sahara Hotel several times in the late 1970s. I was a bit surprised that the Sinatra show could be had for the price of a two-drink minimum. That was around US$27. The room wasn't full by a long shot, and it disturbed me to see that the master was not quite on his game. At the time, Sinatra was in a valley as far as his career was concerned.

It happens to all of us, and if you're around for more than 10 minutes in this business, no matter how big a star they hang on your dressing-room door, it will happen to you. In Lake Tahoe, Sinatra aborted a couple of jokes that he lost interest in telling, and he sang a couple of songs from lyric sheets.

That Little Magic Name Tag

Ten years earlier, in 1974, while en route to Australia, I was bunking down at Helen Reddy's house in Brentwood, California. 'Your timing's perfect, Baz,' she said. 'I'm booked to appear with Frank in a huge show called Sinatra in Concert with Friends at the Universal Amphitheatre. It's a fundraiser for the Cedars-Sinai Medical Centre. You're welcome to join us if you wish.'

I wished. The amphitheatre was filled to the bleachers, with the cheap seats going for US$100. I was sitting middle centre in a US$1000 seat, compliments of my mate Helen. The front row stalls were US$5,000 and US$10,000 apiece, and every chair was occupied by the backsides of the biggest stars of the day. Johnny Carson and Burt Reynolds were there, as well as many other stars who wanted to be on the A-list. The skinny kid who had stared up at the Geelong cinema's ragged silver screen was in seventh heaven. Cary Grant was the master of ceremonies. Gene Kelly would perform the entire sequence of 'Singing in the Rain', with a fully rain-drenched set. The great Jack Benny would be making his last ever appearance. The only woman on the star-studded bill was Helen Reddy, who had been chosen specifically by Sinatra himself. This was one of the most memorable nights of entertainment in my life, but it was what happened after the show that has burnt itself into my memory.

As a member of Helen's party, I had been given an access-all-areas pass. This small piece of exclusive plastic allowed the wearer to do just that. I wandered up to the heavily guarded stage door, where I came across a large, stern-looking hulk named Jilly Rizzo, the former New York restaurant owner who happened to be Frank Sinatra's long-time close friend and personal bodyguard. Jilly waved me through the stage door. My whole body was abuzz with excitement. I was ushered backstage into an expansive, pale green room adorned with flowers, and filled with tables of drinks and appetising savouries. There were two guys at the other end of the room, and one of them was beckoning for me to come over. The man waving was Jeff Wald, Helen Reddy's husband at the time, and he was introducing me, very casually, to his friend, the world famous actor, singer and dancing legend, Gene Kelly. 'Gene, this is Barry Crocker, a friend of Helen's from Australia.'

Gene expressed great interest in hearing about Australia, and he asked many questions regarding the country and the people, and I was delighted to play ambassador. I even told him about the time I'd tried to replicate his magical jump in *The Crimson Pirate* from the roof of our garage in Geelong!

We were laughing and enjoying the banter when a side door opened, and even before he entered the room, I could sense the presence of the Chairman. Sinatra had entered the room.

Earlier that same year, at one of his sold-out Sydney concerts, Frank Sinatra had paused in his singing to express his disapproval of female journalists, comparing them in a throw-away remark to two-dollar hookers. There was a huge hoo-ha throughout Australia that eventually involved Bob Hawke, at the time the president of the Australian Council of Trade Unions. Sinatra's follow-up concerts were cancelled. Unionists would not refuel his private jet. Other unionists would not allow food to be delivered to his prestigious hotel suite. Frank Sinatra, with all of his wealth and fame, was stranded, together with his entourage, and he could do nothing about it, not unless he apologised for his derogatory comments. A notable headline in one daily newspaper read, 'Ol' Blue Eyes Is Black'.

Since that time, I've spoken to most of those present at the party-like negotiations that took place in Frank's suite at the Boulevard Hotel. I talked to John Pond, the then manager of the Boulevard, and even Bob Hawke himself. The truth is that Frank never did apologise. Enough bonhomie, in the form of complimentary tickets to concerts etc., was dispensed among the politicians and the journalists, and a compromise was reached. The press had a field day: they had a story that sold lots of newspapers, and Sinatra retained his power. Bob Hawke added value to his credibility, and his everyday bloke image would help him when he went on to become the Prime Minister of Australia in the early 1980s.

As a cheerful-looking Frank Sinatra approached our party of three, the drama of his recent escapades in Sydney was still on my mind. I gulped as Jeff Wald introduced me by saying, 'Hey Frank, I want you to meet the biggest star in Australia ...'

'Don't hit me,' I heard myself splurting out. I had no idea what to expect, but Frank rolled back his head and uttered his familiar laugh. Jeff continued, '... Barry Crocker.'

'Hi, I'm Frank Sinatra,' said the Man. After a minute or two of congratulatory chat, Sinatra excused himself, explaining that he had to meet a few friends. He had shaken my hand, and I was thrilled to have shared some DNA with the most popular, the most innovative, and longest-lasting singer in the world.

The 1976 Jerry Lewis Telethon

One of my most memorable Sinatra yarns relates to the Jerry Lewis Telethon, which I was part of in 1976. I was working in Las Vegas at the time that the annual telecast was to be aired. Marcy, the wife of the telethon's producer and director, Arthur Forrest, had caught my show in the Lion's Den at the MGM Grand Hotel. She introduced herself to me, explaining that she'd been talent scouting for new acts for that year's show. Might I be interested? Is Donald Trump interested in fake news? Wholeheartedly, I embraced her offer.

The telethon is broadcast on 180 network television affiliates across the USA and generates tens of millions of dollars every year for the Muscular Dystrophy Association. Jerry Lewis had hosted the telethon every Labor Day weekend since 1966. Normally, the live show lasts for around 21 hours or more. My being asked to join the incredible 60-strong cast was a great coup, oh, and Frank was topping the bill.

I became very friendly with the Forrests. We had clicked immediately. During one of my first evening meals with Arthur and Marcy, after the wine had loosened Marcy's tongue, she blurted out, 'Arthur, you can tell Barry, he's not going to let the cat out of the bag!'

After persistent urging from Marcy, Arthur finally came clean. Since breaking up some 20 years earlier, Dean Martin and Jerry Lewis had not spoken a word to each other, and now Frank Sinatra, who was a great friend of both of these guys, had decided that enough was enough. He had talked Dean, who was then playing the main room at the MGM, into appearing on the telethon. Frank now aimed to get Martin and Lewis communicating again. Sinatra had informed Arthur Forrest that if anyone leaked the news before the event, such a person might have trouble walking for a while. Arthur believed this edict unreservedly, hence his apprehension before divulging the secret to me.

The telethon kicked off at 6 pm on Saturday 4 September, and my allotted time would be 1.10 am on Sunday. In between my spots at the Lion's Den, I sat in my room glued to the television, anxiously anticipating the surprise reunion.

On the TV screen, Frank was in conversation with Jerry, and as most of America watched, he said, 'Jer, I have a friend who loves what you do each year, and he would like to come out and say hello.' Turning his head, Sinatra cried, 'Would you bring my friend out please?'

The studio audience could be heard gasping as Dean Martin, in his full persona of dinner suit, cigarette, and the ubiquitous Scotch whisky in his hand, strolled onto the set to join Frank Sinatra and Jerry Lewis. As casually as if the last 20 years of animosity had never existed, Dean said, 'Hi Jer!' Lewis, totally taken aback, replied with a simple, 'Hi Dean!'

Good-natured but slightly awkward banter was exchanged, and the trio finished the 10-minute spot with Frank teasing Dino and Jerry into singing Al Jolson's 'Rock-a-Bye Your Baby', which they had performed many times in the 1940s and 1950s, when they were the unconquered kings of the heap. Dean messed up the lyrics, even though he was reading idiot cards, but no-one cared.

Something very special had occurred on the Jerry Lewis Telethon, and the international press ran away with the story. Prepared headlines were abandoned in favour of front-page pictures of the reunion, and television stations interrupted their scheduled programming to inform the world about this unprecedented coming together of the two showbiz greats. Taking full advantage of the situation, the network ran continuous commercials advising its audience that the reunion of the century would be rerun at 1.30 am on Sunday. My 1.10 am spot had placed me in the unenviable position of preceding a milestone event.

Two days earlier, I had rehearsed a Tony Hatch arrangement of 'Corner of the Sky' with the magnificent 33-piece Lou Brown orchestra, and my version of the song had never sounded better. Now sweating backstage, I prayed that Lou would get the tempo right for my coast-to-coast television debut in the United States.

Ed McMahon, the endearing sidekick from Johnny Carson's *Tonight Show*, introduced this young Australian singer, currently appearing at MGM's Lion's Den, to approximately 85 million viewers on the LOVE Television Network across the USA.

As I performed, I couldn't help glancing in the direction of the celebrity panel, where the telephones were answered and the donations were read out, and there, sitting next to Dionne Warwick, was Frank Sinatra. I didn't dare look in his direction again, fearing he may be expressing disinterest in my performance, but

44

when I stepped down from the riser, I saw Frank looking straight into my eyes. He nodded his head in approval, as he joined his thumb and his rounded index finger together, indicating the time-honoured circle of triumph. I had been given a pass by the Chairman himself.

I appeared on the telethon the following year and it was wonderful again, but it could never be the same as 1976. For years I would tell the story of how Frank had given me the sign, but some of those wise guys less sympathetic to my feelings would say, 'Yeah, but what was his middle finger doing?'

If you want to see the 1976 and 1977 performances, you can Google them; they're on my YouTube channel.

Immediately after his 1976 telethon, Jerry Lewis tried mending bridges with Dean Martin by writing him a long letter, but Dean never answered it. He wouldn't take Jerry's phone calls, and their bitter stalemate was destined to remain. The only correspondence from Dean was a short 'thank you' note to Jerry for attending his son Dino's funeral. The shared memories of their wonderful early careers would later die with Dean.

Sanctuary Cove Resort

In 1988, the flamboyant property developer Mike Gorr completed a luxurious residential complex on Queensland's Gold Coast called Sanctuary Cove Resort. Each residence possessed its own private jetty on the shores of a magnificent man-made lake. Gorr wore the Queensland 'good old boy' costume of Hawaiian shirt, shorts, and long white socks tucked into the obligatory white shoes, and he was a very smart operator. He owned more land next to the complex if expansion should be necessary, and he knew that he needed a gimmick to let the rest of the country know about the paradise he had on offer. Mike needed something that would draw every big-time punter to view his prodigious dream. He foresaw a spectacular event over which the press would go nuts.

A conference with all the big name promoters was called. Mike's first thought was to import a huge international rock star, but that idea soon bit the dust, as the investors acknowledged that the average rock fan wouldn't have the kind of dough needed to snap up any of the expensive units.

It must have taken them all of two seconds to come up with Frank Sinatra. Everyone around the table agreed there wasn't another entertainer anywhere who could generate the rich crowd following that he always did. Sanctuary Cove Resort would be opened officially with a one-off appearance by the biggest star in the world! Negotiations began immediately with Sinatra's people. Over the next week or so, things started to become unstuck. Frank wasn't sure if he wanted to fly all the way to Australia for a one-night stand. Negotiations stalled, and Gorr's backers started talking to a back-up star, Whitney Houston, then the biggest-selling female singer in the world. But Mike Gorr had his heart firmly set on Frank, so a call was arranged for him to speak personally with his idol.

According to those eavesdropping on the conversation, the dialogue went something like, 'Frank, I know it's a long way to come, but for a million bucks, wouldn't it be worth it?'

This offer surpassed Mike's previous one by $250,000! Frank decided it was worth the dough. Gorr, elated over snaring Sinatra, okayed the deal for Whitney Houston to perform on the following night. In addition to the custom-built main show area, there were several other entertainment venues inside the complex. There was a jazz hall, a pop music stage, and an open-air variety arena, where a two-hour show would be staged each night of the five-day festival. Mike had asked me to be the host of this two-hour festival, and I had jumped at the chance, as I would be introducing many of my friends, including Billy Field, Kerri-Anne Kennerley, Daryl Somers, James Morrison, and my most adored musical mate, the energetic Ricky May, who would top the bill as far as the locals were concerned.

Both Ricky and I were desperate to see Sinatra on stage, but every ticket had been sold, and all of the exclusive house seats had been snapped up by politicians and millionaires. Ricky and I would have to devise a way to catch the show. That night, we joined the swell of punters surging towards the wire entry gates. We were both of the same mindset, realising that the best way to attain our goal was by diversion and confusion. As a boy, I had scrambled under the tent at Worth's Circus to get in for nothing. Thirty-odd years later, I was feeling that same rush of cheeky adrenaline as my large New Zealander pal and I prepared to con our way into a Frank Sinatra concert.

There are times when a bit of celebrity status can come in handy. Recognising us, the bloke collecting tickets welcomed our approach, and the unmistakable Ricky went straight into, 'Hey, how are you man?' as he shook the ticket collector's hand. I barrelled in with, 'Boy, what a night! Keep up the great work!' We allowed ourselves to be pushed along by the surging bodies, indicating that our imaginary friends behind us were holding our tickets.

We were soon spewed out into the dimly lit arena, caught up in a writhing mass of humanity. Our scam had worked to perfection. Now, we would split up, in case anyone was onto us, although it was usually pretty hard not to spot Ricky in a crowd!

I made my way towards the front row, hoping to spot a friendly face who actually owned a legitimate ticket. 'Hey Barry,' yelled a voice from the third row.

I looked across, and there was my saviour, Eddie Kornhauser, a multi-millionaire property developer from Surfers Paradise. I had worked for Eddie and his brother Jack in the late 1950s and early 1960s, at the Chevron and Cecil Hotels in Melbourne. I told him how Ricky May and I had sneaked into the concert, and he couldn't help laughing.

'Where are you going to sit?' he asked.

'Good question,' I replied. 'How do you feel about me sitting on your knee?'

'Don't worry, Barry, we'll fit you in,' said Eddie.

Eddie had organised six seats, so he told everyone to slide up a bit on their chairs. I finished up with half a bum on half a seat. I had made it! I wondered if Ricky had been lucky enough to get someone to share seating arrangements with him.

The Aussies who shared the bill with Frank Sinatra that night certainly held up their end. Clive James, then at the beginning of his successful British television career, was the man who introduced Frank to the stage. Prior to that, a glowing array of talented support acts gave their all to the crowd including Julie Anthony, Peter Cupples, Billy Field, James Morrison, and the penultimate act, Peter Allen, who really ripped the joint apart. Backstage, it might have sent a shudder down Frank's spine to hear the roars of approval that Peter Allen was receiving.

Frank need not have worried. This was Sinatra's crowd, and, when he stepped onto the stage, he seemed overawed by the three-minute standing ovation he received. Earlier in the day, Frank may have been worrying a little, thinking about his run-in with the press in 1974, but when the publicity people asked members of the media if they'd like their photo taken with Frank before the show, they didn't get a single knock-back. The once skinny kid from New Jersey was noticeably heavier now, and I noticed the autocue monitors that had been set up to help him with his song lyrics. It saddened me to think that he'd deteriorated so much in the four years since I'd seen him in Lake Tahoe, but the voice was still there, no doubt about it.

The concert was an unqualified smash, and after a couple of encores, Sinatra left the stage. The standing audience was calling for more, and with his chaser music still playing, the crowd wouldn't have been aware that the star was already in his limo on the way to the airport. By the time the last fan had left the arena, Sinatra's private jet was winging its way back to the USA, and well away from any female Aussie journalists!

Afterwards, Ricky and I met up at our own little playground to entertain the punters who couldn't get enough of a good thing. With the inspiration we'd received from the master that night, we probably did the best shows of our five-night season. Everyone thought that would be the last we'd see of Frank Sinatra, but like General MacArthur, he would return in a little over a year later, to storm the beaches and create havoc all over again.

The Ultimate Sinatra Event

In 1988, I was cast in a popular American play called *Social Security*, which had been renamed *Mother's Day* for its Australian season. I was to play the husband of the imported English female lead, her name being Katy Manning. Earlier in that year, Frank Sinatra had come up with the idea of bringing Dean Martin out of retirement to join himself and Sammy Davis on a Rat Pack tour of America.

Dean had no desire to sing after the death of his eldest son Dino in a plane crash and he had become a recluse. Frank wanted to get his old pal back on his feet again. Frank loved Dean, and he admitted that Dean had been the real leader of the rat pack, having what the Italians call *coglioni*, in another word, balls!

The tour opened to a full house of 16,000 at California's Oakland Coliseum in March 1988, but about six days later, when the curtain came down on their last Chicago concert, Frank had a go at Dean about his lacklustre performance. Dean showed Frank just how little interest he actually had. After leaving the theatre, he booked a private jet for Los Angeles, subsequently admitting himself into the Cedars-Sinai Medical Centre. The next day, the showbiz papers were informed that Dean had had to abandon the tour, due to the recurrence of an old kidney problem. The immediate shows were cancelled and the tour promoters went into damage control, but on 15 April it was announced that Liza Minnelli would be taking Dean's place. The sell-out tour would go ahead, under the title of The Ultimate Event.

I had been thrilled to hear that the show was heading to Australia, but I would never have believed that I'd be sitting front row, in Sinatra's very own house seats, compliments of Liza Minnelli. This good fortune came about through my relationship with my new theatre co-star, Katy Manning. By the time Sinatra, Davis and Minnelli hit Sydney, Katy and I were an item.

Katy came along at the very moment I needed her. As our romance progressed, she told me that she and Liza Minnelli, the multi-talented daughter of the great Judy Garland, had been school friends since they were 11 years of age. Growing up in London, the girls had become best friends, sharing make-up, clothes, boys and puberty. Years later, Liza became godmother to Katy's twins, a girl named Georgie and a boy called Jonathan, known usually as JJ. Aunty Liza, as they referred to her, hadn't seen the children for some time, and they were now nine years of age, so a great fuss was made to ensure that Katy and her children would be in the front row on the opening night of The Ultimate Event. Liza told Katy, 'Oh, if you like, you can bring your skinny friend as well.'

As we sat there chatting, Georgie told me she was excited about seeing Aunty Liza perform again. Sammy Davis opened the show, and JJ was suitably impressed because Sammy performed an impression of JJ's favourite singer, Michael Jackson,

As Thaddeus T. Hopper, in the Geelong Musical Comedy Theatre's *Katinka*, 1952.

In the den of my Sydney apartment. Photograph by Greg Bonham.

The Utimate Event, Sydney Entertainment Centre, 1989. Frank initially soaked up the adulation (top left). Later, he lurched towards me at the bottom of the stage stairs.

Backstage with Katy, Liza, Sammy and the twins, JJ and Georgie – the shot I so desperately wanted, sans one!

Sammy Davis Jr at the Humanitarian Awards Variety Club event, Sydney's Darling Harbour Convention Centre, 18 May 1989.

With Deepak Chopra at the Bee Gees concert in Sydney, March 1999.

Oh those peepers!

My favourite image of Bazza.

TV Week cover, 1972.

Posing with the MGM lion during my first stint at the Lion's Den cabaret room at the MGM Grand, 1975. Destroyed by a fire in 1980, it was replaced bigger and better in a little over a year!

Above: With Barry Humphries, entertaining guests at my 50th birthday celebration in The Rocks, Sydney. Will Dower is on the drums.

Below: Relaxing with Shirley Bassey after her show at the Capitol Theatre in Sydney, 1996.

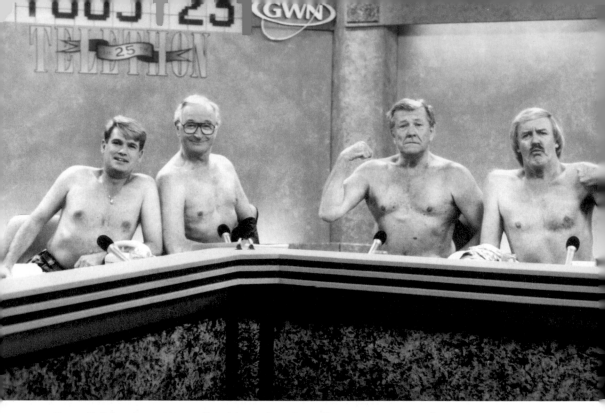

Simon Gallaher, Stuart Wagstaff, Bobby Limb and myself, stripping to raise a few extra bucks on a dare.

Helen Reddy, me and Ricardo Montalbán.

Me and the gang, Perth telethon 1986.

With Cliff Richards.

President Bill Clinton meets Katy and 'Banjo' at Burswood Casino, Perth, 2002.

Barry Crocker's Banjo, performed at the *Banjo Paterson Festival*, Orange 2001.

Dean Martin, Frank Sinatra and Jerry Lewis reunited at *The Jerry Lewis Telethon*, Las Vegas 1976.

ostensibly for the little boy. Liza closed the first half, dedicating her song 'Ring Dem Bells' to her godchildren. Liza was lovely, as usual, and Sammy had sounded really cool as far as the two kids were concerned.

After interval, the house lights dimmed, and, following the Chairman of the Board's overture, Frank was into it, still using the monitors, but seemingly on song, well-deserving of the enthusiastic applause that he received. After the second number, as usual, Frank would call out an attractive lady in the audience and present her with his famous monogrammed orange handkerchief. Ladies of a certain age were excitedly hoping it would be them, but much to their disappointment it was young Georgie Manning-Harris, who was shrinking shyly into her seat.

'Barry why is he looking at me?'

And holding out the much desired handkerchief Frank said, 'I'd like you to have this.'

Georgie embarrassedly slid even further down into her seat, 'Barry why would he want me to have a handkerchief?'

Me, under my breath, 'Just go get it Georgie!'

'But I don't want to.'

'I'll give you a hundred dollars for it!' That did it; taking the prize, she quickly returned to the safety of her seat, and when the laughter and applause quietened, she said, in a rather too loud whisper, 'Who is that man?'

Me: 'That's Frank Sinatra.'

Georgie: 'Yes, but who is he?'

Me: 'He's the greatest singer in the world!'

Georgie: 'Well, he can't sing!'

When Mummy and Aunty Liza explained later the significance of the handkerchief, there was no way my generous offer would ever be considered!

At the end of Frank's set, he called back his two co-stars. The plan was for the three of them to sing a combined medley of some of their various hit songs. Liza had arranged the medley especially, with strict instructions that only Frank would be singing his songs, and in his established keys.

Liza's arrangements were highly creative in their structure and they were certainly very musical, as each song interweaved with the next. Unfortunately, Frank appeared to be getting tired with the whole process. He was losing his concentration and timing. Several times he missed his cue. Liza was trying to flash him instructions with her eyes, but he looked a little absent and he would goof yet again! Sammy, being the ultimate professional, had the idea of singing Frank's part until he'd picked it up. This happened a few times too many for Frank, who was being hugged by Sammy in that ingratiating theatrical way that Sammy had developed, together with lots of forced laughter.

The crowd thought it was all part of the act, and joined in the fun and mirth, but Frank Sinatra was definitely not laughing. Our party had been instructed that, when the last song was finished, we were to make our way to the side stage steps closest to the dressing rooms for an organised exit as a group. As the chaser music struck up, I led the way for the 10 or so people in our group, including Sinatra's wife Barbara, who'd been sitting next to us. I reached the steps first, and it was at that moment that I heard the words that were to be seared into my brain forever.

'I want that fucking nigger off my show!'

No-one could have been more disappointed than me. Not only did I witness the apparent betrayal of a man's close friend, but my carefully planned photo opportunity disappeared along with the exhaust smoke of Sinatra's limousine.

50

Katy and Liza had arranged to get the stars and their immediate fans together for a family shot backstage. My ultimate picture of the ultimate event had become a non-event. The twins were taken home, and I went back to my place. Katy would join Liza at her hotel for a bit of catching up. The next day, Katy informed me that what had happened was not a rare occurrence.

With Frank's medication and the booze, his vindictive outbursts had become fairly regular. Back at the hotel, Sammy had joined the girls for a nightcap in Liza's suite. About an hour later, Frank wandered into the room, dressed in his pyjamas, with a huge smile stretched across his dial. He had no memory of the obscene racist insult towards his old pal. Maybe he was showing the early signs of short-term memory loss?

For all that, he is still my favourite popular singer. In my soul, even with all the heartache and pain, I still wish I could have been Frank, if only for one day!

That Ol' Fading Magic

Frank Sinatra's last show in Australia was the Diamond Jubilee World Tour in 1991. He employed the singing husband-and-wife team, Steve Lawrence and Eydie Gormé, as second stringers. Sammy Davis Junior had died, and Liza Minnelli had had enough of Frank's tantrums. For the tour, Frank also brought along his son, Frank Sinatra Junior, to conduct, or should I say 'follow', the band. The younger Frank had been unsuccessful in his attempts to replicate his father's vocal achievements, but the senior Frank felt obliged to give his son something musical to do. Observing Frank that night, I felt the magic had finally gone for Sinatra. He wandered about the stage aimlessly, and he couldn't take his eyes from the monitors.

If something went wrong, like the tempo, or if anything else was not to his liking, he would abuse his son, who would smile calmly and hand the senior Sinatra another cigarette and a glass of back-up bourbon. The tour may have made money for someone, but the loyal punters, like me, could see a star approaching the end of a long career. But, even with the failings of age, when Sinatra hit the right notes, our memories were stirred and we would forgive him. He had been worth every penny we paid to see and hear him.

After Sinatra's eightieth birthday show in 1995 Ol' Blue Eyes finally retired from performing.

Dean Martin once said, 'Have you ever noticed that when someone retires, two years later he's dead?' Sadly, Frank didn't prove him wrong.

CHAPTER 3

Return of the Don and the Sizzling '70s

Cyclone Tracy Concert 1974

On Christmas Eve 1974, Cyclone Tracy hit Darwin, shocking the entire country with the extent of its devastation. For over 150 years, Australians had suffered through droughts, floods and bushfires, but they had never experienced anything like this. Emergency aid and funds were needed desperately. Anyone who could contribute towards rebuilding the flattened city, from the ranks of builders, carpenters, plumbers, electricians, health workers and stress counsellors, were soon heading northwards to Darwin.

Dozens of professional entertainers also did their patriotic bit, performing at a televised fundraising concert at the Sydney Opera House. The concert, held on 4 January 1975, was televised on the Seven Network. Maestro Tommy Tycho conducted the 50-piece orchestra that backed the many artists, ready as always to provide their time and their talent.

I was among those appearing that night, together with Brian Cadd, the Claire Poole Singers, Winfred Atwell, Colleen Hewitt, Donald Smith, June Bronhill, Toni Lamond, Roger Woodward, Mary Jane Boyd, Paul Hogan and Don Lane. The renowned David Frost was the host of this one-off special. Collectively, we raised almost $100,000, but even so, it was a mere drop in the ocean. Tracy had destroyed the city of Darwin, causing $837 million in damage, and no less than 71 people had died.

When news of the disaster first reached the USA, the lanky Yank himself, Don Lane, contacted Sam Fiszman, a mutual friend of ours, to ask if there was any way for Don to contribute to the cause. Sam called me to see if there was a chance of bringing Don to Australia in time to participate. I called David Frost, who had had an offer from Qantas to fly anyone he deemed worthy, from anywhere in the world, to join the line-up. David thought Don Lane a great choice, so the deal was done.

Don had returned to the States after his *Sydney Tonight* show had been wound up. He received good press after he appeared at the concert for Darwin, and the bosses at Channel Nine started to look his way again. Don Lane had returned to Australia at exactly the right time. He was offered a second chance of stardom on the Nine Network with his own show, and this time he wouldn't blow it!

With Bert Newton, the Graham Lyall orchestra, and Peter Faiman directing,

The Don Lane Show, emanating from Melbourne, would provide Australian TV audiences with some of their best ever long-lasting memories.

'What are you going to do with the apartment in LA now?' I enquired of Don.

'I guess I'll just lock it up ... who knows how long this new show will last?'

I had more or less been living in hotels during my forays to America, and I jumped at Don's suggestion when he said, 'Bazza, why don't you take over the Burbank apartment, and use it as a base? I'd feel happier if someone was living there.'

I was more than happy to accept his generous offer. Neither of us could know what the future might bring, but Don Lane would go on to enjoy growing success in Australian television, and I would have a pad on Burbank Boulevard for the next three years.

So, out of the clichéd 'ill wind' that was Cyclone Tracy, two very positive things had occurred, at least for two grateful showbiz veterans.

Everything Has a Reason, and Everyone Has His Time

If I had to choose a decade where I felt most alive, it would have to be the colourful 1970s. I'd endured the '50s as a boy inside a man's body, and the '60s had been liberating and exploratory, but by the '70s I had hit my mid-thirties. I was at the height of my powers! The new-found freedom of that decade would see me test myself to the limit, along with my fellow 'disco ducks'. We'd take on the world in order to find out how much juice we could squeeze from it. The domain we frequented had a multitude of opportunities and financial security. There is an old Indonesian proverb, 'Man proposes, God disposes.' Proverbs are fairly reliable, and I would find that God wasn't always on my side in the '70s! 'What goes around comes around' would hit me squarely on the chin several times, and I would experience elation and humiliation in fairly equal portions.

On the positive side, for Barry Crocker the entertainer, the 1970s would deliver two hit movies, 33 gold albums, numerous awards, as well as lots of memorable shows and television specials. On the negative side, I would suffer a broken back, and, as I already may have mentioned, the two women I loved at the start of the decade would leave my life. I recorded six albums at London's Pye Studios with Tony Hatch and Jackie Trent, and the joy of working with the husband-and-wife hit-making team is something I may never experience again. Not only were they dedicated professionals in the music studio, but each weekend they would host wonderful social gatherings at their country homes.

We first met in 1970, when Jackie and Tony were my special guests on an episode of *The Sound of Music*. We were on the same musical wavelength, and when the time came to record in London, we were keen to work together. In the studio, or around the piano preparing for the sessions, we found our creative juices flowing along identical channels. Speaking of juices flowing, Jackie was a natural chef, and each weekend pots of goulash, chilli, curries, and spaghetti would be bubbling away on the stove ready to be served with mashed potatoes, peas and pasta. I found myself in musical and gastronomical heaven. While Jackie and Tony later split, and the 'Two of Us' became solo acts again, their lasting legacy is found in some of the world's most popular music. They composed virtually all of Petula Clark's many million-selling hits, from 'Downtown' onwards, and their output is still heard in musical plays and films today.

Tragically, Jackie passed away on 21 March 2015 aged 74. Tony wed Maggi Clough in 2005 and they are now living happily in Menorca, Spain.

Other good things evolved through my London manager, Sydney Rose. He negotiated a deal whereby I would host three Eurovision variety specials for the BBC. However, there was one provision: the TV producers would have to find me suitable for the position.

'Well, have I got the job or not?' I asked Sydney.

'Yes and no,' he said. 'The variety head wants us to do lunch with him at the Savoy.' The food was delicious, the conversation polite and I'd had a free lunch, but during the entire hour spent in the restaurant of one of the world's most famous hotels, not a single word was spoken about the shows!

'What's happening?' I asked when we got back to Sydney's office.

'Don't worry Barry, that's the way it works at the BBC.'

It was only at the very end of our third lunch that the light entertainment CEO finally said, 'Well, I suppose we should talk about the specials. I'll check with Sydney and we'll call a meeting for early next week.'

Duet with Don Lane on Channel 9's *The Don Lane Show*, mid-70s.

The three intercontinental variety specials were telecast from France, Germany and London's prestigious Talk of the Town theatre. I would play the English-speaking host alongside representatives from the other countries. It was easy and very undemanding work. Sydney also arranged for me to be the guest compere for four episodes of *Saturday Night Live* on the commercial ITV Network. It was a joy to work with the very best in variety entertainment. I had to step up a peg or two, and I relished the challenge.

The ITV producers wanted me to stay for more, but I was committed to returning to Australia. I would be playing the eponymous role in *Scapino*, the Molière farce, at Melbourne's Comedy Theatre. I'd caught English comedy actor Jim Dale playing the part on Broadway to rave reviews, and his performance made me realise exactly how physically demanding the role was. I would be hanging off ropes, scaling walls, jumping, and running across theatre seats. Jim told me he'd suffered some minor injuries, including a broken foot and a hernia! I asked myself if my almost 40-year-old body was up for this kind of torture, but I accepted the role anyway.

Englishman Frank Dunlop was our director, and during rehearsal breaks I loved listening to his stories about directing Spike Milligan in *Son of Oblimov*, a riotous hoot that had played the West End. Spike wouldn't go on unless Frank was in the wings, and he told me that several times during the performance Spike would rush to the side and whisper, 'How am I doing?' Frank said he had been amused at first, but the procedure had become very wearing towards the end. Having worked with Spike, I could empathise with both parties.

The Melbourne cast of *Scapino* included Sean Scully, Max Phipps and Collette Mann. I'd worked hard getting the two-and-a-half-hour script down pat, as I was only off stage for eight minutes, and the physical stunts were challenging. However, despite the rave press reviews, the season lasted only eight weeks. We failed to capture an audience, and that hurt us all. The main thrust of the complaints was that I hadn't done enough singing. Scapino only sings once in the play, performing a bastardised version of 'O Sole Mio', which always received the best response of the night.

It was a valuable lesson to learn. Give the punters what they want, as they had completely missed the point of my attempting to master a Molière play. There was one saving grace from being in a flop. I could jet back to Las Vegas a little sooner for another season at the MGM.

Vegas is a different place now than when I worked there in the 1970s. The people in charge, like Bernie Rothkopff, Bill DeAngeles, and expat Kelvin McWhinnie, who went on to manage Sydney's Theatre Royal, would ride shotgun for the performers. If you played your cards right, you would be made part of a very protective family. If you were in the Vegas coterie, you would be looked after with line passes for other shows, all-expenses-paid red passes, etc. Ten years after giving my last performance in sin city, I was still privileged to be on the list.

With two beauties from *The Sound of Music*, 1970.
Mary-Jane Boyd (left) who tragically took her own life,
and Belinda Taubman (Bauer), who developed a lucrative
modelling and movie career in the USA.

CHAPTER 4

King of Moomba

Who Said I Was Spineless?

Having returned to Australia in early 1976, I expected to be entering the next stage of my film career. But maybe the gods thought I'd been enjoying myself a bit too much, as I started to hit a brick wall or two....

I had sustained a back injury in Las Vegas, overdoing my Tom Jones impression of 'Delilah', and the damage hadn't settled down as well as I'd hoped. It was giving me a bit of a Larry Dooley, as the old Aussie saying goes. The injury had been aggravated when I was carrying some heavy rocks in the garden at Wahroonga. Since I'd survived the season of *Scapino* with nothing more than the odd strain, I reasoned that, at a mere 40 years of age, I should be able to work through the discomfort. A week of cabaret work was coming up shortly at the Revesby Workers' Club, and it was imperative that I recover my physical capabilities. Not only that, I needed to be a hundred per cent fit for the filming of a new feature movie, my real reason for coming home.

I had seen an Australian cast in the London production of David Williamson's play, *Don's Party*, and I was mightily impressed with the piece, especially Nick Tate's performance in the lead role of Don. When it was announced the play was to be made into a feature film, I immediately started lobbying for the part, starting with Bruce Beresford, the director. Bruce put the suggestion to the film's producers, who, although reluctant at first, agreed when David Williamson, who'd seen me in *Scapino*, gave his okay. This endorsement by Australia's most prolific playwright was enough to seal the deal, and I was cast as Don. I can hardly tell you how excited I was, to be working on such a brilliant script with such an experienced cast of professionals, including Graham Kennedy, Graham Blundell, Ray Barrett, Candy Raymond, Veronica Lang and Jeannie Drynan. This was the big acting break I'd been sweating over. There had been a couple of English movie offers, but Australian feature film producers had been steering clear of me. Like Bruce Beresford initially, they probably considered me a one-trick pony, typecast as Barry McKenzie, but now I had the chance to prove them wrong. Yes, I would show the bastards!

The first day of filming was completed without any mishaps, and Bruce was happy with what we had in the can, mainly shots of Jeannie Drynan, who played Don's wife, and me walking in and around Don's house. After having been on my feet all day, I felt my lower spine giving me more than its fair share of curry. Following a quick meal and a shower, I felt a little better, and I set off for Revesby Workers' Club to entertain the punters. The venue was about an hour's drive from Wahroonga, and when I alighted from the car I felt quite stiff. I found myself actually leaning to one side. For the first time ever, Dr Stage deserted me that night. My body was racked with so much pain that I had to sit on the edge of the stage to finish the show. Even after swallowing almost a packet of aspirin to help sustain me, I needed to be helped to my dressing room.

I should have gone home to a soft bed, but I had arranged to meet Tony Hatch and Jackie Trent at the Motor Club in George Street. I had wanted to be there to welcome my friends, as they were thinking of migrating to Australia. Disregarding the crippling physical pain, I felt that I should repay the hospitality they always showed me in England. I threw down an icy bourbon and coke and headed off to the city.

The Motor Club was a dark, multi-floored venue in George Street, and I proceeded to give Tony and Jackie a guided tour. We all know that if you have a sore spot, you'll manage to connect that spot with something eventually, no matter how much you try to avoid doing so. I accidentally kicked a tiny step, and it felt like an ice pick had been rammed into my spine!

I had to abandon the tour, informing the Hatches I would call them the next day, hopefully to arrange a more relaxed get-together. Knowing I had an early morning call for *Don's Party*, followed by another night-time engagement at Revesby, all I really wanted was to go to bed, to seek relief from the agony.

Our home in Wahroonga had been built over six levels, with the main bedroom located on the third floor. By grabbing the balustrades on the stairs, I managed to drag my now throbbing body up the three flights to the main living area. My immediate plan was to climb up one more flight to the kitchen, where I should be lucky enough to find a sleeping tablet. But, when I got to the lounge room, I couldn't move my legs at all. I was paralysed from the waist down. I must have stayed there for five minutes, examining my options, which were zilch, before I called out to Doreen. I hadn't really wanted to wake her, because she had lately been criticising the amount of work with which I had encumbered myself, and now she would be able to wave her finger at me, and say, 'I told you!'

An ambulance arrived. Before I could scream in pain again, my stretcher was loaded aboard, and I was on my way to the Mater Misericordiae Hospital in Crows Nest. While emergency ambulances usually speed along the highway, with sirens blaring and red lights flashing, this ride was entirely the opposite.

Because of my delicate condition, which brought tears to my eyes and a wail from my lips with each bump, we crawled at a blistering 5 miles an hour, to make sure that I suffered as little as possible. The X-rays revealed that I had a split disc in my spine. The disc had broken open, interfering with the sciatic nerves that run from my spine to my legs. This state of internal affairs had caused my paralysis. Test after test was performed to get me up on my feet, from injections to traction, but nothing looked like it was going to succeed. I was unable to place even one foot on the floor, let alone stand.

Phone calls were made, and the filming of my scenes in *Don's Party* was put on hold. Like a fractious movie star, drugged to the eyeballs, I kept saying, 'Just fix me up, I have a movie to shoot!'

Dr Dan, a young surgeon gaining a reputation as a pioneer in treating back pain, came to examine me, and he assured me that he would help me to overcome this crisis. On my second day in hospital, an anxious Bruce Beresford came to visit me. Gazing down at me seriously, he asked, 'How long are you going to be like this, mate?' I grabbed his arm, looked deeply into his eyes and replied, 'Give me five days, and I'll be out of here. Shoot around me, Bruce, I promise I won't let you down!'

Bruce told me he would try to accommodate my wishes, but the film's limited budget allowed only for a five-week production schedule. Outside the ward, in the hospital corridor, Bruce asked Dr Dan about my prognosis. 'He won't be out of here in five weeks, let alone five days,' advised the surgeon, 'and in all honesty, it could be more like five months!'

Bruce was left with a tough decision. Should he place the long-awaited production of *Don's Party* on hold, or should he re-cast the leading part of Don? The decision was a no-brainer, and a hitherto little-known actor named John Hargreaves would take over my much-cherished role. John had already acted in the low-budget film version of *The Removalists*, based on yet another of David Williamson's many successful plays. This unexpected break was an important step in John's burgeoning film career. The filming of *Don's Party* proceeded without me, and this was one local movie production that went on to be an overwhelming success. As for John Hargreaves, he would light up the silver screen on many occasions until his untimely death in January of 1986.

During my first week in hospital, Christine was able to get a call through to me. She sounded absolutely frantic, because, by time the news reached her, she thought I was close to death! My show business career was certainly looking fatal. Dr Dan said my injury was so severe that, even If I spent up to 12 months in traction, there were no guarantees that I would walk again. The image of being strapped to a hospital bed for a year filled me with dread.

'Is that my only option, Doc?' I cried. 'Surely there must be something else?'

Dr Dan took a deep breath, 'There is a new procedure involving surgery, called a laminectomy. Normally, it has a 60 per cent success rate, but there is still the other 40 per cent to consider.'

Surgery involved resetting the broken disc and fusing the vertebra. Before surgery could begin, the sciatic nerve cable had to be realigned alongside the spine. It was a complicated procedure at the time, and I would need to sign the usual papers absolving the hospital of any responsibility in case of unforeseen complications.

'If I go ahead with this,' I enquired, 'how long would I have to remain in hospital?'

'If, and I say if, the procedure is successful, you could be out of here in six weeks.'

'Can you do it tomorrow?' I implored Dr Dan. 'Because, if you can, do it!'

On Tuesday 10 February, I was wheeled into rehearsals for *Hello Broadway*. I'd talked my way into being allowed to leave the hospital for a few hours, in order to practise the songs and routines for six concerts, which would commence a fortnight later at the Sydney Opera House. My laminectomy turned out to be a success, and Dr Dan was pleased with my rapid recovery. There was every reason for me to get back on my feet, because as well as performing in the *Hello Broadway* show, I had been selected to be the King at Melbourne's annual Moomba Festival in March, and there was no way I was going to disappoint my faithful subjects, or myself for that matter.

Hail to the King

Following weeks of confinement in a hospital bed, my singing voice was in pretty poor condition. If you don't use it, you lose it. The hospital staff had allowed me to bring in an audio tape recorder to help whip my vocals back into shape. I softly practised my scales, following the voice instructions of my singing teacher, Stuart Harvey. The larynx regained its strength, slowly but surely, and I was soon ready to undertake proper rehearsals. I must apologise to those marvellous nuns at the Mater, who had to suffer the croaky musical scales emanating from my room each day!

On Wednesday 18 February, I was sworn in as the King of Moomba. During the magnificent ceremony, I was dressed proudly in a full ermine and satin cloak, and my head was adorned with a splendidly jewelled crown. The cane I was normally using for balance was replaced with an ostentatious sceptre. Making my acceptance speech, I couldn't help but think of all those who had played the part before me, everyone from Frank Thring to Mickey Mouse. My delightful Queen was 21-year-old beauty Julie Costa, who would prove to be a most enjoyable consort during my brief reign over the state of Victoria.

But some sovereigns still have to work. Later that day, I was back In Sydney, ready

Crowned King of Moomba, with Queen Julie Costa, Melbourne, 1976.

for the next three days of rehearsals for the Opera House. Since leaving hospital, I had worn a special back brace. It was like a bloke's corset, but the support it gave me was reassuring. I knew I would have to live without it eventually, but whenever I removed the thing, I expected to collapse in a heap. The doctors gave me a series of exercises to strengthen my back, and I was confident that I was winning the fight.

Following the strict rules of the Sydney Opera House, I found myself each night in a wheelchair, being pushed along by a trained nurse. She would ride with me in the lift, and then roll me to the side of the concert hall stage. The nurse would help me from the wheelchair, and once upright I would launch myself out onto the stage. My usual bouncing entrance was now replaced by a sophisticated, tempered stroll as I made my way to the microphone. I acknowledged the applause, and then I would move my head slightly, enough to touch my chin on my bowtie. I surmised that the audience would be thinking this is either the coolest dude around, or he's totally up himself! I survived all six of the concerts intact, each time becoming a little more confident. I bowed my head a little lower, and I moved around a bit more during my solos.

Following up the Sydney Opera House staging of the *Hello Broadway* show, with its cast of Julie Anthony, Frankie Davidson and me, supported by the magnificent Tommy Tycho Orchestra, we travelled down to Melbourne for three performances at the Dallas Brooks Hall. Apart from the shows there, I was already into my ten-day stint as the King of Moomba. The official lunches took their toll on my ravaged body, but nevertheless I had a fabulous time for a man who was still convalescing from a serious operation. I was told by many guests that the well-attended parties held in my suite, experienced by myself through a psychedelic haze of stimulants and pain killers, were terrific!

The Moomba Festival culminated in the Grand Parade through the streets of Melbourne on 8 March. Sitting high on the float, with my Queen beside me, ensconced on our papier-mâché thrones, I felt the stinging jerk of every tram line and pothole along the route. But I was well-fortified with effective painkillers. In addition, my flowing regalia concealed a handy flask of Jack Daniels, and several surreptitious swigs enabled me to endure the one-hour-long torture session on the road. My poor battered spinal column was so relieved when it was all over, and I was glad to abdicate the throne!

Career Reflections

On 24 March, Dr Dan gave me the all-clear to go ahead with my life, albeit with caution. So it was back to the clubs, a tour with the brilliant Henry Mancini, more clubs, a Channel Ten telethon, a Gloria Dawn benefit, more clubs, and more clubs.

Two months later, I was aboard a Pan Am flight bound for Los Angeles, with 16 hours in which to reflect on the events that had coloured my life during the previous five months. The purr of the engines lulled me into a retrospective peace. My mind explored why my quest for a movie career had been thwarted. My priority was meant to be the filming of *Don's Party*, and I had allowed my ego to prove to the world I could do it all. I also considered whether my ambitions had been heading in the wrong direction, contemplating my sacrifice on the cinematic altar to make way for the launching of John Hargreaves's brilliant film career. I knew about choices, and I had certainly made mine.

Over the next three years, I flew back and forth between Los Angeles and Sydney for a variety of assignments. I became the proud possessor of a much-prized Green Card, the credit-card-sized piece of plastic that allows a foreigner to work legally in the United States. It was not cheap, what with legal fees and so forth, but what sealed the deal, apart from my ownership of a recording company, was the fact that I had played a unique character in two hit movies. United States law dictates that if an American performer cannot do what you do, you will be granted a Green Card. Nobody else in the world could be Barry McKenzie!

I mentioned earlier that my favourite decade was the 1970s and apart from the heartache and the pain, there were some pleasurable highlights. I worked in a summer season of the popular musical *See Saw*, written by C. Y. Coleman and Dorothy Fields, alongside the original Broadway stars Michelle Lee and the towering Tommy Tune, whose height was a full head above mine. I wonder what happened when *he* tried to join the chorus line! Three weeks of rehearsals were necessary, in order to prepare for eight performances in San Jose. I was cast as Gerry Ryan, the lawyer who falls in love with Michelle's character. For those not familiar with the play, you may remember the movie version, *Two for the See Saw*, starring Shirley MacLaine and Robert Mitchum. I enjoyed working on this show so much that I cried like a baby when the curtain came down on the final performance.

During rehearsals, Michelle gave me some invaluable advice about opening up my emotions, something which has always been hard for me to achieve dramatically. In one particular scene, the action called for my character to become physically confronting, and I was finding it hard to 'go there'. After I had made a few unsuccessful attempts at the scene, Michelle whispered, 'Come with me.' She led me through the foreboding doorway of the nearest women's toilet. To paraphrase

With Tommy Tune and Michelle Lee.

My only photo with Lee Strasberg, in available light in his office, Los Angeles.

the famous *Star Trek* blurb, I thought I was going boldly where no man had ever gone before. Surrounded by the cool serenity of the white porcelain tiles, Michelle worked on me until I found the key whereby I could release the vital compressed anger for the scene's dramatic impact.

I learned more in those 15 minutes with Michelle than I did in all of my earlier lessons with Lee Strasberg, the fabled father of method acting, at the Actors Studio.

We returned to the rehearsal room and played the scene again. Whether it was true or not, Tommy Tune told me that it was the best he'd ever seen it played. Tommy, a professional dancing star on Broadway, had to teach me a tap routine that my character Gerry performs for Michelle's character in a hospital ward. With my spine having taken a battering, I did find this task a little difficult, but Tommy, God bless him, persevered with me. As a closing night gift, he presented me with a Snoopy dancer's sweat towel, and it still travels with me today.

Australian Rules Grand Final 1977

By 1977, I was back to full working capacity, so you can imagine how proud I felt when Neil Harrold, my Aussie manager, told me I had been chosen to sing the brand new Australian national anthem at the forthcoming VFL Grand Final in Melbourne, between Collingwood and North Melbourne. 'Advance Australia Fair'

Singing our new national anthem 'Advance Australia Fair' for the first time at the 1977 VFL Grand Final.

had been chosen by the sacked Prime Minister, Gough Whitlam, from a selection of songs which included 'God Save the Queen', Banjo Paterson's 'Waltzing Matilda', and 'Song of Australia', written by Carl Linger. I would be the first singer to perform the new anthem at a grand final of any football code.

I was in the middle of a Las Vegas season, and I was flown to Australia first class the day before the match. The adrenaline was pumping as I sprinted onto the oval to sing with the massed bands. Here was I, a failed Geelong football hopeful, returning home in triumph to be part of a special moment In Australian sporting history. There were 108,000 footy fans screaming wildly in my direction, reminding me of my childhood days at the cinema, and I wondered if Spartacus had felt a similar sensation as he entered the Roman arena. This was the first year that television cameras had invaded the players' dressing rooms. While I was performing 'The Impossible Dream', images of the players, resembling ancient gladiators preparing to go into battle, were being broadcast nationwide. When I left the field, I felt almost pumped enough to pull on a pair of boots and play for either side! This illusion faded quickly though, and as I sat there watching the crashing bodies of a high-flying pack, I remembered the words of my old Geelong coach, who had sent me on my way as a kid with, 'You'd break ya legs goin' up, and ya fuckin' neck comin' down!'

Dad hadn't been able to join me at the game, but I knew he was at home watching it on the box. As I followed the action, I pictured three generations of Crockers standing in the mud at the southern end of Geelong's old home ground, Kardinia Park, on a freezing Saturday afternoon. How could any of us ever have imagined that this skinny, blue-kneed kid would one day be the focus of so much attention at a Grand Final? My pride may have encouraged me to shed a quiet tear ... but then again, gladiators don't cry, do they?

For Australian Rules die-hards the game was a draw, for only the second time in VFL Grand Final history. The day after the match, I had to fly back to Las Vegas, so I never got to see the following weekend's replay, when North Melbourne produced a convincing win over Collingwood.

The Studio City Album

After learning the hard way, in 1978, that a man who liked to have his cake and eat it too could be left with nothing but crumbs, I faced starvation in the worst possible way. I had no one to blame but myself when the two Marie Antoinettes in my life advised me, almost in unison, 'Go! Find your *cake* somewhere else!' To help alleviate the pain and guilt, I composed some songs, staying up until the early morning hours, accompanied by my faithful co-writer, namely Jack Daniels. Six of those songs, written in a euphoric, partly alcohol-induced stupor, made it onto the only album that I ever recorded in the USA. With its comically pathetic title, the *No Regrets* album had a traumatic beginning.

John Farrar, with whom I'd recorded in both Australia and England, was a member of the gumleaf mafia, the description invented by the Los Angeles press for the founding colony of Aussie artists who made their way to Hollywood in search of mega-stardom. John and I had previously produced my hit recording of 'Susie Darlin'' together. John's wife, Pat Carroll, and the exciting newcomer Olivia Newton-John, had sung the back-up vocals. John had agreed to work on *No Regrets* and I was very excited, as he had recently finished his contribution to the soundtrack of the movie *Grease*, writing two more million-selling hits for the lovely Olivia. But I was about to be given the 'Big A' once again. One morning, I received a phone call from John, apologising that he would have to pull out of our deal because Universal Studios had hired him to write some of the music for Olivia's new film, *Xanadu*. I was thrilled for him, but my severe disappointment regarding *No Regrets* started to descend upon me like a London fog. John could sense my despondency, and before I could speak, he said, 'Don't worry, Baz, I've lined up a fantastic musician to take over the sessions. Trust me, you'll love him. Jay Graydon's a brilliant guitarist, and he's keen to do your album.'

I met up with Jay at his home recording studio in Studio City, in LA's San Fernando Valley. He looked the typical 1970s musician, with long unkempt hair and bohemian clothing, and he used the word 'man' incessantly. But boy, what richness he brought to my musical knowledge. Knowing from the start that we'd be working on a tight budget, Jay planned the recording of the tracks in a most inventive way. Being an A-grade session player, where the musician is usually paid three times scale, he was booked on the most incredible projects, involving anyone from the newly discovered Randy Crawford to Barbra Streisand. He worked with the absolute cream of musicians, whose adrenaline would still be pumping after the studio sessions. Jay would casually invite anyone who might be interested in a nightcap to join him back at his home studio. '... Oh, and by the way, I'm working on this little project for an Aussie guy, so if you'd like to have a jam on it ... it could be fun, man!

My part of the bargain was to be ready to go at any time between 10 pm and 3 am. When a recording session was finished, Jay would make his offer. I would receive a phone call and be on my way quickly to Studio City for another all-night jam, man! In the daytime, Jay would prepare the basic tracks. He would write sketchy chord charts for the players' instruments, giving them the freedom to evolve their own ideas and improvisations. He hand-built one of the first recording synthesisers in America, which produced some of the sweetest sounds I'd ever heard. In its own way, *No Regrets* turned out to be a ground-breaking album.

No Regrets was released in Australia, receiving favourable reviews but only moderate sales. In essence, the album was an indulgence on my and Jay's part, but it was loved by those who heard it. For aficionados, here is a list of the talented musicians involved, some of whom have gone on to greatness: Willie Arnelis, Steve Forman, David Foster, Dave McDaniel, Greg Mathison, Dave Parlato, Mike Porcaro, Carlos Vega, and the man himself, Jay Graydon.

Jenny: The Main Chance

My social life had been put on hold when I lost my taste for 'cake', and my energy became concentrated strictly into my work. In 1979, I lined up a cabaret tour of Australia, and I hired ex-model and TV presenter Joan McInnes to be my co-star. Joan was not only very attractive, but she had a fun personality and a great rapport with audiences. Joan did her own act, and we shared several duets. The famous winemaker, Sir James Hardy, came to see the show in Adelaide, and he was smitten by Joan. He kept his feelings for her well-hidden, and 12 years would go by before their romance came to fruition. She became Lady Joan in December 1991.

Coming off rehearsals during the Sydney season, I noticed a gorgeous young woman sitting alone in Joan's dressing room. From her demeanour, I could tell that she was unhappy. I walked to the end of the corridor, and then I stopped in my tracks. Something made me return to the doorway. 'Whatever it is, it might never

With Jenny Main and Simon.

happen!' I said. The cliché left my lips so rapidly I thought someone else must have uttered it. She glanced at me and looked away. 'And who might you be?'

I continued, but in a kindly way. 'I'm here with Joan,' she answered. 'Ah well, that explains everything then!' I laughed. I felt compelled to bring a smile to her lovely face, but without much luck. As it turned out, Jenny Main and Joan McInnes had been close friends since childhood, having modelled and appeared together on television in Adelaide. Jenny had recently extricated herself from a troubled relationship, and she was intending, for the moment, to hide herself away from the world. That night I found myself thinking about her ... a lot! This bronzed goddess, with a stunning figure and limpid brown eyes, presented a new challenge, and I decided that I would rise to the occasion.

Within six months of our meeting, Jenny was sharing my life at Wahroonga, together with her seven-year-old son Simon, an independent, gregarious, blond ball of energy. I had been going flat-out for a long time, and it was Jenny who got me off the workaholic treadmill. She loved a party, as she still does, and the house at Wahroonga resonated with the sounds of celebration for any, or even for no reason. I learned to relax a bit more, having had my foot taken successfully from the grinding pedal of ambition. My travels to America and England continued, but now with Jenny accompanying me. Wherever we were headed, we'd spend half the time as a holiday. Jenny made many friends in Los Angeles, among them John and Pat Farrar. She also met Christine Platel, and the two have remained lifelong friends, chatting on WhatsApp until all hours of the morning.

Goodbye to my Father

It was in late June 1980, that I received the call most of us dread. My father had been rushed to hospital after suffering a major stroke, and sadly, he left us on 10 July 1980. My hero and best mate, the one who had always believed in me, even when others lost faith, had gone from my life. My one consolation is that, on the evening before his passing, I had the chance to tell him how much I loved him. That night, I'd spent extra time at the hospital. Although he couldn't respond, he lay peacefully in his bed as I reminisced about our family's lives, memories of Mum, the trials and tribulations, and the joy and love that he and my mother had lavished on their only son. I told him I was flying to Sydney the next day to appear on the Mike Walsh television show, but that I'd be back in Melbourne afterwards to spend more time with him. At the hospital, the nurses wheeled in a portable TV so my father could watch his son singing on the show. About an hour after my performance, I received a call from the hospital. When the nurses had gone into Dad's room to get his reaction to the program, they discovered he had passed away. I will never know if he saw my performance, but I would like to think that he did so. I would have expected him to be proud, for one last time, as I sang about a father and son in the beautiful ballad 'Danny Boy'.

Only four months after my father's death, I was honoured on television with a one-hour special edition of *This Is Your Life*. That night, lauded and praised by my peers, I missed Hugh Crocker more than I can say. I know how proud and justified he would have been that our much-maligned dream had finally come true.

Cottage Tales to Coffin Nails

Work opportunities were escalating, and I used them to help take my mind off the loss of my father. I had even invested in a boutique restaurant at Byron Bay, called Barry Crocker's Cottage Feeling. My eldest daughter, Geraldine, had married a chef named Michael Burton.

Michael's culinary dream was to bring a touch of elegance to Byron Bay dining, but with my generous daughter Gerry feeding every stray musician who offered to sing for his supper, and discerning diners thin on the ground, Barry Crocker's Cottage Feeling lasted barely a year. The people who took over the premises, in the main street opposite John Cornell's pub, converted it into two takeaway shops. They made a fortune! As in the world of showbiz, you gotta give the punters what they want! But I still admire Michael and Gerry for having a go at improving the dietary tastes of the locals.

It Could Be … Me!

In early February 1982, I was chosen by the Lyle McCabe organisation to host Channel Ten's remake of Tommy Hanlon Junior's 1960s television series, *It Could Be You*. Like its predecessor, the show consisted of audience games and quizzes, and each week we would reunite people with their displaced families from all parts of the world. As the host, it was my job to give away thousands of dollars in cash and merchandise. Doing the show was a breeze, and I loved giving away money, particularly as it wasn't mine. *It Could Be You* was extremely popular, with overflowing studio audiences and a long waiting list for seats, as anyone could be chosen to win a wonderful prize.

Life was good, and at weekends there was plenty of time to party with my new love Jenny. Unfortunately, my playing Daddy Warbucks would last for only one year. The cost of prizes and the international flights of the reuniting participants were enormous, and someone, possibly Rupert Murdoch, who owned Channel Ten at the time, probably said, 'We're giving away HOW much …?'

The show wasn't renewed for another season.

CHAPTER 5

The World's a Stage — Telethons and Carols

Great Australian Telethons

Most showbiz people, whether they are singers, comedians, actors, clowns, sight acts or merely talking heads, will have participated in their fair share of television marathons, or telethons as they are universally known. Not only are these events an effective way to raise money for worthy causes, but they provide an opportunity for performers to catch up with each other and have a bit of fun at the same time. I particularly enjoyed the telethons organised from Perth, in the halcyon days when Western Australian entrepreneur Robert Holmes à Court owned Channel Seven. Huge garden parties were always held the day before. The marquees would be overflowing with the glitterati of Perth's social scene as they mingled with the performers due to appear in the latest high-rating television fundraiser.

One year, during table chat, English comedian Jimmy Edwards annoyed a high-society lady by referring to her repeatedly as 'Darling'. She insisted strongly that he refrain from doing so, a warning which the gruff-voiced entertainer ignored. 'Mister Edwards,' she protested for the third time, 'I have asked you not to call me *Darling!*'

'Very well then,' replied Jimmy, as he thoughtfully stroked his famous handlebar moustache, 'I shall call you *Fuck-face.*' The tent immediately cleared.

Robert Holmes à Court was a superb 'doer of deals' and in previous years he had successfully included Sammy Davis Junior as a major drawcard for the telethons. At the time, Robert owned the revered London Palladium, a theatre Sammy had always wanted to play. The entrepreneur secured Sammy's services by offering him a date at the venue as a sweetener. Unfortunately, Sammy was never able to take up the offer.

Robert died of a heart attack in 1990, ironically the same year in which Sammy passed away. Maybe they are both up there, still trying to sort out the deal.

Hi, I'm Michael — I Love You

For the 1985 Perth Telethon, Robert had managed to persuade Michael Jackson, the world's biggest star at the time, to appear. Michael said he would love to take part, but only on the condition that Robert would sell him the bulk of the Lennon-McCartney song catalogue. It was the only inducement he would accept. Robert agreed, and what a crafty stipulation that turned out to be for Jackson. The King of

Michael Jackson with Jenny and me.

Pop never gained so much for so little effort. For starters, he wouldn't have to perform any music on the show, unlike Sammy Davis, who they couldn't get off the stage, Michael's only contractual obligation was to be the goodwill ambassador for the appeal, which involved him muttering a few phrases during the official opening and closing ceremonies. One fan actually counted the number of words that Michael managed to squeeze out, in his familiar whispered tones, when introduced by Robert. The count was 37, and many of those words consisted of the phrase 'I love you!'

Michael had been secreted away from his telethon work mates, and we intended to change all that! At the end of each telethon there was a huge get-together by performers and staff and a splendid time was usually guaranteed for all. After exhausting the supply of hot meat pies and tasty savouries, not to mention the free booze, we performers would normally return to our hotels to get a good night's sleep, before flying back to our respective home bases the next day. Performers find it extremely difficult to come down after such a joyous social occasion, and a few of us would congregate around the lounge to squeeze one last drop of joie de vivre from the evening.

Normie Rowe and I were still in the mood for some fun on that quiet Sunday night in Perth. With the evening still a pup, we decided it would be a nice gesture to show our special guest, Michael Jackson, some real Aussie hospitality. Before I go any further, I must tell you that I had met Michael before in LA and Vegas. We both did our grocery shopping at Ralph's supermarket in Encino, and if we found ourselves passing in the aisles, pushing our respective shopping trolleys, we would exchange greetings, invariably using the same brief words each time.

Crocker: 'Hi Michael!'

Michael: 'Good afternoon, sir!'

'At least we kind of know each other,' I said to Normie, who replied, 'Well, that's good enough for me, Bazza. Let's go!'

The Jackson entourage occupied the hotel's entire top floor. Normie and his wife Jo, Ray Burgess and his wife Jenny, together with my lady Jenny Main and I, all squeezed into the elevator. The doors slid open to reveal a long, dimly lit and empty corridor. Not a lot of thought had been given as to what room Michael might be occupying, and I thought perhaps I could try my Marlon Brando impression. Instead of my screaming 'Stella!' it would be 'Michael, Michael!'. Before I could utter a syllable, and as if out of nowhere, two dark giants appeared, blocking our exit from the lift. 'Can we help you folks? I think you may have come to the wrong floor.'

We tried to explain to the two Darth Vader doppelgangers that we had come to offer our salutations, but we were gently, but firmly, escorted back inside the elevator with the words, 'You're very kind, but Mr Jackson has retired for the evening.'

We felt about as welcome as James Randi might have been in Don Lane's hotel suite, but we bold telethon veterans were not about to be thwarted from the tiddly task of making our presence known. Today, Normie, Ray, and I each claim it was the other's idea to lean the ironing board against the elevator doors and press the button for the top floor. At the time, we could only imagine the surprise that our fun-spoilers experienced when the lift doors opened, and the board hit the deck!

The next morning, as we waited aboard the Sydney-bound plane, feeling slightly remorseful over our childish attempts at humour, we watched Michael's limo deliver him right to the bottom of the entrance stairs. Michael, still in full white stage make-up, was quickly bustled past us, together with his entourage, into the first-class section. The curtains were quickly drawn, the aircraft's engines roared into life, and we were up, up and away.

Normie Rowe's three-year-old daughter, Erin, had been allowed to come on the telethon trip because Michael Jackson was her favourite singer in the whole world. She had become a bit distressed. Erin couldn't understand why she wasn't able to see her idol, even though he was so close. Normie could not settle the toddler down, and old buggerlugs here thought, 'This is ridiculous ... we're all the same, we are just simple human beings.' I took a deep breath and stuck my face into the dividing curtain that separated us from first class.

A suited heavy appeared immediately, and I asked him if I could have a quick word to Michael's tour manager. 'I'll see what I can do,' he said, disappearing. Frank Dileo, the tour manager, could have been mistaken for the archetypal movie gangster. He came to the partition as if to say, 'This'd better not be no trouble, buddy!' I introduced myself, and threw in a few Vegas names, explaining that I'd done my share of work in the States and that I had met Michael a few times already. I explained the current situation, with tiny Erin crying her eyes out, wanting desperately to meet her singing hero. Frank's expression relaxed, and he said, 'Stay there.'

Twenty seconds later he was back and he said, 'Bring her up!' I said to Erin, 'Come with Uncle Baz, I have got a lovely surprise for you.' Taking hold of her small hand, I led Erin up to first class, where I introduced her most favourite singer in the whole world.

As Michael chatted to Erin, I asked if it would be an imposition to take a photo, as a keepsake for the little girl. Michael graciously agreed, even though he had already washed off the white stage make-up. I thanked him for his kindness, and after a while we returned to our own seats. Erin was ecstatic. With a certain amount of pride, I told Jenny what had transpired. Instead of saying 'well done' as I'd expected, she exclaimed, 'What about ME?'

For a moment I thought she was joking ... but she wasn't! So, it was back to Frank Dileo. 'Frank, I have a vested interest here – if I do, I'm sweet. If I don't, let me put it this way, there could be a little wait for some kindness!'

'Stay there!' he repeated. Returning with a lopsided grin, he said, 'Bring her up!'

By the time Jenny Main was enjoying her unique photo opportunity, alongside yours truly, there was a veritable party atmosphere around Michael. Then the superstar asked, 'Could you take my picture with the surfie boy?' I don't know how much of the telethon Michael had actually watched, but he certainly knew who the Iron Man was. I went back and explained to surfing champion Grant Kenny that Michael Jackson had requested the pleasure of his company. Grant shot past us as fast as a surfboard in a Waikiki pipeline, and he still tells the story of how he was summoned to appear in a portrait with the King of Pop.

As our little group left Michael's presence, his suited tough guy announced, 'I could get you guys a lot o' dough for that last shot!'

Camera Shy: Stevie Wonder

Another battle of the camera lens occurred in 1987, when Stevie Wonder was making an appearance at the telethon. I thought that getting a photo of myself with Stevie would be a piece of cake, as I'd had no trouble taking photos of him at the

With Stevie Wonder, Perth telethon, 1987.

earlier tent party, but it would require three days of sweet talk and bravado to obtain the exclusive shot. My body came close to potential harm at that very same party.

Along with several of my contemporaries, I was close enough to the stage to smell Stevie's cologne at the moment his performance began. As he went into his first song, the microphone on the piano began to slip downwards, and the audience couldn't hear his vocal. Looking around, I saw that no-one was coming to rectify the problem. Even the bodyguard standing next to Stevie's piano looked oblivious to the situation. So, being the sympathetic fellow performer that I am, I jumped from my seat with the intention of securing the offending microphone stand. As I flew towards the piano, I became aware of three fast-moving bodyguards lunging towards me, while the man next to the piano placed his hand inside his jacket. When they saw what I was attempting to do, they cooled down. The suave Stuart Wagstaff, who was sitting at my table, admonished me, saying, 'Barry, you fool, you could have been shot!'

Stevie Wonder made several appearances on those telethons, often performing with disabled kids at his feet. He had great empathy with them, and he was only too willing to be available whenever he was asked. He was escorted everywhere by a huge African American bodyguard who never wore even a hint of a smile on his face. The man had a serious commitment to his job, and right from the start he was adamant that getting a photo with Stevie was not on the cards. It took me some time to get this big, good-looking man to crack a smile. When he wasn't working, the bodyguard was either in the studio or the green room, taking part in the fun and the action. I brought him around gradually to my way of thinking, and I persuaded him to arrange a private photo session. In all honesty, I think what really won him over was the sight of me dressed as a ballerina for one of the sketches. When he saw my knobbly knees adorned that way, he had burst into full-blown laughter. The upshot was, after the curtain fell at the end of the telethon, and before the celebratory parties got into full swing, the still-laughing guard escorted me to Stevie's dressing room, resulting in the image which you see in this book.

That night, while we local performers were vocalising around the hotel piano, we were joined, ever so surreptitiously, by Stevie's own musicians and back-up singers. Someone must have thought we sounded okay and sent back the word, because the man himself soon came down and we all jammed on for several hours.

If only the ice could have been broken earlier.

A Diva Takes a Dive: Whitney Houston

When it came to me getting a personal shot, Whitney Houston presented a very different challenge. I expected that, being one of the world's most beautiful women, she would love having her picture taken, but a strong rider had gone out with her telethon contract – no photography. I was smitten with Whitney, not only with her glamorous elegance, but also her incredible voice. There had not been a female singer since Barbra Streisand who was so capable of sending shivers down my musical spine in the manner of Whitney Houston.

The extraordinary Whitney Houston, Perth telethon, 1988.

Imagine my disappointment when the TV station manager, my good friend Kevin Campbell, told me that not only would I not get to meet Whitney personally, but there were to be no cameras present in her vicinity. He, as much as anyone, knew my reputation as an amateur paparazzo, and he warned me to 'leave the bloody camera at home'. Her people had threatened to walk from the show if they saw so much as a lens cap. I was not to be deterred. Like most Aussies, I hated this kind of bullshit being exhibited by overseas stars, even if they were as talented as Whitney. The photos I took of her during the telethon were accomplished with a magician's dexterity. I evolved the hidden camera technique into an art form. The red warning flag, waved in front of this particular bull, had inspired me to try even harder to overcome the rules of engagement.

Whitney didn't come to the after party, but no-one had expected her to. She had toured Australia with John Farnham, and he didn't get to meet her either.

Sometime later, Whitney teamed up with singer Bobby Brown and her world descended into an abyss of drugs and self-destructive behaviour. She embarked on a disastrous tour of Australia in 2010, appearing haggard and bloated, and unable to hit the high notes for which she was famous. Despite recording a new CD, and declaring she was free of narcotics, she was unable to turn her life around. While preparing for the Grammy awards on 11 February 2012, she was found dead in her hotel room bathtub at the Beverly Hilton, lost at the early age of 48. Another shining star, like Garland and Presley, and so many others before her, had burned out before their time.

With Julie Anthony, Carols by Candlelight, Melbourne, 1988.

Carols by Candlelight

For most entertainers, the Christmas season usually brings work with one of the yuletide carol-singing shows across the nation, from major television events like Melbourne's Carols by Candlelight, or Sydney's Carols in the Domain, to local churches and social clubs getting in on the act.

At an estimate, I think I've hosted and sung at a thousand events all over Australia, maybe more. I had the pleasure of hosting the very first Carols in the Domain in Sydney in 1982, and I have hosted five more over the years. I've featured many times on other carol-singing shows across the various states, and I am always thrilled to perform my own composition, called simply 'Carols by Candlelight', on these special nights. In the past, at the end of the festive season I would carefully pack away the Chrissie music, ready for the following year. In those days, with time seemingly going at the speed of a bullet, and even Superman possibly having trouble keeping up with my schedule, I'd throw the charts on top of the music pile, and before I knew it, it would be 'Here comes Santa Claus, Here comes Santa Claus'.

When the weather is mild and pleasant, Australia can be a wonderful place for outdoor concerts, but we shouldn't forget that it can also be a 'sunburnt country of droughts and flooding rains'. Many Christmas carollers have suffered through the extremities of the climate, not to mention a whole lot of other inconveniences. From swallowing the odd bogong moth or dragonfly, to being smacked in the face by a lump of dirt in an outback wind, possibly containing a fair smattering of cow crap, and being caught in a tropical storm while performing on live television, I've lived through the best and worst. Over the years, I'd find the best policy was to expect the unexpected. Here's a tip – it was always advisable to 'go' before you left for the venue. The portaloos were always attended by a constant stream of anxious little Christmas fairies and elves from the dancing schools.

The carols were always a wonderful end to my year. Problems were temporarily forgotten, and people of all shapes, sizes, colours and religions would come together to celebrate in a shimmering sea of tinsel and flickering candles. The kids' expectant faces never failed to give the old ticker a touch up, and the world was at peace for those few hours of musical togetherness. I can't help wishing it could be like that always; now I catch the new generation of talent on the tele and see what they can bring to the Christmas table.

I mentioned before about being ready for anything when performing at the carols, but nothing in my wildest dreams could have prepared me for what happened in the NSW south coast city of Wollongong one year. The event was called Carols in the City Square. We were playing to about 5,000 good folk, all singing along to the usual Christmas songs. As my Christmas pièce de résistance, I had a regular surprise for the kids, meant to be a bit of fun for their mums and dads as well. It went like this: As the big smart compere, I can't seem to get the words and melody right for 'Rudolf the Red-Nosed Reindeer' and I ask if any kids in the audience might help me out. The ruse always went down well, and the stage was usually besieged by kiddies of all shapes, sizes and ages. Over the years, I'd become adept at choosing the most suitable little personalities to lift onto the stage. I'd pick energetic, pretty, or unusual children. There was nothing worse than having a kid jump onto the stage and then clamming up, which would then make it hard going for both the audience and me. I'd usually have eight to 12 kids join me, and once they were in position I'd ask their names.

I'd try to get the boys to interact with the girls, which of course caused embarrassment and red faces on stage, but much laughter from the grown-ups. Hands I'd clasped together between the two different camps were wrenched apart in mock horror, and I'd always joke, 'Well, it looks like the engagements off!' I might work off an unusual name that I couldn't quite pronounce, much to the amusement of those involved. I'd switch the kids around, pairing them off in order of exuberance. When the chatty part of the sketch was through, we'd get down to the serious business of the kids teaching me the song.

I'd go from child to child, giving each a chance to show off his or her wares. If one made a mistake, I'd stop the band and blame the musicians for messing up a lovely performance. I'm sure you get the picture. The parents of the toddlers had a wonderful time, and they'd invariably leave with happy memories to share with their kids later on; 'Do you remember getting up in front of 5,000 people ...?'

Over the last couple of decades or so, extra words have been added to the lyrics of Rudolf, such as:

Rudolf the red-nosed reindeer,
had a very shiny nose – like a light bulb!
and if you ever saw it,
you would even say it glows – like a light bulb!

For the routine, I'd usually pick the smallest boy in the group to sing the 'like a light bulb' line. No matter where I'd be in the group I'd always rush back to him for his big moment. This night I felt I'd cracked the jackpot. For my light bulb man, I had the cutest, most perfect little five-year-old, with blond curls, the bluest of blue eyes and a perfect face. But whatever I said or did, he'd freeze on me, and he wouldn't utter the magic phrase. I kept going back to him time and again. The number was getting laughs, but finally I stopped the proceedings and the song ground to a halt. I knelt down, level with his face, and asked gently, 'Won't you say "like a light bulb" for Barry?' I placed the microphone close to his lips, and with 5,000 people focused on him, he said, 'Fuck you!'

The place went absolutely berserk. I had to clarify that I'd heard right, and asked one of the bigger kids, 'What did he say?' The big kid answered with some relish, 'He said, fuck you!' By now his parents were rushing to the stage, frantically waving for him to say no more. The audience erupted in sustained laughter for a good three minutes. Moments like these only come along once in a career, and with my very best Jack Benny stance I waited for the reaction to subside. The cherub stood demurely on the stage, totally at ease with the world, oblivious to the sensation he'd caused. When I regained the audience's attention, I cried, 'One more time!', and, with my band of handpicked carollers, I finished the song with a rollicking chorus. Only this time, much to the amusement of the crowd, every time we came to the 'like a light bulb' line, I would run as far from the cherub as possible.

Promotional shot with Tom Burlinson, Georgie Parker and Jackie Love for Carols in the Domain, Sydney.

CHAPTER 6

From Banjo to Katy

Banjo Enters My Life

It was in 1983 that I had my first taste of the works of 'Banjo' Paterson. I was sailing along quite merrily, playing the clubs after *It Could Be You* had bitten the dust, when I had a call from promoter Bill Watson, with what he described as an interesting proposition. Bill was known as a promoter of rock concerts and boxing matches. He was one of the veterans of the entertainment industry and had pioneered big, concert-type attractions, so naturally I agreed to meet with him. You shouldn't judge a book by its cover, as they say, but this time you could've knocked me down with a bookmark! This so-called rough diamond had written a play about the life and times of Andrew Barton ('Banjo') Paterson, and he wanted me to star in it as the young Banjo. As we chatted, I soon found myself gobsmacked by what I learned about the varied life of Bill Watson.

Bill's home base was in Sydney, but he'd spent his teenage years on a farm in Gippsland, Victoria, where he'd ploughed fields and ridden steers and horses at local gymkhanas and rodeos. After graduating from Sydney Boys High, he became a journalist and wrote for *The Sun*, *The Mirror* and *The Telegraph*. Bill had secured sponsorship for his Banjo project from the makers of Meadow Lea margarine, along with Trans Australia Airlines for our travel, and Budget Rent a Car for other transport requirements. I was flattered by Bill's offer, but I wasn't sure if wanted to do a play, let alone a tour. I must have sounded a bit iffy, because he said, 'Look, take the script home, and hopefully you'll enjoy it, and give me a call tomorrow.'

Bill called every day for a week, hoping for an answer. I had left school at 14 and I had never studied poetry. All I knew then about Banjo Paterson was that he'd written the words of 'Waltzing Matilda'. I was enjoying my relaxed lifestyle with Jenny Main, and I thought that if I agreed to the project it would become a tough assignment. I even mentioned the names of other actors to Bill, suggesting that maybe one of them could do a better job. But Bill was convinced that I was the man for the part, and in the end it was Jenny who suggested I take up the challenge. So, the weight of opinion convinced me, and I agreed to tour with *Banjo the Man*.

The play was directed by Graham Corry, with an ensemble cast of five actors. Rehearsals began in early July 1983, in an old church hall in Surry Hills, Sydney. The cast included Brian Harrison (playing the old, dying Banjo), Rainee Skinner (in the roles of Street Lady, Alice Paterson and Christina McPherson), Andrew James (as Mate, Henry Lawson, Harry Morant, Visitor and Winston Churchill), Don Chapman (cast as Jules Archibald, George Robertson, New South Wales Lancer and Rudyard Kipling), and me in the role of Banjo as he aged from 19 to 61. The tour opened on 24 July at the Albert Waterways Hall, Surfers Paradise, and over the next few months we played towns like Caloundra, Bundaberg, Rockhampton, Cairns, Townsville, Toowoomba and Brisbane.

The theatres we played, and the accommodation in which we stayed, were sometimes hit and miss, but the public gravitated readily towards the wonderful writings of Banjo Paterson. We often played to sold-out houses, so Bill and his business partner, comedian Johnny Holmes, actually made money. *Banjo the Man* was well-received and quite profitable in the Queensland towns we played, and Bill was inspired to look to broader horizons. One night at the pub, he announced that after Queensland, we would be opening the show at the Seymour Centre in Sydney. I really liked Bill, but I had reservations about this latest decision. I had strong apprehensions that the show in its current form wasn't quite ready for the big-time. Apart from minimal lighting, the set consisted of about four or five transparent screens on which we projected the various locations depicted in the play. The images were watercolour scenes painted by Bill's sister, Dolly Olsson. The rest

Bill Watson, author of *Banjo the Man*.

of the stage was covered in black flats and curtains, to allow the actors to enter and exit. It was all very simple to assemble and dismantle at the various venues; in a word, practical.

In my heart, I felt that such practicality was not going to be adequate for the sophisticated city theatre scene, and I came straight out and asked if we would be building a whole new set for Sydney. Bill looked at me as if I'd asked him to explain brain surgery. His eyes glazed over and he asked, 'Why would I want to change something that's been working so brilliantly for us?'

I could certainly see Bill's point of view. If *Banjo the Man* could continue its run of good luck without any more money being spent, the potentially large Sydney audiences would bring a motza in profits for the investors. 'In all honesty Bill,' I said, 'the screens are quite shabbily made, and they'd stand out like dogs' balls in proper lighting, and they're far too small for the Seymour Centre ... and the lighting needs reworking. If you use this set in its present form, the Sydney critics will have your arse. Not to mention mine!'

I'd had a wonderful time on the road, making some lifelong mates, but I had to trust my intuition. I made the unpopular decision to leave. And so, before the show made it to Sydney, my association with Bill, his lovely wife Julia, and his partner Johnny Holmes, came to a sad end.

Banjo the Man had only a short run at the Seymour Centre, and as far as I know, the show has never resurfaced. This was one time that I hated being right. The production had been my first taste of Banjo Paterson, and 17 years later I would thank my lucky stars that Bill Watson had insisted on my being Banjo, the man.

To bring in the new year for 1984, Jenny and I jetted off to Las Vegas, the entertainment capital of the world. It had been five years since I had last worked in the city of a billion bulbs, but as I mentioned earlier, if you'd worked there before, you were treated like royalty. Jenny and I had passes to all the big acts, including Wayne Newton, Paul Anka, Siegfried and Roy, and more.

Leaving Las Vegas

After exhausting Las Vegas and ourselves, the time had come for us to leave the glitter and glam, so we headed back to Los Angeles. Watching the dusty desert recede in my rear-vision mirror, I felt in my heart that this might be the last time I would experience the decadent gambling city. When I first planted my feet on Nevada soil in 1965, Las Vegas was owned by a friendly business corporation known as the Mafia. The town had been built with the help of mob money, designed to be a place where the high rollers could bring their broads for a little fun, a little gambling, some good food, and maybe, to keep the little ladies happy, catch Frank Sinatra's Rat Pack doing their thing at the Sahara. This was the playground of the Cosa Nostra.

These days, the area is renowned for its monumental, theme-based hotels, with each trying to outdo the other for a share of the millions of tourist dollars on offer. One can visit London, Paris or ancient Egypt, all within a few blocks of each other. The hotels even have carefully supervised areas where small kids can enjoy themselves, playing ostensibly harmless toy poker machines, while the parents get on with the serious job of losing their life savings. No, I prefer the Las Vegas of the 1970s, when it was policed by the Mob and the singing movie stars were the main attraction. It was a relatively crime-free zone, as no-one dared to mess with the Mob.

Now Vegas is another corporate city, and the evening air sings with emergency sirens, providing apparently limitless opportunities for crime scene investigators.

Who Loves Ya, Baby?

Helen Reddy had invited Jenny and me to stay at her new home in Brentwood, Los Angeles. Her expansive estate was located at the upper end of Tinseltown, with neighbours like Jimmy Stewart and Barbra Streisand. Apart from the tennis courts and the swimming pool, a full-sized movie projection room had pride of place, and for me, being able to watch newly released Hollywood movies, with some not yet publicly screened, was a super treat. After a few days of 'rest and wreck', Jenny and I set off for San Francisco and Lake Tahoe, where we caught Frank Sinatra's act, as mentioned earlier. Helen had generously offered us the use of her Tahoe cabin, and we took the leisurely route up the coast, stopping wherever and whenever we felt like it, doing all the touristy things. We stayed in the picturesque seaside town of Carmel, where Clint Eastwood once did a stretch as the mayor, and we visited the magnificent Hearst castle, with the giant swimming pool in which Errol Flynn and many of his peers had bathed. Our minds boggled at the cost of US$3,000 per week needed to heat the pool, and that was back in the 1940s! We were shown the secret passageways, rumoured to be used by the film stars of the day to swap beds in the middle of the night. The culprits would meet up again the next morning, attending their places at the mile-long breakfast table, looking as pure as the driven snow.

Jenny and I had a wonderful break, but I was itching to get back to performing. There always seemed to be a limit to my being idle, with a little voice inside me saying, 'Yes, this is all very nice, but let's get back to doing what we're supposed to be doing!' Perhaps it was this compulsive work drive that led to the erosion of my relationship with Jenny. I threw myself wholeheartedly into each new venture, be it a TV show, concert tour or cabaret, while the noisy parties continued at the house in Wahroonga.

In 1986, I was asked to be part of the entertainment team for the opening of the Townsville Casino, and it was there that I experienced another case of six degrees of separation. On opening night, the casino was swarming with dignitaries, pollies, the usual millionaires and their special guests. The overseas guest of honour was the chrome-domed American film and television star, Telly Savalas. The *Kojak* star's duties consisted of no more than mingling with the crowd. After the show, which was performed inside a strange, tunnel-like cabaret room, we were asked to join Telly and his entourage in the bar for a *tête-à-tête*. Telly had been married four times already, and I was soon introduced to Julie Hovland, his wife since 1984. I enjoyed chatting with this charming lady, but I couldn't wait to inform Telly that I'd recently performed on a New Zealand telethon with actor Kevin Dobson, who played the part of detective Crocker on *Kojak*. But here's the real synchronicity ... bear with me ... before meeting Julie, Telly had been in a long-term relationship with an actor named Sally Adams in the 1970s. Although they never married, they had a son called Nicholas, who became the half-brother to Sally's daughter Nicollette Sheridan, who starred in the first five seasons of the high-rating American TV series, *Desperate Housewives*. Okay, here's the pay-off ... my stepson Simon, Jenny Main's son, and Telly's stepdaughter Nicollette, would eventually meet, and together they became one of Hollywood's hottest couples in the 1990s. If only we could have anticipated that in Townsville in 1986!

Shaken and Stirred at Tasmania's Casino Royale

There's definitely something about me and gambling joints. In 1973, I was the first Australian performer to be employed at Hobart's Wrest Point Casino. The famous Wrest Point Hotel, a longstanding landmark, had been fully refurbished and issued with Australia's first casino licence. For all the true-blue Aussie gamblers who had hidden in dark alleys, private clubs and back rooms for years, this was Christmas! You couldn't get near the place. They were 10-deep at the tables, all too eager to have a legal punt.

The casino licensing regulations stipulated that restaurants and top-class entertainment must be provided for the customers. The showroom, set up with both long tables and private booths in the style of US casinos, was opened by Jerry Lewis for the first season, followed by the highly pitched ukulele song-meister Mr Tiny Tim, who was pretty hot at the time. I was the third attraction in this wonderful performance area, and when I arrived I was shown to a beautifully furnished double room, which was to be my accommodation during the season. The manager apologised profusely for not giving me the penthouse suite that both Jerry and Tiny had occupied during their respective stays, but it transpired that Jerry had used the back of the ornate entrance door as a dartboard, and he had cut a hole in the newly laid luxury carpet to practise his putting! Tiny Tim had his moments as well. In his famous falsetto, he demanded that 144 fresh towels be delivered to his room each morning! I have no idea how he used the towels, but a gross of blanched cotton each day surely had to involve something grossly indecent. By the time I arrived, the management had decided not to take any more chances with the penthouse.

Letters after my Name

On 8 June 1987, with the approval of Her Majesty the Queen, I was appointed a Member of the Order of Australia (AM) for services to the performing arts and the community. Other award recipients that day were Edna Edgley, a showbiz doyenne, Vic Patrick, my early boxing idol, T. J. Smith, the leading racehorse trainer, and Douglas McClelland, the parliamentarian. This was a prestigious ceremony, a

milestone in my life, but I couldn't shake off a sense of loss as I stood amongst these Aussie icons, freshly adorned with our honours. I would have loved dearly to introduce Vic Patrick to my dad as an equal on that day. I'd lost count of how many times Dad and I had sat around the wireless, listening to the commentary on one of the great stoushes between Vic and opponents like Tommy Burns and Freddy Dawson. I imagined how proud my mother would have been, mingling with all of those politicians, all praising her son for his achievements. I would have given anything for my parents to be with me on that day, but the passage of time had taken that possibility from my grasp. Whimsically, I like to think that they were there in spirit. Their wedding picture holds pride of place over the framed Order of Australia citation on the wall in my study.

Dancing with Edna Edgley, also appointed an AM.

Unfortunately, having the revered letters after my name did not stop the cracks deepening in the facade of my relationship with Jenny. For some time, Jenny hadn't been happy with the way things were going between the two of us and she went off to visit friends in America. So, on a very windy Australia Day in 1988, it was my daughter Erica who accompanied me to the forecourt of the Sydney Opera House for the award celebrations, in the presence of their Royal Highnesses, the Prince and Princess of Wales.

In the '80s 'Greed is good' spouted *Wall Street*'s fictional Gordon Gekko, and most entrepreneurs followed his advice. Women's hairstyles were feathered, wet or flattened, men's mullets were the go, breakdancing happened, and melodious music seemed to be on the way out. Work had been very acceptable for me so far, but I found myself becoming a little choosier. Variety shows still had their place on the television airwaves and I was asked to host many of the big award shows and beauty specials, like the Miss Australia Quest, which, of course, I still found very rewarding.

Jenny returned from her American holiday, but the nasty tension that had been developing since 1987 showed no real sign of improvement. I had hoped that her time away from me would loosen the uncomfortable rigidity between us, but the situation had only developed into one of inflexibility.

Lessons from a Dynasty

Pernickety is a good way to describe Jenny's attitude towards me. She had become very critical of even the simplest things, asking, 'Why are you driving so slowly?' or 'Does the television really have to be so loud?' It felt as if an invisible wall had been raised up between us, and I knew I would have to break down this barrier to get to the truth. Jenny was obviously missing America, perhaps far more than I expected her to be. When she was chatting with friends at our dinner parties, she displayed exuberance and cheerfulness whenever the topic turned to the States. When we were alone, the icy wall would go up, and her mood would become sombre again.

I arranged a beautiful dinner at an inner-city restaurant for the two of us. After a little while, with the lubrication of the wine, I felt brave enough to ask the burning question, although my heart already knew what the answer would be. 'Jen, I know you're desperately unhappy ... please be honest with me, is there someone else?'

Jenny fiddled with her silver tablespoon and moved her wine glass around. Her eyes welled up with tears and, looking away momentarily, she answered simply, 'Yes.'

Oblivious to my personal misery, the diners around us laughed and chatted. I swallowed my emotions, in what I perceived was a sophisticated approach to the not-unexpected revelation. My feelings were very far from sophistication. Inside my soul, the caveman raged. I wanted to scream, 'Who? Why?' But this was the 1980s.

Before Doctor Phil and Jerry Springer came along, TV shows like *Dallas* and *Dynasty* had shown us how to handle these uncomfortable situations, so I sat quietly as Jenny unburdened her motives to me. She had met a stranger on the streets of Los Angeles. The handsome man told her how beautiful she was, besieging her with flowers and attention. We discussed the seriousness of this instant love affair, and yes, she was *very* serious. We drove home to our separate bedrooms in Wahroonga and I thanked Jenny for her honesty, while wishing deep inside that she had lied to me. But this was for the best. I had survived a broken romance or two before, and I would get over this one too, eventually.

Around 4 am, I awoke from a disturbed sleep. Something compelled me to pick up the telephone extension beside my bed, and I found myself eavesdropping on Jenny's conversation with a mystery man. With not a small amount of guilt, I was allowing myself to listen in on two people who were obviously into each other. Hearing the sexual innuendo, with Jenny expressing her desires, and talking about plans for the future, I started to feel an intense emotion in the pit of my stomach, which slowly moved to my sternum, proceeding to fill my chest with anguish. I wanted to scream into the handset, 'I've heard everything, you arseholes,' in a vain attempt to end my own mental agony and embarrass the crap out of the cheating lovers. But instead of exploding, I softly replaced the phone and lay silently in a black prison of regret and anger. Wanting desperately to pick up the receiver and listen again, I resisted the urge. I may have wept, but I have wiped a lot of what happened that night from my memory.

My own ambitions and actions had caused more than a river of tears to flow from others, so how dare I allow myself to wallow in a well of self-pity? This was payback time, and it had been brought about by me not keeping my selfish eye on the ball. I should have noticed the warning signs, but I'd become slack when it came to paying attention. It was all too late now, and my princess had escaped from her confining tower. Ten years would pass before I confessed to Jenny that I had overheard her conversation that night. At first, she appeared to be embarrassed, but we remained friends. It was impossible for me to dislike her, even at the time of our break-up, and by the time I admitted my eavesdropping, a lot of water had flowed beneath the emotional bridge.

Speaking of water, the Los Angeles cowboy, as I had dubbed him, turned out to have feet of soggy clay. When Jenny returned to the States, reality set in. She discovered that he was an opportunist, expecting that in meeting Jenny he had struck the gravy train. Finding out that she was not the rich bitch who could give him the life of infinite luxury about which he had fantasised, the cowboy hitched up his spurs and disappeared from her life as quickly as he'd entered it. Very soon afterwards, Jenny entered into a more substantial relationship that would keep her in the USA for some time.

Katy Enters the Scene

For nine years, Jenny and I had been going around and around on the carousel. Now I would submerge myself in work, and Dr Stage would never let me forget to make the most of my other lover, the one that I have never neglected – my audience.

Following my resignation from Channel Ten in 1968, my future seemed most insecure, but a man by the name of Bruce Gyngell came along to rescue me, steering me back on the right track via Channel Nine. Now, 20 years later, I would find a new deliverer from doom, in the form of that previously mentioned little Pommy sheila named Katy Manning.

About six weeks before Jenny and Simon flew out for Los Angeles, I started rehearsals on a play called *Mother's Day*.

The Kerry Jewell–produced play, known in the USA as *Social Security*, had won awards in New York, and this would be its Australian debut. The cast consisted of June Salter, Terry Bader, Peter Collingwood, Sarah Kemp, Katy Manning and me. Katy and I were cast as husband-and-wife art dealers David and Barbara Kahn.

My first reaction to the departure of Jenny and Simon had been one of confused self-pity. Simon was now 16, and although I had been his stepfather for nine years, he had accepted the split without too much angst. As any teenager would, he thought a trip to America would be an exciting adventure.

I was shortly to find that Katy, a bolt of blissful British cheer, would kick my arse, pointing me back on the road to happiness and creativity. I had been introduced earlier to Katy in Perth when she was appearing with Martin Shaw in the play *Otherwise Engaged*. Our meeting had been a fleeting one at the theatre's stage door. After a quick, nice-to-meet-you, she had disappeared in a cloud of smoke down the lane, scrunched up on the pillion seat of her date's Harley Davidson. A few days later we were re-introduced at the 1986 telethon, she didn't remember our fleeting theatre encounter, and I have teased her over her memory lapse ever since.

Katy has one of those smiles that can light up a room. When I showed up for our daily rehearsals, I looked forward to getting an injection of her happy vibes to lift the dark moods that I was feeling much too often. There is usually a mother hen in close-knit theatrical communities, and Katy took on that mantle readily. She did her utmost to solve the little personal problems that occasionally arose, firing up the whole company with her energy and vivacity.

We opened *Mother's Day* at Newcastle's Civic Theatre on 20 June to a very appreciative audience. Afterwards, we headed to a restaurant to celebrate. As the evening wore on, the usual inhibitions relaxed, and Mr and Mrs Kahn were seen cuddling each other, but our excuse was that we were still rehearsing our roles. Old trouper June Salter announced to the assembled throng, 'Now there's two for the tour!'

Katy and I were both still in dying relationships at the time. Carrying only a single suitcase, Katy had come to Australia in the early 1980s for the sake of the health of her children, Georgie and Jonathan. The twins had been born prematurely, and they suffered from a debilitating bronchial illness. Doctors had advised her that a warmer climate would be advisable, so Katy and the kids waved goodbye to England, along with her lucrative acting career.

When she arrived here, Katy knew only one person, Roz Wertheim, a make-up artist who had migrated earlier. Although she was a well-known TV and theatre star in Britain, on arrival here, to finance the requirements for two poorly children, she was forced to take on menial work to pay the bills. In a large department store, she played the part of a cheese salesperson, with a fake Norwegian accent and blonde plaits. The job lasted for only a day, as several customers asked her, 'Aren't you Jo Grant?' having recognised her from her role in the phenomenally successful BBC TV sci-fi show *Doctor Who*. Katy had played the role of Jo Grant to John Pertwee's *Doctor Who* for three years, and her character, amazingly, would resurface 40 years later in an episode when Matt Smith was the current *Dr Who*. Katy's long career started in television performing in some ground-breaking drama series. This would lead to her co-starring in several West End theatre productions, including a season of Tom Stoppard, also Shakespeare at the Young Vic. Among her other credits, she would star in the West End productions of *Why Not Stay for Breakfast* and *There's a Girl in My Soup*, and she was Miss Damina in the comedy film *Don't Just Lie There, Say Something!*

Her disastrous cheese-selling attempts would soon be forgotten as she returned to her chosen profession in Australia. She appeared with Jack Klugman and Tony Randall in *The Odd Couple* and with Andrew Sachs in *See How They Run*. And, as mentioned earlier, starred along with Martin Shaw in *Otherwise Engaged*. Now Australian theatregoers were discovering her considerable talents, and she had every right to be satisfied with her selfless decision to bring the twins to their new home.

I relaxed into a warm and playful liaison with Katy. We spent most afternoons going to the cinema or taking long walks together. I allowed myself to emerge into a happier world, overwhelmed by Katy's attention and the friendliness and respect of my fellow actors. But, when we all got back together for the Sydney season, I found dark clouds of despondency descending yet again. I was still coming to terms with the demise of a nine-year romance and I had allowed myself, little by little, to slacken in my commitment to the play. I would often arrive late for the half-hour call, upsetting Katy and the other cast members. It was then that I came to experience the other side of Katy's smiling persona.

Theatrical tradition demands that actors should be present backstage at least 35 minutes before the curtain call, so the producer knows they have a full cast on hand. If an actor is sick, or delayed on their way in, they are expected to telephone the stage manager. If it is an important show, arrangements are normally made for an understudy to take over. *Mother's Day* didn't have any understudies, and I would selfishly let the side down by consistently turning up late and unprepared. Professional actor Katy was allocated the task of bringing me into line, and she certainly did that to the best of her ability. One night I arrived even later than usual, and my procrastination became the final straw that not only broke the camel's back but sent the rest of the herd grumbling for vengeance. At my home earlier that evening, I had been reflecting in Jenny's bedroom, breathing in the last remnants of her fading scent. My mind had dissipated all sense of time, and I arrived at the theatre with less than 15 minutes to spare.

The other, more punctual, players were glad to see me, relieved that I had made it in the nick of time. As I hurried to don my stage clothes, I didn't have the chance to enjoy my favourite part of the evening's ritual, when I would normally receive Katy's welcoming smile. As the cast members entered the stage, I detected a glare from Mrs Kahn ... The audience enjoyed the performance that night, and I soon rose above my earlier melancholy.

'Can I have a word?' Katy asked, as we made our way backstage. 'Sure,' I replied, following her through the back door, out into a dark, damp alley in the heart of Kings Cross. She turned to face me, and it was at that moment the resoluteness of her hard-set expression made its impact. 'How dare you,' she started. A diatribe followed that would have made Ava Gardner blush, as Katy ripped into me with vitriol.

The admonishments spewed freely from her tight-lipped mouth. I was picking up phrases like 'Lack of professionalism', 'Selfishness', 'You are either on the bus or you're not', 'You lack a big star's dedication', followed by, 'You're being a pain to yourself and to everyone else!' She suddenly softened with, 'If you want to pick up your problems outside the stage door, after the show, then I will be happy to listen.'

Her tirade was so one-sided, with me standing there somewhat dumbfounded, I was surprised that nobody called the cops.

Throughout the reprimand, I heard myself pathetically stuttering the odd 'Yes, but ...' and 'You don't understand ...' and although I protested to a degree, I knew that Katy was right. I had allowed my personal problems to intrude when dedication to the performance is indisputably the first rule of theatre. An actor needs time to get into the skin of the character he is about to inhabit for the duration of a play or musical. I had made myself known as a 'Mr Slackarse'. Speaking personally, I have always felt that half an hour is more than sufficient, possibly because of my cabaret years, when one has to be ready at a moment's notice. Some actors may need longer periods in which to absorb the persona that they are going to inhabit for the following few hours. Katy likes to be in the theatre an hour or two before curtain call, and there are others who might take even longer, two to three hours in some cases. Of course, if prosthetics need to be applied to an actor, more time may be needed.

In my *Mother's Day* slackness, I had abused the wonderful discipline of the theatre, but Ms Manning gave me a brutal first-hand refresher course, without charging a fee to yours truly. *Mother's Day* toured Australia and New Zealand, mostly doing well and keeping afloat by amortising the profits from the good weeks with the bad. We ran out of steam on the Gold Coast, and the company was in debt by the time it limped back to Sydney.

'Our Don Bradman' performance, Sydney Entertainment Centre, 1988.

For Katy and me, the tour cemented a relationship that lasts to this day. We have remained together, not only as a couple, but as show-business partners as well. The next play we would enjoy as a union would be the two-hander, *Educating Rita*.

A Royal Command

So many memorable things coloured my life in the year of 1988. I lost a lover, gained another, and I was honoured to appear in the most glamorous Royal Command Variety Performance ever staged in Australia. I also befriended one of the most outrageous ladies that I had ever met. But yet again, the scales of joy and sadness would balance out, and my equilibrium was challenged with the heart-rending loss of a dear friend. It all started out in magnificent fashion when I was asked to perform in the most anticipated Royal Command Concert in years. Their Royal Highnesses, Prince Charles and Princess Diana, were the guests of honour at the Sydney Entertainment Centre.

I was thrilled to join illustrious stars from all corners of the planet, sharing the stage with Peter Allen, Olivia Newton-John, Rolf Harris, Kylie Minogue, Jackie Love, Pamela Stevenson, and Jeanne Little. The rock line-up was impressive, with Jon English, John Paul Young, Icehouse and Angry Anderson. The hugely popular American country singer John Denver was also part of the line-up. Over the years, I have sung in seven Royal Command concerts, but this one was the most exciting and prestigious of them all, due in no small part to the presence of Charles and Diana, the world's most publicised couple. The world had fallen in love with Princess Di, and we artists couldn't hide our own excitement at the prospect of meeting her. Unlike the 12,000 people in the audience, we would have the chance to swap dialogue with her at the end of the concert.

The theme of the show was Australiana, with everything relating to our past and present, and even John Denver sang a song he had composed for his Australian wife. The song chosen for me was 'Our Don Bradman', a bouncy hit from the 1940s, written in praise of our greatest batsman. Privately, I'd been hoping that the producers would choose a big ballad, allowing me to show off my vocal range, but instead I was surrounded by a dozen cricket-uniformed chorus boys, choreographed by Ross Coleman. Admittedly, the infectious number succeeded beyond my expectations.

At the presentation of the artists after the show, I was sandwiched between tiny Brian Rooney, who had played Ginger Meggs, and Jeanne Little. Prince Charles didn't linger very long with me, as we'd spoken to each other at earlier command performances, but then the princess appeared in my vicinity. After she spoke to little Brian Rooney, who had been almost overlooked because of his minuscule stature, her attention turned to me. Her first words were, 'It's so nice to be able to stand up straight and look someone in the eyes.' And what charming blue eyes she possessed! Diana made you feel as if you were the only person in the room. The tilt of her head, together with her upward gaze gave the impression of a shy lover sneaking a furtive glance at the object of her affection. It was easy to see why the world was so besotted with her, like no other princess before or since. Today, as I view the footage from that evening, I am surprised at the amount of time I was allowed with the lady, and one day I must get a lip reader to decipher what we were saying to each other. I do recall that we discussed the significance of my jacket emblem and other trivial snippets, and my overall feeling was that Diana was quite happy to continue our conversation. All too soon, a hurry-up glance from her husband ended the moment.

A couple of mildly amusing things happened relating to that concert. The first incident occurred before the show, when the police dog squad arrived to search the building for explosives. At the first sighting of the canines, most of the rock musicians scattered to the furthermost corners of the complex!

The legendary, now disgraced, Rolf Harris was mortified when he discovered that he'd performed his entire spot with his fly open. When I watched the replay later, I could clearly see the splash of white shirt in the middle of his crotch. Rolf wasn't overly amused when I told him I thought he'd been preparing to perform his Jake the Peg routine.

Scepticism, would be my initial reaction when I found out years later that my showbiz mate Rolf Harris (and another mate, Bill Cosby, too) had fallen into the naughty jar. Evidence would seal their fate.

I first met Rolf when he appeared on *The Sound of Music* in 1969. He was already a huge star, not only in Australia, but England as well, and they couldn't get enough of his talents. I found him to be gregarious, open and an all-round top bloke. From that *SOM* meeting, our paths would cross many, many times in the following years, always having a joke and chewing the showbiz fat. His much-admired showbiz fame, would be snuffed out like the flame on a candle when the damning revelations came thick and fast.

Rose tries out as a 'lap dancer' – two for the price of one.

From An English Rose to a Filipina Rose

In 1983, Rose Lacson had arrived from the Philippines into Perth, Western Australia on a three-month working visa. She was soon employed as a maid to Langley Frederick George 'Lang' Hancock, earning $180 per week. Lang was one of Western Australia's wealthiest men, having made his vast fortune from mining in the Pilbara, one of the world's richest iron ore deposits, which he had discovered in 1952. Rose observed that Lang, then in his seventies, didn't seem to care much about his grooming or personal appearance. Using a little flattery, she influenced him to dye his hair black, upgrade his wardrobe and discard his walking stick. Lang was well aware that Rose's presence in the household was responsible for brightening his outlook, and when her visa was due for renewal, she had no problems in extending her stay. Lang and Rose were married on 6 July 1985. She was 39 years younger than her husband. I became involved in their lives in 1988, when Rose booked me to sing at Lang's seventy-ninth birthday party, to be held at their home in the affluent Perth suburb of Dalkeith. Rose had enjoyed my television appearances, and she had chosen me to take part in a lavish prank to be played on her husband. As she said, 'What can you give a man who has everything?'

Rose arranged for an expensive wax replica of herself to be made, with the quality you would expect of a mannequin in Madame Tussaud's gallery. Rose and the wax look-alike would be dressed in identical red evening gowns, and at a specific time in the evening, a curtain would be opened to reveal the two Roses, seated side by side on a bench. It would be Lang's challenge to pick the real Rose from the fake. My part in this intricate scam would be to stand beside the two Roses, while singing 'The Impossible Dream'. The plan sounded simple enough, but I soon found out that, with Rose, things are never that straightforward.

Picked up from Perth airport, I was driven, in a white Rolls-Royce, straight to the elegant Dalkeith Hancock home. Rose welcomed me with open arms, thanking me profusely for coming such a long way, and I thanked her, as she had been most generous with my fee.

I was offered afternoon tea and shown to the 'pink room', a room usually occupied by Rose's daughter Joanna; a place for me to be hidden away so I could be part of Lang's big surprise. The room was lavishly decorated in every shade of pink that you could imagine; fully mirrored, Danny La Rue would have been in heaven. Later, when Joanna came home from school she was thrilled that her room was being inhabited by the guy who *really* sang the *Neighbours* theme! When I next saw her, the schoolgirl had morphed into a very glamorous facsimile of her mother; the 14-year-old could have easily passed as a 24-year-old.

The evening arrived. The guest list was filled with the cream of Perth society; there were politicians of all persuasions, although the conservatives vastly outnumbered the others. Former Premier of Queensland Sir Joh Bjelke-Petersen was seated very close to the guest of honour and the inhabitants of the rich list were also there in droves. A rib-tickling moment came for me when the early guests began arriving; Rose had covered the entire room with rose petals, including the spa that was level with the floor. A few of the guests, who were not familiar with the home, had done a kamikaze dip into the water. Hiding away in my pink room, each time I heard a kersplosh I visualised the scene that was unfolding. Rose would take care of the wet ones, decking them out in some of her own finery.

But now the time had arrived for the eminent birthday gift for Lang. Towards the end of a magnificent feast, and after lots of people had said all the right things during their toastings to Lang, it was time for Rose's pièce de résistance. All eyes turned to the curtain on the upper landing, where I was hidden with my companions, the two identical Roses. The room was hushed into silence. Then Rose surprised me with an announcement from behind the curtain: 'Langley Hancock, now comes your biggest test. You say you love me, but can you pick the real me from my double? If you fail, Barry will take me away with him, so choose carefully! Are you ready? Raise the curtain!'

The curtains parted, and as Rose and her replica sat in the same cross-legged position, I sang 'The Impossible Dream'. Looking out at the mesmerised party guests, who did not quite believe their eyes, my gaze was drawn to a bemused Lang Hancock, who had a half-smile creasing his leathery features.

When the song finished I said, on cue, 'Well Mr Hancock, which is the real Rose?' With a languid flick of his hand, he pointed to the real Rose, who immediately sprang into an animated dance of joy, squealing in delight. 'Barry, carry me to my husband!' she instructed. 'What?' I thought, with a surge of panic. This bit wasn't in the contract, but what could I do … walk into the pool? Taking a deep breath, I picked up my hostess, praying that my fragile spine would hold up, and I carried her down to her spouse. Lang didn't move a muscle throughout the whole rigmarole, obviously playing along to please his Rose. I placed her in his lap, and she told him, 'I'm your birthday present, darling, you have won me fair and square!'

Regardless of the slightly bizarre nature of the evening, it seemed that everyone had a fun time, and I'd certainly experienced one for the top shelf. While preparing for Lang's party at Dalkeith, I had complimented Rose on their beautiful property. 'This is nothing,' she said, 'Wait until you see the house I'm building at the moment.' I had no idea that the house in Rose's vision would become one of Australia's most controversial buildings. Whenever we'd meet at functions or airports over the next couple of years, I would ask her how the new house was progressing, and Rose was only too happy to give me an update.

Coincidentally, I was about to appear in a show in Perth when I heard that Prix d'Amour had been completed. In a flash I rang Rose, who immediately sent a car to collect me. The Rolls-Royce driver explained that we were now in Mosman Park as we swung into Wellington Street, and I saw Rose's dream house. Yes, it did remind me of Scarlett O'Hara's mansion 'Tara' from *Gone with the Wind*, as I'd been told to expect by others, but frankly, someone here really did give a damn. The photograph you see of the front of the house was taken through the car window as we drove up. Rose had opened the front door before we arrived, eager to display the results of her handiwork. From what I understood, she'd had her say in every decision, from the architectural design and furnishings to the colour of the wheelie bins. As Rose led the way across the polished marble and parquet dance floor, I felt as if I had entered a palace. In the centre of the dining room was a magnificent inlaid Italian marble table which could seat 14. I was so taken by its craftsmanship that for a moment I didn't notice the massive central chandelier, which wouldn't have looked out of place in the Paris Opera House. I asked if I could take photos, and Rose gave me carte blanche.

'Wait!' she declared, calling for a maid to find Mr Hancock. Lang suddenly appeared, as if by magic. 'I'm showing Barry the house,' Rose explained. 'Let's

Prix d'Amour.

have a picture together.' Her being Rose, it couldn't be a regular shot. She told us that she would like to sit astride both our knees. Afterwards, Lang disappeared as quickly as he'd arrived, and I didn't see him again for the rest of the visit. I was escorted proudly through six bedrooms, five bathrooms and seven sitting rooms, each with its own exclusive colour scheme. I was shown the eight-car garage, then given the privilege of viewing Lang's private den. 'This is where Lang does all his work,' Rose explained.

She then led me into the massive master bedroom and waving her hand over the king-size bed she chuckled, 'And this is where I do all of mine!' I couldn't help but smile at the innuendo. It was this kind of simplistic honesty that others criticised over the years, but I bet if Lang had heard her say it, he would have laughed too. As we were winding up the tour, she caught me completely by surprise when she asked, 'Would you do me the honour, Barry, of being my first guest in the guesthouse?' I had already booked into the Lansley Plaza Hotel, unpacked all my gear and laid out the music to prepare for my show at Burswood Casino that night. Having to collect my stuff and move to Prix d'Amour was the last thing I needed before a performance, so I thanked Rose and told her that normally I'd be delighted to accept, but the show had to come first. 'I'll get the chauffeur to help you with your gear,' she pleaded. But I begged off, saying 'Next time for sure.'

In hindsight, I wish I'd accepted her generous offer; I could have claimed the privilege of being its first inhabitant. But the building became a part of Australian

history when Lang Hancock, who occupied it last, passed away in the guesthouse in March 1992, at the age of 82.

Over the years, Rose and I have remained close. Perhaps it's because we both come from less than well-to-do backgrounds, and we understand the struggles that one often has to go through to hang on to what he or she has achieved.

When Rose built Prix d'Amour in 1990, her detractors called it a joke. But when the building was demolished in March 2006, and the land subdivided into 10 housing lots, she earned a profit of almost 20 million dollars. I have happy memories of the times spent in Rose's house, and I will always miss the 'Tara' look-alike edifice. After Lang's death in 1992, Prix d'Amour became a bitter battleground for the Hancock family members, with claim upon counterclaim of foul play. Following a coronial inquest, the eventual finding was that Lang Hancock died of natural causes, from a heart attack, and not from the perceived pressures placed upon him by his wife. To escape the prying eyes of the Perth citizenry, Rose plumped for a change of vista, moving to the other side of the country. Friends advised her that she would fit nicely into the upper-class Melbourne suburb of Toorak, where she purchased a multi-million-dollar home. The sojourn turned out to be quite short.

As Melbourne socialite, the late Lillian Frank told me, Rose was never going to cope with 'the hoity-toity bitches of Toorak', and she soon returned to her beloved Perth.

In this homogenised, politically correct, devoid-of-true-characters world, Rose is

Ricky and I 'mirror singing', a musical game we played around the world.

a diamond amongst the rhinestones. As far as I am concerned, she can make waves for as long as she wishes.

Ricky May

On the first day of June 1988, I was awakened by a wailing voice interrupting my early morning reverie. Footsteps were running towards my bedroom door, and a female voice was crying, 'Barry, Barry, Barry.' It was still dark as I peered sleepily towards the illuminated clock beside the bed. It was 6.30 am. I knew this wasn't a part of any dream when Jenny burst through the doorway, half-screaming, 'Ricky's dead! Ricky's dead!' Tears were streaming down her face, and between giant sobs she explained that she'd picked up the early morning phone call in her room. A radio station wanted a quote from me on the sudden death of Ricky May. Not, 'Have you heard the bad news?' or any such politeness, only the request, 'Has Barry got a quote?' That first day of June would now always be remembered by me as the last day of May. I had not only lost a great mate, but my mirror singing pal and I would never again have the chance to share a stage.

Ricky's death would really affect me. 1988 proved to be a year of love and loss, elation and disappointment, success and failure, and every possible emotion in between.

I had covered a great distance, both physically and emotionally, and it was

With Katy, *Educating Rita*.

'I Am Woman', with the cast of *Fast Forward*.

With the Doug Anthony All Stars: Enmore Theatre, *The Big Gig*, *The Money or the Gun* 'Stairway to Heaven', as The Five White Blind Boys, 1990.

Still keeping up appearances during my mystery illness: With (top row) Bronwyn Bishop, Shirley MacLaine, Andrew Peacock and Katy. Bottom row, with Kerri-Anne Kennerley and Jan Adele, 1993.

Razzle Dazzle.

Donnie Destry in *Razzle Dazzle*.

Toni Lamond (Sherry), me (Donny), Noeline Brown (Leonara) and Leo Sayer put some 'dazzle' into the 'razzle'.

Mephistopheles, *Reefer Madness*, 2008.

Eureka. Commissioner Grey (Michael Cormick) kneels over the body of Paddy (me), who has just been kicked to death by publican James Bentley and his henchmen.

Celebrating my 69th birthday with the *Eureka* cast at Her Majesty's, Melbourne, 4 November 2004 – a tradition kept for all birthdays during the season.

Graham Kennedy had been talked out of his retirement to appear on my 1976 *Barry Crocker Special* for the Ten Network. I was honoured that he'd accepted. He'd later return to television on his late night *News Show* and *Coast to Coast*, then *Funniest Home Videos*, but after that he retired for good.

Tania Zaetta (third from the left) and 'The Hoff' (second from the right), visit the *Rocky Horror* cast.

With Katy and the Bee Gees in Kings Cross, 1988.

Selfie at St Mark's Square in Venice during Simon's trial.

soothing to end the year by joining my mates on Channel Nine's Carols by Candlelight. I'd always enjoyed the peaceful atmosphere brought on by the festive season, and although it felt good to see the candles, the children, and the faces of my fellow performers in the joyous finale, I would have been so much happier if Ricky May could have joined us for one final Christmas session.

When There Were Clubs and Pubs

It might have been wise for me to think of slowing down a little, to 'take some time to smell the roses', but my old mentor, Ike Delevale, had always advised, 'If it's there, grab it, because next week it might not be.' In the late 1980s, we entertainers never had it so good. Big venues like Sydney's St George Leagues, South Sydney Juniors, and the Gold Coast's Twin Towns Services Club were offering one- and two-week seasons to performers, sometimes even longer. Every RSL and rugby league club had its own showroom.

These days, entertainers consider themselves lucky if they can score one booking a week. In this digital age, it is almost impossible for live acts to compete with home entertainment packages, online computer games, iPads, 3D movies and the myriad of electronic toys on offer. In the same way that vaudeville and live theatre were largely replaced by the movie industry, followed by the movies having to co-exist with television, the entertainment industry has latterly found itself having to deal with modern technology in the form of computers and the World Wide Web.

I found myself traversing the country, taking on anything and everything that was on offer. I went to New Zealand for a one-night stand, to open the new Park Royal Hotel in Christchurch. Guests were flown from all over the islands to take part in this prestigious opening. My role in the celebrations was to provide the after-dinner entertainment, scheduled for approximately 9.30 to 10 pm. I had selected a fairly serious and classy choice of music to entertain these distinguished guests, and after rehearsals, I went off to do a little sightseeing, before returning to the hotel to prepare for my performance. Around 6.30 pm I consumed a light dinner, as I'd generally eat very little before I performed. I turned on the television and waited for my call. However, I wasn't aware that the guests had started the day very early, with a hearty welcome breakfast, followed by a sumptuous three-hour lunch. The invitees had enjoyed the finest wines in-between speeches from the hotel owners, builders, politicians, in fact anyone who had anything positive to say about Christchurch's glorious new showpiece.

At 5 pm, the time came for the dining room to be cleared, in preparation for the pièce de résistance, a lavish four-course dinner. The guests had been advised that cocktails were available in the outer lounge, and that dinner was to start at 7.30 pm. 9.30 pm came and went, as did 10 pm and 10.30 pm. I started sending out a few distress calls, as I didn't want Cinderella to leave during my show. Preparing to perform, you aim to build up your energy level so that you hit the floor firing on all cylinders. I'd been fired up about three or four times, only to be told that the main feast was running a little behind. Jet lag was now invading my brain, and it was a struggle to keep firing on the one sputtering cylinder I had left.

Finally, a little after 11 pm, the word arrived, 'Yes, Mr Crocker! We're ready for you.' The stage had been set up at the end of the sparkling new foyer, and in my naivete, I imagined there would be seating. But no, the audience was expected to stand, or maybe dance, during my performance. Management had thought this would be the better way to go, but they hadn't envisaged the 200 wobbly-on-their-tootsies and off-their-faces guests with whom I had to contend. These revellers had been hard at it since breakfast. They were tired and emotional, and most of them appeared quite inebriated. In all fairness, the crowd seemed ready to give this interloper from across the Tasman a hearing. I got through a couple of songs and told a few jokes, but it was clear that fatigue was creeping in on them. Many were shuffling from one foot to the other, or glancing around furtively for somewhere to sit, impressing on me that I would have to do something big, and very soon, in order to hold their attention.

Every once in a while an entertainer makes a bad choice which ultimately turns out to be the right choice. Now, it was my turn … The biggest song I had in my repertoire for that night was my closer, 'The Impossible Dream'. I decided it was time to hit 'em with this, as it was sure to capture their undivided attention. To introduce the song, I'd usually recite some of Don Quixote's words from *Man of La Mancha*: 'Oh, maker of empty boasts. On this, of all nights, to give way to vanity. Nay, Don Quixote, take a deep breath of life and consider how it should be lived. Call nothing thy own, except thy soul. Love not what thou art, but only what thou may become …' This is accompanied by dramatic opening music, in order to set the scene.

As I was coming to the middle of the intro, an elegantly dressed couple in their fifties, right in front of the stage, took my mellifluous words as their cue to start dancing. A better way of describing it would be to say they tried to start dancing, because after a couple of vigorous spins, the highly polished wooden floor won the day, and down they went in a tangled heap, as if they'd been crash-tackled by Johnny Raper. But you know what they say about babies and drunks. They bounce! This pair, all arms and legs, helped each other to their feet and continued from where they'd left off, and, not surprisingly, down they went again. By now, I'd completely lost my audience as it cheered on Christchurch's own Fred and Ginger. Everybody joined in, trying to dance to my dialogue. Over the years I've worked all types of crowds, and I have learnt that at moments like these an on-the-spot decision is needed. I turned to the band and said the three little words that saved the night – 'The Elvis medley!' Suddenly, everyone from senators to salesgirls were bopping along to the rock'n'roll rhythms, and I ad-libbed my way through the rest of the set, totally ignoring the sophisticated program that we'd rehearsed. We reached the magic midnight hour, and since no prince with a glass slipper showed up to ask embarrassing questions, I felt that my mission here was duly accomplished. The band played on into the early hours and I marvelled at the stamina of the guests as they boogied into the night. Before falling asleep, I couldn't help but smile, knowing my head would feel a whole lot better than those of Fred and Ginger in the crisp morning air of a new day in the City of Churches. As far as management was concerned, the evening had been an enormous success. I was presented with a handsome cheque, and that afternoon I winged my way back to Oz. Elvis may have left the building, but he saved my bacon that night. Footnote, the hotel that I'd opened in October 1988 would be demolished after the 2010/2011 earthquakes and is now called The Crown Plaza.

Professing to Be Frank

I first became aware of Willy Russell's work in 1989, when Katy Manning was booked to appear with *Cop Shop* actor Peter Adams in Peter Williams's production of *Educating Rita* at Sydney's old Phillip Street Theatre. Driving home after opening night, I told Katy exactly how impressed I was by the message and structure of the play, not to mention the two wonderful performances. 'You know,' she said, 'you could play Frank.'

'What?' I shot back, 'I think you might be stretching it with that. There are a lot of words, big words, some I don't even understand. Frank is a professor, for God's sake. Don't forget I left school at 14.'

'And don't you forget you're an actor!' she admonished.

I didn't think too much more about her suggestion, but within a year I was performing the role of Frank Bryant opposite Katy in a new season of *Educating Rita*, produced once again by Peter Williams. I firmly believe it was Katy who'd convinced Peter to give me a go. Thank God her faith in my dramatic talent didn't let either of us down. We toured Australia intermittently for two years, during 1990 and 1991, and it was an absolute joy to share the stage with Katy as Willy Russell's Frank and Rita, two of the best characters ever written for the theatre.

Tribute to Sammy Davis Junior

In 1989, the Variety Club made its presentation of the 1988 Humanitarian Award to Sammy Davis Jr at the Darling Harbour Convention Centre in Sydney. The event, the biggest on the Variety Club's calendar, was held on 18 May to a main hall

Sammy Davis Jr and an all-star Australian cast, Convention Centre, 18 May 1989.

that was filled to capacity, overflowing with the royalty of Australian and overseas show business. I would be the ring master for the night, leading a colourful parade of 50 Janice Breen junior dancers as we opened up the show with 'Join the Circus', followed by the Variety theme song, for which Tony Hatch and Jackie Trent had kindly given me co-writer status. The night was a splendid tribute to the talents and humanitarian achievements of our special guest. It was a black tie event, and for once the edict was adhered to, and how splendid we all looked. The evening was fully catered, with only the best of food and wine laid out on the tables.

The late Kerrie Biddell, Angela Ayers and Greg Anderson, the electric horseman, took their turns performing in-between courses. The moment for which the audience had been breathlessly waiting came in the form of a loud drum roll, followed by the announcement: 'Ladies and gentlemen, would you please welcome to the stage, MISTER SAMMY DAVIS JUNIOR!' The band struck up the familiar theme tune from *Hawaii Five-O*. Picked up by the white spotlight, the diminutive star dashed in from stage right, to the accompaniment of a mighty round of applause and a standing ovation. For the next hour, Sammy regaled the crowd not only with his songs, but also little bursts of gratitude, anecdotes regarding his friends, and stories of the good things in his life. He belted out the numbers that we'd come to expect, 'Begin the Beguine', 'What Kind of Fool Am I', 'Candy Man', 'Lady Is a Tramp' etc., but then he surprised everyone with a rendition from 'Phantom of the Opera,' a show that was comparatively new at the time. Sammy's much-demanded encore was one of his early hit records, 'The Birth of the Blues'. As a surprise treat, Barry Newman, the show's producer, had written a special anthem for the night entitled 'You're the One'.

As Sammy was about to make his exit, he was held up in the wings by Kerri-Anne Kennerley, who led him back gently towards the spotlight. 'Mr Davis, may I have a moment of your time,' she began to sing, and finished her lines with 'You beat the band'.

I entered on Sammy's right, and my lyrics consisted of, 'You're the one they call the hoofer, you're the one they call the star, you're the one who's kind of magic, draws the crowds from near and far, you're at home on a movie set, or a big time Broadway run, and tonight at Darling Harbour, you're still the one!'

Jackie Love then took up the lyric, and soon the late Norman Erskine, Julie Anthony, Paul Martell, Danny McMaster and Danny La Rue joined in the musical tribute. Sammy was seated centre stage as this band of gypsies surrounded him, assaulting his senses, while he soaked it all in, flashing a huge grin on his pearly whites.

Jack Thompson gave an inspiring speech about what led the man to be honoured with this most coveted of awards. Video messages were shown above the stage, from American stars such as Bob Hope and Angie Dickenson, and Tom Jones popped up on the big screen as well. They all gave the usual salutations to their friend and apologised for their personal absence. Jack Thompson introduced a past International Chief Barker, Michael Samuelson, who placed the Golden Heart award into Sammy's hands. Sammy did go over the top a bit, becoming emotional and weeping freely as he gave his acceptance speech. I had been a loyal fan of Sammy's since I was 17, but over the previous decade I had become a little tired of him sucking up to his peers, with his constant repetition of phrases like, 'Let me sincerely say, sincerely, you're my man, man!' He didn't really need to carry on in that self-belittling fashion. There was no reason for the fake laughter, the drying as we call it, whenever he was being interviewed on television, nor for the incessant hugging of anyone within arm's length.

Sammy was then celebrating 60 years in the business, and I'd followed his career for almost 40 of them. He had long ago become the benchmark for the development of my talents, and I longed to emulate even a modicum of his success. I never missed the chance to catch every show that Sammy brought to Australia, in the same way that I never missed Sinatra. From his first tour, organised by promoter Lee Gordon in 1959, to The Ultimate Event with Frank and Liza in

1989, I had been a devoted fan. When I was living in New York in 1965, I went to see his Broadway show *Golden Boy* many times. I paid top bucks in LA to catch him in *Stop the World, I Want to Get Off*, the exciting musical created by Anthony Newley and Leslie Bricusse.

However, one time, I became a bit disillusioned with Sammy when he appeared at Sydney's old Hilton Hotel Showroom. After his performance, the other invited guests and I were taken to a small lounge, adjacent to the lobby, to await Sammy's greetings. After waiting about 15 minutes, we were all chatting happily away when two very large African Americans entered the lounge. One of the gentlemen gained our attention by clapping his huge paws loudly. He announced in a booming bass tone that Mr Davis was about to enter, and then, to our surprise, he requested that we all remain standing, and that we refrain from sitting down until Mr Davis was comfortably settled in his own chair first. My heart sank at this perceived reverse discrimination. I would like to believe it was only the bodyguards playing at cops, because Sammy was soon drying, that is, bestowing his forced laughter upon us, and hugging everyone in sight.

On the night of the 1998 Variety Club award, nobody was aware that, shortly before his attendance, Sammy had kept a vital appointment with the doctors at the Los Angeles Cedar-Sinai Medical Centre. He was suffering from an inoperable throat cancer. The medics had advised him to begin treatment immediately, but he had promised the Variety Club he would be In Sydney to receive his award, and not even throat cancer would keep him away.

When I learned of his dire medical battle, I felt ashamed for supposing he was faking his tears that night. Sammy knew that he would never perform again in Australia. He returned home for his radiation therapy, and he worked doggedly right up until the time the pain from his illness could no longer be overcome. He may have thought he could beat it, but the years of heavy smoking, cocaine abuse, and drinking with his Rat Pack cohorts had already determined his destiny. A spectacular American television special was held in his honour. Sitting with his wife and family in a front booth, all of his friends entertained *him* for a change, and although the star could no longer even speak, he did team up briefly with Gregory Hines for one last tap dance. At that very moment, he looked as if he could not have been happier.

Most may think that he must have died a wealthy man, but he was bankrupt. It was estimated that for over 20 years he gambled and squandered more than 50 million dollars. The awards in Australia had been held on 18 May, and if you factor in the time zone when the 64-year-old song and dance man died, on 16 May, his passing over took place only one day less than a year after he accepted the Humanitarian Award in Sydney.

Performing in *Educating Rita*.

CHAPTER 7

Feet Back on the Ground

The 1990s began with the joyous birth of my second grandson, Aaron, in January 1990. My second daughter, Martine, was now on her second marriage to Anthony Williams, an American serviceman with the US Navy Air Force. Little Aaron would stand out from stepsister Bianca, and stepbrother Lee Nacson, for his father was an African American, and everybody was delighted when this coffee-coloured new arrival joined the ranks of the Crocker clan.

I had to interrupt my busy schedule of cabaret work to take on the task of *Educating Rita*. Katy's prediction had come to fruition. Having allowed her to convince producer Peter Williams that I was the man for the job, it was now time for me to put up or shut up. Although I was more than slightly terrified, having a mere two weeks to digest the complicated script, the production opened at the Seymour centre on 28 May. Once again, I was taking on a formidable challenge, with a fair amount of prodding from Katy, but I would never regret it.

Not only did we play to good houses, but *Educating Rita* was also placed on the university syllabus, so we played daily morning and afternoon sessions. It could be like walking a tightrope, as far as some of these teenager-attended presentations were concerned. Surviving with our confidence intact, not to mention our professional integrity, would often be a matter of how strictly the students' discipline had been enforced by the accompanying teachers, hopefully prior to the opening of the proscenium curtain. Mayhem could reign, with interruptions and comments coming from youthful audience members who may have preferred to be somewhere else. Jaffas might be rolled down the aisles, thus bringing titters from the less-mature adolescents. All theatre actors have their own horror stories of battling these marauding future leaders of society. An unexpected humorous comment, stage-whispered by some smart-arsed student, can provoke unrelenting chaos, causing any serious drama to become a carry-on comedy in a nanosecond. Worse still, the odd loud fart can turn a hitherto studious theatre audience into a cheering football crowd! We didn't know if it was the tantalising subject of *Educating Rita*, set in a school with a male teacher and an attractive female student that held the expected havoc in check, but very little interruption was ever experienced during our sessions. However, there is a moment at the end of the play where an unrequited moment of sexual tension rises between the professor and Rita when she offers to cut his hair. Cleverly written, it is never really resolved if this is the beginning of a relationship between the two, or actually the end of their journey together. Whenever we reached this moment, we were aware of squirming in the seats, accompanied by the soft murmuring of ooohs and aaahs. Finally, during one matinee, we did get our long-feared moment of interjection when a very loud male voice called out, 'Go on, give her one!' Everyone in the theatre erupted into hysterics, including, may I add, the two actors on stage. The curtain came down, and when it arose again, the entire audience, still roaring with laughter, gave us a standing ovation.

There is nothing like doing live theatre, so they say. It was a memorable moment, but, to me, the most endearing and touching thing about the experience is that some 30 or so years later, I'd still get adult men or women coming up to me to recount how much they enjoyed their introduction to the theatre, courtesy of Katy and me and *Educating Rita*. Intermittently, over the next two years we took *Rita* to places like Wollongong and Brisbane, and we did a season at the Sydney Opera House, where Japanese tourists, taking in the show as part of a package deal, would sit with confused expressions as they waited patiently for the dancing girls to come on! Katy and I really loved the piece, and we had the added privilege of being able to work together. She paid me an absolutely wonderful compliment by lauding my performance as Frank.

London Calling

This would also be the year when three grandsons would be added to the quickly expanding Crocker clan. After Aaron's arrival in January, my eldest daughter Gerry's first son, Caleb, was born in July, followed by the arrival of my son Barry's first child, James, in October. It has been most interesting to observe the boys' development into young men since 1990. Each has his own distinct personality, and vastly different interests.

As winter approached, I had this overwhelming urge to visit England again. Katy was working in a new play, and I had a vision of whipping across to the Old Dart to catch up with friends, see what the West End had to offer, and also, to help pay for the trip, find an agent over there to arrange some work for me. It all seemed easy and uncomplicated, but it would turn out to be the opposite.

When I arrived in London, the weather was absolutely delightful, as English summers can sometimes be. I had been invited by Basil and Claire Sellers, whom I'd originally met through Jenny Main, to be a guest at their opulent Belgravia home. Basil was once one of Australia's most successful businessmen, and he was also a cricketing tragic. Through Basil I would meet one of my boyhood idols, the flamboyant Keith Miller. As far as I was concerned, Keith had been the Errol Flynn of cricket; as a boy in Geelong, I always imagined I was him as I bowled and batted on a field in Kardinia Park but, let's face it, my talents turned out to be in a different field altogether from the cricket one. While staying with Basil and Claire, I had the opportunity of catching the best of what the West End had on offer.

Veteran thespian Richard Harris gave a most outstanding performance in *Henry IV*. There was one moment when he stopped the action, and the entire audience was stunned into breathless silence. We all thought he'd lost it. 'I've had enough of this!' he declared loudly, wiping off his make-up as he moved to the front of the stage. But it turned out to be a part of the play within the play! I did not take a breath until he revealed the plot, and I've never experienced a moment like that in any actor's performance since that day.

The inimitable John Malkovich delivered a spine-chilling portrayal of a psychopath in *Burn*, and I saw the late, Dennis Waterman in the comedy *Jeffrey Bernard Is Unwell*. Ben Elton's *Gasping* was very provocative, based on the premise that one day we may have to pay for breathing air, which may come to pass! I caught the lovely Eric Sykes in the old classic *Run for your Wife* and he was quite chuffed when I visited him after the show. I went to see Australian actor Michael Kormick in *Phantom of the Opera*, and I said hello to him as well. It was a given that I would catch Willy Russell's latest smash hit, *Blood Brothers*. It was fabulous! A few years later, I'd see Helen Reddy play the lead on Broadway, where she absolutely blitzed them. My only complaint would be that these beautiful theatres were built for a different generation, and with seating that had cramped my elongated frame. Oh and the air-conditioning? There isn't any!

Panic Attack

The Sellers had been wonderful hosts for the previous couple of weeks, but I knew I'd have to find my own digs. I was expecting a prolonged stay in England. Tony Brady, my Australian manager, had pulled the old mates act with a London agent who booked several shows for me, mostly up north. I'd worked for clubs and other entertainment venues in the 1960s and the 1970s, and the memories weren't all that pleasant. I thought, okay, this is the 1990s, and things will be much improved by now. The list of clubs came through, but I didn't recognise any of them. I put aside the schedule and went out in search of affordable accommodation. The first places I looked at, the ones in my price range, could best be described as dreadful, dank, dark, and dangerously malodorous. Fagin would have turned up his considerable nose at these crappy rip-offs. Initially, I thought they weren't even fit to house wild pigs, and then I decided that they were. The apartments that didn't offend my sense of decency needed the income of an oil sheik to afford the keys. Anyone who has tried to chase down reasonably priced, quality lodgings in Greater London will attest to my frustrations.

I was sent from one disaster to another. I was becoming somewhat desperate, as I really did have to move. The Sellers had kindly extended my stay by a couple of days to help me in my search. Finally, I settled on a compromise, so on 2 September, I moved into 1 Princess Mews. I think the word mews is from the Shakespearian, meaning minuscule. It was like being Gulliver in the land of Lilliput. As I had experienced in the Shaftesbury Avenue theatres, there seemed nowhere to stretch. I had to accept this constricted arrangement because, frankly, it was the best of the bunch. I would have to accept the tiny shower with its previous occupants' hair plugging the drain, the two battered cooking pots in the windowless kitchen, the ancient tele; it was as if Steptoe and Son had furnished the place, and all this for the equivalent of $1000 a week (and this was in the '90s!). My planned working holiday started to take on the aspects of a real holiday abroad. Not that I would have chosen my current surroundings if I were inclined to take holidays. I pacified myself with the knowledge that the impending cabaret bookings would help to take the strain off my wallet.

The first of my bookings was upon me, and I rented a car for the trip north to Cleethorpes in Lincolnshire. I hopped into my rented vehicle, which had to be parked three blocks away, due to the fact that only owner-residents merited free parking at the mews. Undaunted, I set out in the fresh morning air. It was late afternoon when I reached the Beach Haven Club, being stopped by a boom gate at the entrance. There, a stern-faced middle-aged lady had to be convinced twice, because I wasn't on her list, that I was indeed the entertainer performing that night. After checking, Nurse Ratched thrust a tagged key into my hand muttering, 'You're in bungalow 17,' before slamming the booth's window shut. Winding around the complex I found bungalow 17. The asbestos and wooden structure consisted of a bedroom, small living room, and a shower and toilet that smelled like a mixture of chlorine, urine and vomit. The old double bed was home to a much-stained mattress, two rolled up blankets, along with two pillows, sans covers; a note on the bed read 'If sheets or pillowslips are required, call this number'. Suddenly my London mews didn't seem so bad.

Deciding to book into a small hotel in town, I headed off to rehearsals. I found I was top of the bill at the old-style variety concert with singers, sight acts, compere and a small ballet. It amused me that on the poster advertising the show, my billing was the man who sings the *Neighbours* theme. The band played well, the show was spiffing, I even had to sing an encore of *Neighbours*. I was happy to return to the clean sheets of the hotel for a good night's sleep before setting off for the next gig.

When I arrived for the second show in St Leonard's, Lincolnshire it hit me right in the gut that I'd made a terrible mistake. This was no stroll in the park where I could pick up a few easy quid to cover expenses. I had no complaints as far

Julie Anthony, Eddie Natt and 'The Hat'.

as the audience reaction was concerned, but the thought of traipsing around Britain, working in such demoralising conditions, brought on what I would later recognise as my first panic attack. In the 1960s, I could have seen the situation through, but not anymore. When one has already been there and done that, repeating the experience only saps one's self-confidence.

There were about five days to go before my next planned show, at the other end of England. I had some time to figure out a way to escape my obligations, and sitting in my little mews bedsit, I realised that I had to get out before any more damage could be inflicted upon my spiritual and artistic ego. I used the fact that my closest boyhood friend, Ron Brockenshire, was dying of mesothelioma. Ron, a carpenter, was only a year older than I was. I had been informed that he didn't have long to live, so I called the agent who had booked me to explain the situation to him, and I begged off the remaining work. This didn't go down well at all, as he'd heard very positive vibes back from the earlier shows, and if his artists performed well, this was good news for his future business. He did not want to let me out of the contract, but I insisted that I had to be on the plane home on the approaching weekend. He turned understandably nasty, threatening to sue. I told him there were a thousand acts that would be begging to take over my gigs. I also said I wanted no payment for the two completed shows, and I expected this would provide some compensation for him. This whole shameful scene would not read well down the line, but my whole being was screaming to leave.

I advised the mews owner that I'd been called back to Australia urgently. I told him I would pay the extra week's rent and he could also keep the bond money. I'd been in touch with Ron's wife Noeline to inform her that my plans had changed, and that I would be coming home earlier, but I was going to stop off in Los Angeles for a day or two, to say hello to my dear friend Helen Reddy. I told Noeline to tell Ronnie to hang on, but when I reached Helen's home, there was a message from Noeline telling me to take my time. Ron had passed over while I was in the air. I still had an aching feeling about using his terminal illness as an excuse to escape London, but knowing him as well as did, I could hear him saying, 'Baz, don't let the bastards beat ya, go for it! No worries.'

La La Land

The California sunshine seemed to soothe and to calm me. The laid-back atmosphere at Helen's home was precisely what my constitution needed, to help deliver me from the panic attacks that had occurred towards the end of my stay in England. As usual, Helen was the perfect hostess. I could sleep in as long as I wanted, the larder was open for any delights I might find to my liking, and in the evenings we'd share lavish dinners in Hollywood's finest restaurants. In addition, she would take me along to special gatherings, where some of the great film stars of the past would congregate, once a month, at the 213 Party.

This higher echelon of stars who had their peaks during past generations, would congregate once a month in order to reminisce and catch up with each other's lives. Time marches on, and most of the people in the photographs are no longer with us, and therefore the ranks of the 213 are somewhat diminished. Helen had been invited along to one of these gatherings by Army Archerd and his wife Selma, and she asked if she could bring her house guest. 'Absolutely!' said Army, then one of Hollywood's most influential columnists, who wrote a daily column for *Variety* from 1953 to 2005. I was introduced to each and every one at the party, and each and every one of them made me welcome, only too pleased to embrace this interloper and chat away. Many of them were interested in life Down Under, and I was delighted to impart my knowledge.

As you can see by the photos taken that evening, I was in my element, mixing shoulder to shoulder with faces I'd been admiring on the big screen for as long as I could remember. Craig Stevens, who had played Peter Gunn in the television show, was there with his wife, Alexis Smith, along with Cesar Romero, mostly

remembered as The Joker in the 1960s *Batman* television series, and Ricardo Montalban, of *Fantasy Island* fame.

Eventually I knew this recuperation had to end. I thanked Helen for bringing me back to sanity, before I went off to board the Qantas jet in time to catch Katy's opening at the Sydney Opera House on 25 September, where she was starring in Nöel Coward's *Blithe Spirit*. Katy had been chosen to play the role of Elvira the ghost, along with an impressive cast, including Rowena Wallace, Donald McDonald, and June Salter as Madame Arcati.

I had arrived home way ahead of schedule so Tony Brady let the local venues know I was available for work again, and the bookings started to arrive, building once again to a packed Carols by Candlelight season to finish off the year.

After a lovely Christmas with all of the family, followed by the New Year celebrations, Katy flew out on 13 January 1991, bound for Britain and America.

The rest of 1991 turned out to be one of my busiest periods. There were cabaret and concert appearances, with seasons of *Educating Rita* in Wollongong and Brisbane. Katy and I shared a fabulous apartment right on the river in Bris-vegas. Each evening, we would watch the sun going down. Reclining there on our balcony, we'd visually imbibe in the combination of the city's neon lights coming to life, blending in with the fading of the late afternoon glow. As the varied sources of lighting merged, contrasting with the liquid black licorice of the winding Brisbane River, the effect was nothing less than breathtaking. I wanted to stay for ever on that balcony, but we knew we had to drag ourselves away from our reverie. The evening performance at the QPAC Theatre was beckoning.

It was a pleasure for me to make an appearance on the hit television comedy series *Fast Forward*. In a send-up cabaret scene, I was required to sing Helen Reddy's biggest hit, 'I Am Woman'. The joke went down a treat and Steve Vizard asked if he could use the gag as an introduction to his Agony Aunt section on his show. I agreed.

The final realisation of the jest came to fruition at a Hats Off concert at Star City in Sydney in 2005, held to raise funds for the Oz Showbiz Cares/Equity Fights Aids charity. I was asked to reprieve the old joke. When I finished singing 'I Am Woman' in front of the packed house, Helen Reddy herself stormed from the wings, grabbed me by the ear, and dragged me off the stage to tumultuous applause. Helen, who had retired from showbiz by then, was doing her old mate one more favour.

At Christmas, the carols took me across the country yet again, and before I knew it we were singing 'Auld Lang Syne', and 1992 was upon us, with the promise of plenty of work for both Katy and me.

On 22 February, we were invited to the Governor's garden party at Government House, to meet the Queen and Prince Phillip. Katy is a true monarchist, and she bought the biggest hat I've ever seen, lapping up the royal occasion perhaps more than anybody. But I had to laugh at that hat! Shuussh. Even she admits that her headwear was a bit over the top (where else would it be?), and I have been forbidden to use a picture of it in this book – as if I would!

Early in the year, it was a real joy when my son Barry and I sang 'The Heat Is On' on Ray Martin's *The Midday Show*. Barry had been working as director of lighting at Channel Nine for some time, and every once in a while Ray would feature my boy, having him perform a solo, or even a duet with me. On this particular day, I was amused to peruse the show's rundown sheet which read 'Heat Is On', sung by Barry Crocker and his father! His very proud father, that is.

During his time at Channel Nine, Barry had become more and more involved with the church he had been attending, and felt he needed to participate more in what he strongly felt could be his future, so after 15 years he would leave Nine to pursue his dream. He became a Pentecostal pastor, and through his church duties, travelled to many distant countries. Spreading the word, he travelled to places like Hong Kong, Cambodia and many more. Barry Jr always had a hankering to go back to America and put inquiries in through the church, to bring this to fruition. The papers came through confirming that everything was in place for him to go; so along with his wife, Suzie, and children James and Faith, they moved to America, taking on a job that he believed he was destined to do. He was originally given a five-year contract as Worship Pastor and Creative Arts Director at a Los Angeles church, where he organised the pageants and the choirs, a regular feature of the church's musical offerings. He impressed the church elders enough to be allocated his own worship centre, as head pastor of the Hope Church in Santa Monica. Barry and his wife, along with the rest of his family, would build a new congregation from scratch.

Barry would also travel to the Far East to establish his church in destitute communities, helping to bring much-needed technology to the masses. They, along with local church members, would build new dwellings for the locals, and establish clean drinking water wells. During the worldwide 2019–21 pandemic, his church was honoured for their work in feeding and clothing the poor in Santa Monica. He had finally fulfilled his dream, and I couldn't have been more pleased for my son.

When he turned 60, leaving Los Angeles and the Hope Church behind, he decided that he needed to take a new direction in life, and along with Suzie, they are now running a vacation rental business in the township of Crestline in the San Bernardino Mountains, California. The company called The Dogwood Cabins is situated close to Lake Gregory.

A footnote to the California Crockers, Barry Jr's son, James, is now a fully commissioned Pentecostal pastor with *his* own church in Los Angeles, and recently became father to a son, Henry Hugh Crocker; ah, the dynasty continues on.

A Matter of Health

Every once in a while a positive run of health can come crashing down with a thud, and I experienced this when I started to feel slightly under par, with the sort of symptoms that usually appear during a bout of the flu. On 8 July, I was fulfilling a promise I'd made to my two daughters, Martine and Erica that I would be the guest speaker at the Hillsong Conference in Castle Hill. At the time, they were both members of the church, and they wanted me to speak to the congregation about the art and joys of singing. This annual get-together, where people come from all over the country, was a much heralded event, and after my little speech and a couple of songs, where I had been warmly acknowledged by the packed auditorium, I decided to head home. The girls waved me off as I headed home to Wahroonga, only a 20-minute drive away. While driving along Castle Hill Road, I had trouble focusing on the road ahead. I was losing sight in my right eye, and my overall vision seemed to be deteriorating quickly. I pulled over to the side of the road. It was as if I were wearing kaleidoscopic spectacles. Glowing, zigzagging, prismatic images were spinning around the perimeters of my field of vision. I sat in the car and waited a good 25 minutes before my erratic eyesight returned to a level acceptable enough for me to resume driving. I was glad to get home and get a cup of hot tea into me, but this episode wasn't over yet.

The next morning, at about 4 am, I awoke with an awful start and sat bolt upright in bed. My entire body was drenched in sweat, and I was shaking uncontrollably, with an overwhelming feeling of despair. In my 58 years of life, I had never experienced anything like this before, and I thought I must be suffering a heart attack. I found myself alone in Dr Ludiwici's waiting room, in order to make sure I would be his first patient for the day.

David Ludiwici was a little perplexed, he had never known me to be up this early, but he could see that I wasn't my usual chirpy self. He performed all the standard tests, including blood pressure, miniature torchlight to the eyes, ears, nose, and throat, checked my reflexes and placed his cold stethoscope on various parts of my skinny chest, listening intently for any extraordinary rumblings within the vicinity of my heart. Apparently, there was nothing wrong with me. Physically, I was A1. The doctor suggested that I may have simply had an anxiety attack.

'No!' I protested. 'I had them in England, and they were nothing like this.'

'I'll prescribe some Anginine,' he said, 'and if you feel any pain in your chest, pop one of those. In the meantime, I'll book you in for some tests at the Sydney Adventist Hospital, in order to be sure.' I hate to confess this, but I've had that unopened bottle of Anginine sitting in my medicine cabinet since July 1993, and I really must get around to throwing it out.

At the SAH I had an angiogram test which proved all was well with my heart, but I had an amazing circumstance present itself while undergoing the procedure.

Before the doctor arrived for the test, the head matron in my ward approached my bed. 'Mr Crocker, I believe you may know my mother,' said the matron. 'Her maiden name was, Rogers, Merle Rogers? She tells me you used to be in the Geelong Musical Comedy Company together.'

Was it the medication? I thought I must be dreaming, resisting a compulsion to pinch myself in an effort to see if I was awake. Merle Rogers was the most beautiful girl in the GMCC, and I had been too deathly shy to ask her out, although I had wanted to do so when Doreen and I had briefly broken up. Merle's daughter filled me in with what had transpired in the intervening years, and all at once I felt connected. I knew my body was in good hands, and I was ready to take on the probe.

But they hadn't finished with me yet. I would have CAT scans, MRI examinations, and X-rays. After the results were all assembled and compared, the medics all came to the same conclusion, repeating ever-so-authoritatively that there was nothing wrong with me physically. But why was I feeling so poorly? As a last resort, I was booked into the SAH again for more pathology tests, and there was also a rescheduling of chest X-rays. Some of my friends had tried to frighten me with horror stories about certain pathology tests.

When it came time for mine, having subsisted on fluids for the previous three days, I entered the hospital ward feeling decidedly weak and vulnerable. Now let me say this, before we go any further; I don't care if you're a pop star, a sporting hero, or next in line to the throne, there is no way for you to retain even a semblance of dignity when you are lying on a stainless steel table on your side, with a flimsy backless gown tied loosely around your neck, and a masked stranger preparing to insert a metal-and-plastic tube into the sanctity of your rectum. This is the dilemma faced by a patient awaiting the application of a barium enema. You may laugh, my friends, but sooner or later, it could possibly happen to you. My exposed rear end was facing the apparatus when a cheerful middle-aged sister, whose name was Sue, looked over me and reassured me with the words, 'You've brought a lot of joy to a lot of people, Mr Crocker! They'll be coming for you shortly.'

My stomach warbled, like a slow-leaking inner tube, as I contemplated Sue's ominous words. Was she trying to tell me something? I tried to think of all the people to whom I may have given joy. I wondered how much joy I would bring to them if they could see me now, lying naked on a steel table with a hose shoved up my anal orifice. Sue had brought in a copy of the day's *Daily Telegraph* to keep my intellect occupied while I waited for the medical technicians to commence their unenviable work. It was 16 August, the birthday of Bruce Beresford, Madonna, and Geoff Thompson. It was also the fifteenth anniversary of Elvis Presley's death.

They gave me a knock-out needle before I was wheeled along various two-toned corridors towards the operating theatre. As the trolley was moving, and as in every hospital movie you've ever seen, I had the patient's-eye view of the fluorescent ceiling lights passing over my head. I was chattering, in an increasingly drunken manner, to my wheelers, when I thought I recognised an enchanting female face looking down at me. 'What are you doing here?' I emitted, wondering if I was still awake. 'I work here!' came the beautiful lady's reply. The overhead fluoros started melting into one another, and, in my last second of consciousness, I knew that the last person taking part in my degradation was Sohodra, a qualified nurse and the wife of popular singer Kamahl, my friend and competitor.

Throughout all of the tests, no evidence was found of what had instigated my initial illness, but I did suffer further anxiety attacks, and over a period of months I lost between two and three stone in weight. Katy remained strong and supportive. She forced me to attend openings, and to continue with my social activities and obligations. I wanted only to hide away from the world. I surprised myself by continuing to work in all fields of entertainment, and I maintained a reasonable appearance, courtesy of the low lighting in most of the clubs I played, although my suits really were hanging off me.

Goodbye Wahroonga

To alleviate the stress of keeping the house and garden going, those around me were suggesting that I should seriously think about downsizing my abode. Erica, my third daughter, and I were sharing a very large house. With her own water business she was up before dawn, and didn't return until the evening, so we saw very little of each other. It came to pass that my beautiful Wahroonga dream home was placed on the market, and I began the hunt for a suitable apartment. Very few of the properties that I inspected met with my satisfaction, and there was always the comparison with my lovely bush paradise floating in the back of my mind. Simon, my stepson, came up with the perfect solution. At the time, he worked in the used luxury car business, and his wealthy boss had decided to upgrade to a larger apartment in the same central city building.

Simon was onto it straight away. He arranged for me to inspect the two-bedroom unit, which looked right out onto Hyde Park. The position was perfect, close to all the action. The view from the balcony of the park's tree-lined expanse would remind me of Wahroonga. Negotiations were started. I aimed to sell my house in time for a Christmas changeover that would suit both of the parties concerned. Much dedicated labour was required to re-establish the gardens' past glory, and the work was particularly hard going for me, considering the delicate balance of my health.

The property didn't achieve the anticipated price when a young family eventually took it over, but I loved the way the excited children raced around the house and garden, as my own young family had done back in 1967. In the 26 years that followed, so much joy, and some sadness too, had been shared within those walls.

On 24 December 1993 all the members of the family sat down to share our last Christmas dinner at Exeter Road. We had watched each other grow and change in that house, we had laughed together, and we had cried together. Leaving the house was the biggest challenge of them all. We spent the rest of the festive period sorting out 26 years of accumulated memories, packing it all into boxes, crates and cases. Doreen and the kids took it in turns to push me along, urging this inveterate hoarder to throw a lot of space-taking ephemera away. My offspring had split into several camps, with their own houses and apartments, so a lot of my discarded stuff soon found a new home.

The new year arrived and it took from January 3 to 6 to move me into my new home. It has been said that, on a par with a death in the family, or a divorce, or a bankruptcy, moving house is a most stressful experience, and I readily agree with that opinion. Katy had missed all the drama. She had been on her annual Christmas trip to England to visit her mother.

Breaking New Ground

Feeling, a little healthier now, it would be Katy who would steer me onto a new path yet again, insisting I take up the offer to join the Doug Anthony All Stars for a one-off spot on their ABC television show *The Big Gig*.

Katy had caught the comedy singing trio live in Adelaide, where she was appearing in Neil Simon's *The Odd Couple*. The boys had been taking part in the South Australian Comedy Festival. After their own show closed each night, Katy, along with her friend and co-star, Penny Whitely, took her seat in the front row of the comedy festival, where she laughed herself sick at the antics of the DA All Stars. Over the community pool table, the parties introduced themselves to each other. The three young men, especially Tim Ferguson, were big *Doctor Who* fans, and they were impressed to be meeting Jo Grant, aka Katy Manning, in the flesh. They confessed to Katy that they were secret Barry Crocker fans, not for the Bazza McKenzie movies, but they had been taking note of my cabaret shows for years. The ABC television corridors in Melbourne had been decorated with very large stars of the past posters. The boys had fallen in love with the safari-suited lothario that had once roamed the old studios, and they claimed me as their main inspiration.

My first reaction to the prospect of joining the boys on national television was that of inestimable terror. Here were three of the trendiest new stars on Australian television, welcoming an old-timer like me into their midst. I risked the chance of being sent up no end, and I let Katy know it. Barry Humphries had once advised me, 'If you don't go over the top, you'll never know what's on the other side.' So with nervous apprehension jingling in my belly, the Doug Anthony All Stars and I met to discuss our forthcoming television spot. I was surprised at how the three articulate young men differed from their media personas, where they came across as foul mouthed, aggressive and anti-establishment. They had been university students together in Canberra, having met through the student revues. We started working on the script.

I thought that these guys would have a preconceived, well-written layout, but all they had was an idea at best. Their method was to start off with a premise, and then ad lib until something formed that resembled a funny sketch. Paul McDermott, the perceived leader of the group, had seen the Five Blind Boys of Alabama, an all-blind African American blues singing group, performing on television, and he thought that a white version of the band could raise a few laughs. Initially, I couldn't understand how this would be all that funny, and I was thinking the irreverent attitude of these three youngsters was even a little sick. Nevertheless, the Five White Blind Boys were going to make their appearance on national television, and I relished the task ahead. From the days of Crocker and Clark, I was enthused by the idea of improvisation before a live audience.

Comedian Paul Livingstone, universally known as the clownish Flacco, was brought in to make up the quintet. Up to the very minute of our entrance on nationwide television, we were still working on the shaky script. The studio audience went along with the joke, and there was one unrehearsed moment when I removed my conspicuous dark glasses, proclaiming loudly, 'I've seen the light, I've seen the light, and it blinded me!' I then walked into a wall.

I could hardly believe the positive vibes created by my appearance with the DAAS team. At first, when introduced to the audience as the show's special guest, I thought the roar that followed was a send-up, but no, I had been accepted as one of the team. Popular television presenter Andrew Denton was impressed enough to invite us all to be a part of his new program, *The Money or the Gun*.

Upon my arrival at the ABC studios that day, I was greeted by the boys in the rehearsal room, all expressing looks of abject consternation. None of them had come up with anything innovative enough for a decent sketch. 'Everything's been done, Bazza, we're stuffed,' Paul McDermott proclaimed.

Were they doing a leg-pull? I'd expected that I would walk in and add a few little touches of my own. There had been a running musical gag on Denton's show each week. Every high-profile showbiz act would perform its own rendition of 'Stairway to Heaven', the iconic hit song made famous by Led Zeppelin. It had been rocked, swung, recited, and bent in every which way by the inventive minds of the many artists who had tackled the song.

Composer Robert Plant had never explained the real meaning of the lyrics,

Katy and I with the Doug Anthony All-Stars.

which start off quite normally, mentioning a lady who's sure all that glitters is gold, and she's buying a stairway to heaven. But the song soon muddies up by telling the listeners about a bustle in your hedgerow, and they must not be alarmed, pointing out that spring cleaning is due for the May Queen. An idea came to me in a flash. I would utilize the personality of Professor Frank from *Educating Rita*. The boys were slightly desperate by then, ready to grab at any straw that was offered. They jumped at my suggestion. I would explain the true meaning of the lyrics after each line had been sung. The other guys would sing, and I would explain. On air, my ad-libbed explanations were more nonsensical than the original song lyrics. I spoke in edifying gobbledygook!

At the end of the song, I said something like, 'There you have it folks, the true meaning of "Stairway to Heaven".' Paul looked at the camera, then at Tim and Richard, then up at me, crying, 'It all sounds like bullshit to me, Barry!'

The audience exploded in laughter. An idea plucked from the air had triumphed!

The DAAS disbanded in 1994, but they would later reunite briefly for my appearance on *This Is Your Life* in 2005. Katy's determination in getting me to move forward, as opposed to dwelling on my past achievements, led to appearances on many of the younger demographic's television shows, and I was asked to record with alternative music groups. I sang lead on 'Crazy Little Thing Called Love' with Front End Loader, and I warbled on 'Six Days on the Road' with The Celibate Rifles. I recorded with The Robertson Brothers on a song they'd written, called 'Ticker Tocker Shocker Man', which made great use of the rhyming slang that my surname regularly invoked. As with the DAAS, I'd been a little reluctant at first to co-inhabit the recording studios with these groups, expecting their members to be wild and undisciplined, but nothing could have been further from the truth. These young people were accomplished musicians and we all had a good time putting down the tracks. It was fun to appear on Channel Nine's *Hey Hey It's Saturday*, singing lead with The Badloves on a rendition of their hit single 'Green Limousine'. My other, more conventional work was flowing along in tandem with the new stuff.

Liza with a Katy

Prior to that year's televising of the People's Choice Awards, Katy had flown out to join Liza Minnelli in New York. The diva had called Katy urgently to help her with several assignments. Being the best mates that they were, there was a trust between the two that Liza shared with no other person, so I warily had to accept the situation.

In January 1995, I was visiting Katy in California, rekindling our relationship at the beautiful home of Chet and Dallas Clark in Santa Barbara. Katy, apart from helping her old pal Liza, was writing her first play, titled *Not a Well Woman*. She'd been away from home for several months, so we had a little catching up to do. We walked and talked for hours, soaking in the scenery and enjoying the appetising delights of the many eateries. In one of the many jazz clubs, Chet and I jammed together, to the enthusiastic applause of the locals. However, our idyllic holiday was disturbed by Liza Minnelli's constant phone calls, and Katy felt obliged to return to Los Angeles. Liza relied on her former constant companion, Katy, to be on hand whenever anything became a bit too overwhelming. The two ladies had travelled together all over the States and Europe, but Liza was becoming so dependent on her friend that Katy's own career was suffering as a result.

Nevertheless, a lot of pleasurable moments were spent in Liza's pad in West Hollywood. There was a Minnelli family tradition going back to the days of Judy Garland, when Saturday night parties were held, gathering around the old piano for a good old-fashioned singalong. Liza was determined to keep this tradition going, and her parties were the hottest ticket in town. Every would-be star and his pedigree dog wanted to be seen there, testing their vocal chords in front of their peers. Mel Torme's son, Steve March, was a regular, as were the sons and daughters of many older stars, hoping to be discovered by the likes of Cy Coleman, who had written *Barnum* and *Sweet Charity*. Some of the other attendees were Whoopi Goldberg, Natalie Cole and Michael Douglas. On a couple of occasions, I joined in and contributed a couple of songs as well.

No-one cared who the hell I was, but the deeply suntanned George Hamilton kindly told me that I had a good voice, and I should think about a singing career. Thanks, George!

Liza would naturally dominate the evening's singing. After performing her songs absolutely magnificently, she would whisper to Katy, 'D'you think I was okay?' Liza's remarks brought home to me the reality that even the most accomplished stars can sometimes need reassurance. Over the next two years, Katy and I spent more time apart than together, due to the demands placed on her by Liza Minnelli's heavy workload. Katy was certainly living the high life, but she was losing out by neglecting her own career, and her self-penned play was put on hold for the time being.

And All That Jazz

In March 1995, my first *great*-grandson, Wade was born. Now I had positive proof that I must be getting on.

In 1996 I recorded *BAZAZZ*, my first jazz CD. Although I'd recorded over 25 albums prior to this, they'd all been mainly show tunes and popular songs, but jazz is basically at my core. The first time I recognised the sounds of augmented chords, my musical soul had found its home. On the album, I worked with the great jazz pianist Dave MacRae, the father of pop diva Jade MacRae. Dave's main claim to fame was his composition of the music for *The Goodies* television comedy in the 1970s. I'd finally succumbed to recording something that would feed my soul, as jazz has always been a hard sell. It's almost impossible to describe the feeling a singer gets when an improvisation that he's created blends together with a beautiful song, but I'll try ... for those who love their sweets, a freshly baked pavlova, and for druggies, a bliss bomb.

After a six-week tour of New Zealand with *Fiddler on the Roof*, I finished recording my second jazz CD, titled *Reflections*. Several of the songs were my own compositions, and I worked once again with Dave MacRae. The CD was perhaps my most personal since *No Regrets*.

A Firework Spectacular

In 1977, I had been the first singer to perform 'Advance Australia Fair' at a football grand final of any code at the MCG, and since then many performers have followed in my wake, but 1996 would be special, as it was the 100-year anniversary of Australian Rules. The organisers had pulled out all the stops by inviting many of the singers who had graced the hallowed turf before to join in the celebration of this milestone. Among those who shared the stage that year were Olivia Newton-John, John Farnham, Glenn Shorrock, Normie Rowe, Diana Trask, Venetta Fields, Mike Brady, and country music legend Slim Dusty.

Two days of rehearsals and prerecording had the entertainment section of the show looking polished. We rehearsed the firework spectacular that would make up the centre piece of the show, but without the actual fireworks. We were simply instructed to stay away from certain areas of the stage during a particular part of the routine. I would learn a valuable lesson on the day of the grand final: when working with fireworks, always demand a demo beforehand!

When the cue was given for the explosion, a dazzling spectacle was created, as if David Copperfield himself had made all the entertainers disappear into thin air. Speaking of thin air, that's exactly what we were forced to breathe, with our lungs totally overpowered by smoke and ash, and for a brief moment I thought there was going to be a mass suffocation of many of Australia's top entertainers. We all covered our mouths and noses with our hands, but the black cloud was all-enveloping as we gasped, coughed and spluttered. If the strong wind, which had earlier deflated a giant plastic effigy of Wayne Carey, hadn't come to our rescue, it would have been a rather nasty beginning to a grand final! The television director pulled the cameras away from the doubled-over asphyxiating stars, definitely not looking their most glamorous on this occasion. There was a lot of 'That was close!' and 'I thought we were a goner!' but no-one said, 'Let's get the pyrotechnic bastard who almost killed us!'

It was Grand Final day and the air was palpable with good will. Earlier that day, we entertainers had joined some of history's football greats, along with members of the Olympic team, for lunch in the main grandstand. It was a profound moment to sit with some of my past heroes and to be able to chat to them as equals. The two teams playing that day were North Melbourne and the Sydney Swans, my second team after the Geelong Cats. Will Dower, who had been my drummer on TV and in cabaret for many years, was a huge Sydney fan. As Katy was still overseas, I invited Will to have my spare ticket. This was heaven for a mad footy fan like Will, who had played Aussie Rules in Western Australia. He was blown away to be mixing with his idols and the Olympic champions. I took photos of him with Cathy Freeman and the Oarsome Foursome. I enjoyed my usual banter with Bobby Davis and Lou Richards.

All was right with my world this last Saturday in September. Only one thing spoiled the party, apart from the gun powder, and that was seeing the Swans get thrashed.

A Crocky Horror Show

In August 1998, my first great-granddaughter, Amber, was born to my granddaughter Camilla.

In October 1998, I took over from Red Symons as the narrator in *The Rocky Horror Show* at Sydney's Star City, and it was a joy to catch up again with Tim Ferguson, who was playing the transvestite Frank-N-Furter. Also in the cast were Wilbur Wilde, whose hilarity swept through the corridors, Totti Goldsmith and Jay La'gaia. I loved being with the theatre crowd each night, and it made me realise how much I'd missed the experience. I was reluctant to leave the show when Red returned from his five-week absence.

Earlier, in 1996, when there was nothing on the horizon for me in theatre, I had my first crack at writing my own piece. At Woolloomooloo's old Tilbury Hotel, there was a series of reviews for Sydney's divas called Almost a Legend. Toni Lamond, Maria Venuti, Jeanne Little, Kerrie Biddell and Judi Connelli were some of the names who played the venue. I talked the owners into letting me be the first man to have a go. So I became the only male Almost a Legend diva.

The piece I'd written was called *The Observatorium*. The premise was set in the future, when the world's population explodes unacceptably. In this mythical scenario, each individual reaching 50 years of age is called into an observation room, called the observatorium, where unseen assessors judge the worthiness of the candidates to remain living. I'd prerecorded the voice of an electronic god, with me impersonating the booming camp voice of actor Frank Thring. The god would pass judgement on my performance. I had timed the passages of dialogue so I could have arguments with the electronic voice. I was harshly lit, with a single spotlight shining down from above. The god would demand of me why I should be allowed to continue in my chosen profession, and not be jettisoned into space to make room for others? This device, of course, gave me the chance to tell the story of my life through comedy and song. The alter ego voice would be constantly denigrating me, but in the end I would triumph, as I would be judged by the assessors in the dark, namely the audience, by their applause, and therefore be allowed to remain on the planet.

In the end, the Thring god turned

Rocky Horror gets a visit from David Hasselhoff.

out to be myself, challenging my own fears and trepidations. My message was that we are constantly questioning our own worth. I had a satisfying short run at the Tilbury and a couple of weeks at Sorlie's Dinner Theatre in Frenchs Forest. Creating this piece, had whetted my appetite to do something bigger and better in the future.

An Evening with Pavarotti

Sydney's new 190-million-dollar giant Superdome at Homebush would have its unofficial opening on Saturday 4 September 1999, and I was asked to sing the national anthem. The official opening would be performed by Premier Bob Carr in November. Once more, as with the Sydney Opera House, where I'd performed in the main concert hall months before the Queen's official opening, I had been lucky enough to be first on the podium. I was beginning to think, are they using me as a test dummy?

On Saturday 6 November, Katy and I visited the Superdome to see the famed Luciano Pavarotti performing selections from the celebrated operas. The difference between the protocols that surround a performance by the classical artist and we cabaret and concert performers is really quite fascinating. Where we are simply introduced and burst out onto the stage for our hour or so in the spotlight, the etiquette that accompanied the Evening with Pavarotti was truly revealing. After the lead violinist instigates an elongated tuning session with the orchestra, he leaves the stage, only to return almost immediately to a round of applause. The lead violinist then motions his hand toward the side and the conductor enters, once again to the sound of much applause. At the conducting podium, he and the lead violinist shake hands. By now a hush has fallen over the audience, and the air of expectancy erupts into rapturous applause when the spotlight spins to catch the great tenor's entrance. Once on centre stage, Pavarotti shakes hands with the conductor, and then with the lead violinist. The orchestra follows, with a lengthy introduction of several bars before the voice opens up. In cabaret, we use that opening as our entrance music, so we can start singing the moment we hit centre. On this particular evening, Pavarotti sang a beautiful bright aria that was greeted with great warmth by the audience. 'Great opening,' I thought, but then the singer turned and left the stage, closely followed by the conductor. Had something gone wrong? The sudden break was graciously accepted by the audience. When the applause subsided, the conductor returned, once again to an ovation, and the tenor came on for his second rendition of one of the classics. This had been my first ever attendance at a recital. I had been to the traditional opera many times before, but operas keep on going until the fat lady sings.

This ritual of leaving the stage after each song was very new to me, and I shudder to think what would happen if I'd dared to try this rigmarole in my act. There was also a female guest star who sang the odd duet with Pavarotti, but that didn't alter the rhythm. When they finished their piece, she would lead him off, and the routine would pick up again from there. There was only one time in the whole concert, when the illustrious tenor stayed on for two songs in a row. There is a theory that tenors have to spit a lot, and that is why they leave the stage. To add credence to the supposition, maybe that is why Pavarotti always carried that oversized handkerchief.

Me and Jezebel

My stepson Simon, who had gone to Los Angeles to work for Katy and Liza in a business they were putting together, arrived back in Australia to spend Christmas with the family. He brought along his actor girlfriend, Nicollette Sheridan, well known at the time for her long stint on the US television series *Knot's landing*, playing Paige Mathieson from 1986 to 1993. Simon was demonstrably proud of his new lady. Much later on, in 2004, her career would take off like a rocket when she was cast as Edie Britt in the smash hit series *Desperate Housewives*. There was a lot of catching up to do for Simon, and we managed to get a lot of the family together, not only for a lavish lunch in Double Bay, but we all went to the new concept opening of Andrew Lloyd Webber's *Cats*, held this time in a giant tent and subtitled *Cats in a Tent*. It had been a hectic interlude, and we poured an exhausted Nicolette and Simon onto the plane back to the USA. The next time I saw my stepson, the circumstances would be very different.

The year 2000 was upon us, and it would turn out to be perhaps my most creative year. In February, I found myself directing a two-hander play called *Me and Jezebel*. When I had first read the script, I knew the character of Elizabeth would be perfect for Katy, and I talked the producers into casting her. Then they surprised me by letting me take over the whole rigmarole. I had directed before, including my sketches, short pieces and television spots, but never a full length legitimate piece of theatre. I would have to rise to the challenge, directing the American star who had played her part many times already. Kelly Moore was an accomplished female impersonator, playing the lead role in this based-on-fact story of the time legendary actress Bette Davis went to visit one of her fans for a few days, and finished up staying on much longer.

This production would be tough on my actors. Glebe's Valhalla theatre was undergoing a drastic refurbishment, and we would be rehearsing there to save costs. The building was being transformed into two separate venues, as opposed to its original one, and we would have to put up with noisy building workers on the site. Our 200-seat theatre was complete, but the larger room under construction below was throwing out not only the constant sound of jackhammers, but a fine dust storm was constantly encroaching upon us. There was no air conditioning as yet, and we were still in the summer months. Katy Manning rehearses one way only, and that's flat out. Following her lead, I began to treat my actors like galley slaves, in order to keep the scenes rolling along. There is never enough time before opening night. I had to do my job to the utmost, because the writer of the play, Elizabeth Fuller, would be attending the opening. At the end of each day, I almost had to mop Katy up from the stage. I thought, one day Katy won't be there, I'll find only a puddle. Luckily, our American star was a very agreeable person, accepting the situation gracefully, and it was heartwarming and enlightening to be able to bring new nuances to his performance. Ever since the Valhalla experience, if I complain about anything when Katy is directing me, she only has to say, 'Valhalla!' and I retreat into my shell to think about my cruelty to her.

On Thursday 2 March, Elizabeth Fuller joined the 200 celebrity first-nighters to see what we'd done with her play. They spilled out into the foyer for the after-show party, and photographers bustled for the best shots. Congratulations were coming thick and fast for the producers and me. Elizabeth confessed that she started crying five minutes into the performance and her tears did not cease until the curtain came down. She told us that ours was the best production ever mounted, and she felt privileged that Katy brought her character to life with so much humour and passion.

Off the back of the fabulous reviews and the positive audience reaction, we envisaged a long run, but the production turned out to be undercapitalised. The producers were trying to stage two productions, the other an elaborate musical,

Me And Jezebel, Valhalla Theatre, 2000.

in the same theatre, at the same time. The more expensive show was planned for the larger Valhalla theatre, only two weeks after we'd opened. The idea looked good on paper, but the American producers, who travelled with the bigger piece, were demanding set changes and new production schedules. The larger production would drain the capital from the lesser *Me and Jezebel*, leaving us with no advertising budget whatsoever. No matter how good a show may be, if people don't know it's on or where it's playing, there's only a grim prognosis for its prospects of success.

Word-of-mouth promotion would lift our pathetic attendances a little, but the slowly increasing houses would come too late, as by then the bigger production had collapsed in debt. Both Katy and Kelly played the last week for no salary, in the hope that we might save the show, but many others weren't paid at all, and there was no option but to close the production down. We had lasted exactly one month, closing on 2 April. I made an offer to finance the play and take over its future, but my proposals were quickly rejected. Elizabeth, who was devastated by the show's unanticipated early demise, had plans of her own to deliver our production to theatres in Connecticut and other New York outlets, but theatre availability snookered the deals. However, I wasn't yet finished with *Jezebel*, not by a long shot.

CHAPTER 8

Rediscovering Banjo

In 1998, Katy and I attended the christening of Pauline McFetridge's grandson Jack. Pauline later became the chairperson of Miss World Australia, but back then, together with Tony Hatch, Jackie Trent, Penny Docherty, Max Markson, Barry Newman, Katy Manning and me, she had a big hand in producing the Heart Awards each year for Variety, the children's charity. Pauline knew that I had once appeared in the play, *Banjo the Man*. She asked if I could do Banjo Paterson's 'Bush Christening' at the party, as a special treat for the guests and little Jack. The poem was received enthusiastically. One guest cried out, 'Can you do *The Man from Snowy River*?' I felt almost guilty to decline, as I had never learned the poem in the five-hander all those years before. Even so, it got me thinking, the way the assembled guests had shown such interest in the works of Banjo Paterson, arguably Australia's most popular poet, as long dead as he was. *Banjo the Man* had provoked such a positive reaction on its early tour around Queensland, that when I'd finished with the show, I put together a little 12-minute montage of his poems, songs and stories, to be included in my cabaret act. Whenever I chose to perform it, the tribute to Banjo was always a popular highlight in my show.

After the christening, as we drove back into town, I shared my thoughts with Katy. 'Do you reckon I could get a one man show out of Banjo Paterson?' I asked her, somewhat rhetorically.

Deliberating for a moment on the question, she replied, 'Why don't you give it a shot? It's not as if you have anything to lose.' I took my senior advisor's remarks as a positive, and so I began my two long years of research and writing to bring *Barry Crocker's Banjo* to fruition.

Some things fall into place with a seamless fluidity, while others can be like having teeth

Katy and I celebrate our season at Sydney Opera House.

pulled out with rusty pliers, a pain from start to finish. I am thrilled to be able to tell you, dear reader, that the former held sway and not my childhood dentist!

My first important discovery was that Andrew Barton 'Banjo' Paterson had been to school a mere 200 metres from where I now resided. He had attended Sydney Grammar in College Street, Sydney. I thought there wouldn't be a great chance of the school's personnel helping with my research, but what the hell, I could only try. Almost apologetically, I phoned the school and asked to be put through to the headmaster. Dr John Valance took my call, and instead of the rebuff I'd expected, he had his secretary make an appointment to see me as soon as possible.

As I entered the historic stone building, with its lead-lined stained-glass windows, mahogany-panelled walls and heavily embossed doors, I felt distinctly out of my comfort zone. This intimidating complex of higher education had always been for the privileged classes, as far as I was concerned. Not for a moment had I ever expected to see the inside of such an institution, and yet here I was, about to engage in a serious discussion with its prestigious head. The boy who had left school behind at the age of 14 felt a fluttering of butterflies in his stomach.

I tapped on the secretary's open door somewhat shyly. 'I'll let the headmaster know you're here,' she said. 'He shouldn't be too long.'

I wanted to turn around and hurry back towards the entrance, but the secretary said, 'The headmaster will see you now, Mr Crocker,' and she opened the door to his room. There was a mile of polished oak bookshelves filled with heavy tomes, and a large desk piled with paperwork. It was like visiting the set of *Goodbye, Mr. Chips*. I was greeted with a warm handshake and a smile from a lively man in his forties. He welcomed me in, pointed me to a chair and asked kindly if I might care for a cup of tea or coffee. After the pleasantries, I outlined my plans to write a one-man play, based on the life of Banjo Paterson. Dr Valance thought it an inspiring idea, and marvellous publicity for the school. Letting the populace know that this college was where Mr Paterson received his education couldn't be bad at all. He suggested we visit the school's archival facilities. He introduced me to the head of the archive division, a lovely lady with the unusual name of Ily Benedek. She told the headmaster she would be glad to look after me, and I bade John farewell, thanking him for his time and his generous enthusiasm for my project.

'Now where would you like to start, Mr Crocker?' she asked. 'I've long been most fascinated with the life of Banjo Paterson, and if I can offer you any assistance with your project, it will be my great pleasure.' As we chatted, she showed me all kinds of Paterson memorabilia that she had accumulated over the years. It was then that I noticed a constant procession of students filing in and signing a huge book near the front entrance.

I asked Ily what they were doing. 'Oh, today is the last day of the school year, and the final-year students are signing out for the last time in our Records Almanac.'

A thought struck me, and I asked her, 'Do you have the book that Banjo signed? In or out? Both, if possible.'

There was something intrinsically special about the viewing of Paterson's own signature, and I found myself touching it with my fingertips, and pondering the significance of the course on which I had embarked. In the meantime, Ily's assistant, Anne Jasman, was photocopying a plethora of pictures and printed materials that we thought might be of use.

The constant stream of signing-out students fascinated me, and I asked Ily what usually happens on the last day of school. She explained that the boys were called to the big school, the main hall of learning, for farewell speeches and so forth. Usually, an Old Boy, as former students are known, would give a talk on what might lie ahead for the students. They would be reminded always to uphold the Sydney Grammar School motto, *Laus Deo*, meaning 'Praise Be to God'.

I asked Ily if it was possible, considering his achievements, that Banjo may have been a guest speaker at one of these end-of-year assemblies. She told me she wouldn't be able to check that out, as the presence of guest speakers was never recorded. But *Laus Deo*, for these people had given me the premise for the play. In my vision, Banjo would address the assembly in 1940. Knowing of his heart condition and realising that this could be the last time he would speak publicly, he would open up his life to the boys, dismissing the myths, and for the first time let the world in on the truth, revealing the real Banjo Paterson. It had been a fortuitous day. When I accepted the invitation, I'd had no inkling that this was the last day of the school year. If I had made my request to visit a few days later, I would have lost several weeks with my research, having to wait for the school to reopen, but fate had leaned in my favour.

In 1983, when I had toured with *Banjo the Man* throughout Queensland, the earlier play had presented a flawed and biased version of Banjo's life and character. Paterson's nieces, who owned the rights to his work, had editing licence as well. They could, and did, censor anything they found untoward. They had wanted to perpetuate the image of a nice old bloke who had had some stirring adventures, and along the way had helped to write 'Waltzing Matilda', the song most identified with the spirit of Australia.

I'd always felt a bit sorry for Bill Watson, the author of *Banjo the Man*. Bill had tried to touch on the juicer bits, but his work was nipped in the bud. He'd given in to literary pressure because his priority was to get the play up and running. Although the piece was roundly accepted, I always felt there was much more flesh and blood to this man called Banjo, and my detailed research would eventually confirm my instincts.

The Real Banjo Paterson

To complement the hefty amount of documents I had obtained from Sydney Grammar, I went out and bought as many unbiased biographies as I could find. The first major revelation was that young Andrew Barton Paterson had a badly impaired right arm. When he was only eight years of age, the boy had a bad spill from his pony on the family farm, Illalong. His mother was shocked when a doctor, after inspecting the injury, told her that the arm had already been twisted and mangled when Andrew was a mere infant. Mrs Paterson would blame a young Aboriginal servant girl who had 'always been rough with the child'. When he reached his early teenage years, the seriousness of the damage became evident. After he endured many painful operations, medical specialists told the young man that any attempt to realign the damaged bones would only cause even further deformity. He would have to get on with his life, grin and bear it. Generations of the family before him had been in the armed services, with some reaching high-ranking positions. His boyhood dreams had always been of joining the military and experiencing the glories of the battlefield. Andrew came to terms with the fact that those dreams could never become reality and he was temporarily devastated. But he had other talents. Later on, after talking to his influential journalist friend James Fairfax, Andrew became the inaugural war correspondent for *The Sydney Morning Herald*, taking up the coveted position at the start of the Boer War In 1899.

There was a fair amount of inferred sexual misconduct with the women in Andrew's life, but the families had closed their doors and pulled down the shutters, in order to sweep the innuendo, rumours and half-truths under the carpet. I made it my mission to unlock those doors.

In his youth, Andrew had been self-conscious about his physical affliction, always carrying his arm behind his back. To counter the untoward impressions of his disability, the family made a lot of his great success as a young solicitor. However, at Sydney Grammar he never did officially pass the required leaving certificate. On the occasion of the exams, he was gripped by a near-fatal bout of typhoid fever. His parents couldn't afford the mandatory apprenticeship fees demanded by established law firms. However, he was taken on as an articled clerk by a family friend, solicitor Herbert Selway. Andrew's grandmother, Emily Mary Barton, was known to have useful connections, and some thought she may have called in a few favours.

For a man who craved action, the companionship of affidavits and legal briefs would give him little pleasure. If he couldn't experience the life of the outdoorsman, he would write about it, starting with the poetry he sent in to *The Bulletin* and other magazines, under the pseudonym of The Banjo. The sudden burst of fame saw him pursued by the ladies of Sydney society, and he conducted many affairs, including an unrequited liaison with the author Miles Franklin. He eventually became engaged to a young lady named Sarah Riley, from a monied family in Geelong. The relationship lasted for seven years, ending only after the couple undertook a disastrous trip to Dagworth Station in Queensland, in the early months of 1895.

ABP and Sarah had been invited by her brother Frederick to visit his property in Winton. When they arrived, Frederick told them that they were all invited to a huge party at Dagworth Station, on the Diamantina River. The property was owned by the wealthy Robert MacPherson, who was playing host to his two younger sisters up from Victoria. The siblings were recovering from the aftermath of their mother's death, and one of the sisters was named Christina, a most attractive and musically talented young woman. She would entertain the other guests on an autoharp that she had found at the station. Already an amateur pianist, she soon taught herself to play the abandoned instrument.

Ready to go as Banjo Paterson, Perth, 2002.

It was at Dagworth that the song 'Waltzing Matilda' would come to fruition by the pairing of Christina MacPherson's music with Banjo Paterson's lyrics. Bob MacPherson's live-in lover was Josephine Penée, a vibrant woman of French heritage. Outrageous, unruly parties were held at Dagworth, with libertarian frivolity being a major ingredient. Later biographers touched upon these hedonistic social events, but none explained why the poet, in his later years, would not enter into any discussion regarding the writing of Waltzing Matilda. Instead of traipsing in the well-worn tracks of those busy researchers before me, I knew I had to suss out the living descendants of the main characters. It would take many hours of phone calls and lots of frustrating dead ends, but my efforts would eventually pay off in spades when I met up with Diana Baillieu, the great-niece of Christina MacPherson, as well as Dr Barrington Thomas, the grand-nephew of Sarah Riley, and a lady named

Jean Johnson. Jean Johnson was the granddaughter of the out-of-wedlock liaison between Bob MacPherson and his lover Josephine Penée. Jean told me of the incredibly tangled triangle that comprised the various relationships at Dagworth.

The merde hit the fan the moment Banjo caught sight of Christina MacPherson. He was besotted with her, even though he was betrothed to Sarah Riley. He would lock himself away with Christina to pen this whimsical story about a swagman, ostensibly for the entertainment of the current house guests. He never imagined the piece would find an audience beyond the confines of Dagworth Station, believing it to be his worst writing ever and embarrassed that it had garnered so much attention and controversy. Banjo's attachment to Christina would send the crestfallen Sarah to bed with the vapours.

The reason Paterson would always avoid talking about 'Waltzing Matilda' is that he felt ashamed of what happened at Dagworth Station during that fateful trip. Christina and Sarah had been school friends in Victoria, but after the 'incident' they never spoke to each other again. Various family members told me there were indications that Christina and Paterson became lovers. When she became aware of the erotic affair, Sarah called off the engagement, and she would flee to England, not to return until ten years later. Christina returned to her hometown of Warnambool.

Neither woman was destined to enter into matrimony. The most disgraceful indignity for Banjo came when he was ordered from the property at the wrong end of a shotgun, pointed in his direction by Bob MacPherson.

There were so many incidents, good and bad, to explore and I set about pulling the real story together. I decided that the 76-year-old ABP, having been invited to be guest speaker at the end-of-term assembly at Sydney Grammar, would relate his story from start to finish, warts and all. He would tell of not only the glory, but also the disappointments, his own subterfuges, the pain, and the betrayals. With research and constant revision, it took me the best part of two years to come up with a finished manuscript. I included several songs from the period, in addition to 'Waltzing Matilda', and I wrote the music for one of Banjo's poems, 'Road to Gundagai'. Clive Lendich at Pymble Music worked tirelessly at recording and editing all kinds of sound effects to enhance the play's atmosphere.

Unfortunately, when I timed it, the play was running at roughly three-and-a-half-hours long, but I had chosen to learn the whole thing in order to assess what worked, what didn't, what would hold interest, and what wouldn't. I booked the tiny Stables Theatre in Kings Cross for the one-night-only preview on 29 December, after Katy and I managed to trim the running time back to about three hours. My musical director, Craig Gower, would act as sound and lighting supervisor. I dragged in some friends and people from my management agency, and about 20 of these 'guinea pigs' scattered themselves around the theatre's wooden benches. The performance would be somewhat limited, with no ambitious lighting, and minimal sound, but that's what these private showings are all about. The big question was, did we have something to offer, or had I wasted two years of my life?

The theatre's prior production had used a completely black backdrop. The airless summer night was stifling, and there was no air conditioning. I hadn't expected such an absolute scorcher on that particular night. By the time we were halfway through the second act, the people in my melting audience were fanning themselves with anything they could utilise. Paper flyers were a godsend. With the heat exacerbated by the matte black backdrop, I was aware that eyes were starting to droop. Maybe they were all hoping it would be a brief second act, and that Banjo might hurry up and die!

Praise be to God, they all held in there, and everybody stayed for the question and answer session. I needed desperately to know the audience's opinions, and we learnt a great deal from the exercise.

I had originally approached the renowned Rodney Fisher to direct the play, but he wanted to change the story's viewpoint, concentrating more on the military sections of Banjo's life. It was my contention to flesh out the man, rather than concentrate on the written history, so Rodney and I parted company. After that difference of creative opinion, I talked Katy into being the show's new director. This was her chance to get back at me for *Me and Jezebel*, and Katy relished the idea.

After discussing all the positives and negatives from the Stables experience, we knew it was time to 'kill the babies', a terrible euphemism for slashing once-cherished anecdotes and stories from an overly lengthy piece. One has to be ruthless enough to cull the extraneous bits for the sake of the whole work, acting with surgical precision, so to speak. Katy and I would fight over the play's content, but she usually won the day, being the possessor of an uncanny instinct in knowing what was best to keep and what to eliminate. There were so many stories that had to go. Regardless of our reluctant but necessary editing process, I was grateful to have discovered so many interesting personalities along my journey for the truth.

In early 2000, I'd been fascinated when I watched a demonstration on television by a commercial artist named Ian de Gruchy. This man had turned the Melbourne Town Hall into a Holden car, all with the use of photographic slide projection. Thinking of Ian's process, I now envisaged turning a whole stage backdrop into a story. The next day, I phoned Ian in Melbourne to find out if he could bring my visualisations to reality. We had a fruitful meeting, and he assured me that everything in my conception was probable! Three giant screens would have to be constructed, along with all the mechanical apparatus needed to lift them up into the flies. Six powerful projectors would have to be purchased, to throw the various images onto the screens. Ian de Gruchy designed the construction layout for all the heavy equipment. Ian, Katy and I would go through volumes of photographic material, seeking that perfect image. Ian travelled about the country with his camera, shooting scenery and historic buildings, and he also took pictures of Sydney Grammar School's exterior. The headmaster gave us permission to shoot its esteemed interior, which remained much the same as in the days when Banjo was a student. This period of constructing a show, whether it is for television or theatre, can be laborious, tiresome, backbreaking, and terribly exciting. I was fortunate to have a team around me that was as enthusiastic as I was.

Banjo Treads Warily

We reached the point where we were ready to test the six projectors and the computer program for the meshing together of the assembled images. The slide vision and the timing had worked well in Ian's studio, but now we needed to see how it all worked in situ. In January, we hired Carlton Hall for the night, in Melbourne's North Carlton. The special screens were still under construction, so Ian, with his ingenuity, had hung taped-together large white bed sheets, roped to the side walls, facilitating a crude replica of what was yet to come. As with our Sydney experiment, we invited about 20 friends to make up the audience and give their thoughts and opinions. We devised a rather simple setting, consisting of a chair and a table, and adorned with a few props, such as a water jug, a drinking glass, and scattered papers and pencils. I charted an elementary lighting layout for Ian's apprentice Simon to follow, and Craig Gower was once again in charge of the separate computer disc system that held all the prepared music and sound effects. We assembled behind the bed sheets at the back of the hall and wished each other the best of British luck.

Like a rugby scrum breaking apart, we went about our business. Katy would call the show from the theatre's audio-mixing desk. Surrounded by Ian on his computer, Simon on lighting control and Craig with his mini-disc system, Katy called for 'Lights', and we were underway! I was certainly impressed at the way the bed sheets turned into the interior of Sydney Grammar. I heard the recorded voice of the 1940s headmaster at this end-of-term assembly, announcing, 'Gentlemen, would you please welcome: Mr A. B. Paterson CBE.'

I entered from stage left, wearing the first incarnation of Banjo's make-up and suit and the production was underway. I would like to say that all was smooth sailing, but we suffered our share of mishaps. Towards the end of the first act, two of the projectors started to malfunction, throwing out the blending of the images. Ian decided to abort them, so we had four projectors doing the work of six. Gaps were now left in the sequence of images. In the second act, one of the bed sheets decided it wasn't meant to be used as a projection screen and left its moorings in protest. Regardless of these not unexpected mechanical mishaps, we soldiered on to the end of the play, when we were rewarded by strong applause and positive feedback. We knew more 'babies' would have to be sacrificed. Our projectors would have to be serviced more efficiently. Cues needed to be tightened, and some of the sound effects would have to be modified, but we were on the way to accomplishing the dream.

Each year, to celebrate his birth at Narambla, 8 kilometres out of Orange in western NSW, a popular festival is held to celebrate all things Banjo Paterson. This year, on February 14, 15 and 16, our new play on the life and times of Banjo Paterson would be presented at the Orange Civic Theatre, to coincide with the annual celebrations.

On 13 February, the day we departed for Orange, my granddaughter Jessica presented us with another great-grandson, whom she named Ezekiel. Ezekiel's arrival turned out to be a good omen for the show, as everything worked according to plan.

We had a decent-sized stage, full lighting, a sound desk and, most importantly, an audience that had actually paid to see the play. The punters gave us an exciting reception, and each night, after the show, I mingled with the knowledgeable audience, some of whom were only too happy to tell me how I'd mispronounced this word, or that name. I was getting my information straight from the mouths of the horses. Katy and I visited the old brick factory where Banjo was born, about 5 kilometres out from the town, and as icing, the committee asked me to cut the cake!

In my play, when ABP is addressing the students, he points out, 'As you go out into this world, gentlemen, you will find that you have absolutely no control over directing human circumstances or events to your own liking, regardless of how successful or wealthy you may become.' In the play, the words pertain to the discussion of the early death of Banjo's father, but in my own reality, while constructing the play, I was faced with a terrible and crushing calamity of my own.

CHAPTER 9

Family Affairs

Drug Charges

Once before I had been startled by my ex, Jenny Main, when she burst into my bedroom in the early hours of the morning to tell me that Ricky May had died. This time when the phone rang, it was early evening, and I could sense the deep pain in her voice. 'Jenny, what is it?' I demanded. There was a pause, an intake of breath, and then she whispered hoarsely, 'Simon has been arrested in Italy, on drug charges!'

This was April of 2000, and it was only four months after Simon and Nicollette had celebrated Christmas with the family at Wahroonga. When I arrived at Jenny's house, her partner Peter opened the front door. He led me upstairs, where I found Jenny sitting on the edge of her bed, drained of all emotion and her hand still resting on the phone handset, as if she were waiting for a call to tell her the nightmare was all an elaborate hoax.

Simon had been on a business trip to Italy, having started a cosmetic company

Simon and Nicollette Sheridan.

with two partners in Los Angeles. On his London stopover, he was advised by friends to get in touch with a certain man when he arrived at his destination, someone they felt could clue Simon in to important business and social contacts. The two men spoke on the phone and arranged to meet for coffee at a beachside pizzeria in Lignano. The Italian police had been tracking one Alex Bruell, and when he turned up for the meeting with Simon seven unmarked police cars and 21 officers were waiting for them in the car park.

Both of them were handcuffed, and when the police opened Bruell's car boot, they found 333,000 ecstasy pills. Alex and Simon were arrested in the car park, driven to the police station, and charged by the International Drug Trafficking and Anti-Mafia Association with the possession of prohibited drugs. Simon used his one permitted phone call to tell Nicollette that a disastrous mistake had been made, but she was not to worry, as he felt sure the matter would soon be cleared up. After two days without any word from Simon, Nicollette decided to phone Jenny. Through AAP next day, the headlines screamed:

'Australian social celebrity arrested on massive drug charges in Italy'

'From high life to agony of ecstasy link'

'Hollywood star's Australian boyfriend arrested in Mafia ecstasy sting'

Inevitably, my own name was dragged into the feverish savaging mounted by the press. Being Simon's stepfather, I was good copy, but I could do without this sort of publicity.

Back in America, Nicollette had hired Robert Shapiro and Giuliano Carretti to chase down the case. Shapiro was the defence attorney in O.J. Simpson's infamous murder trial, but the two high-profile lawyers would soon drop out of the proceedings. Their fees were far too prohibitive.

Following our triumph there in February, we were invited back to the Orange Ex-Services Club to give two more performances of *Banjo* on 15 June 2001. It would be a fast trip up and down the hill, for I had to leave for Italy on 17 June. Jenny had been fighting Simon's cause, virtually on her own, in Padova, and her son's trial was scheduled to start on 19 June. By being there in person, I aimed to give her my support, to lessen her load in this long and protracted mess.

This would be my first trip back to Italy since 1964. Back then, for me, Italy had been a wonderful enjoyable experience, but now, 37 years later, the only emotion I was feeling was that of nervous apprehension. By the time I arrived, Simon had been interned at Casa Reclusiane in Padova for 14 months, spending 22 hours each day in his cell. One day, there in the exercise yard, six Tunisian and Moroccan Muslims decide to clean up three white Christians, one of whom happened to be Simon. The attack didn't come as a surprise; blood was spilt! Simon acquitted himself well, and suffered little injury, but the fight was an excuse to punish him further and he was transferred to the notorious Casa Circondariale Di Tolmezzo in Udine, the home of hardened Mafia killers.

Simon would spend the next four years of his life in two of Italy's most infamous prisons.

On my arrival in Padova I was quickly taken to the hotel where Jenny had been ensconced since her arrival more than a year earlier. The Art Hotel al Fagiano nestles in between some ancient buildings on the cobbled Loco Tossolini in a quiet area of Padova. I'd like to say its boutique – but it's just small! I found the owner and staff friendly, and Jenny, who has been living there for eight months, came with me to explore room 44, my new home for the next little while. The room was simple to say the least. The bathroom was an ingenious example of space-saving, with the toilet bowl almost under the sink. The shower recess was minuscule, and I realised that if I dropped the soap, I'd have to open the door to pick it up! The reason Jenny had chosen the hotel was because of its reasonable rates and proximity to the jail where Simon was incarcerated.

I would learn that Jenny and I were expected to be in Trieste for Simon's first trial at the infamous Tribunal Di Trieste, (approximately 183 kilometres away). The picturesque train trip there would momentarily take my mind away from the *real* reason we had been summoned. The large grey building, that had housed the Gestapo during World War Two, stood monstrously before us, and as we entered this ominous abode a feeling of dread sent a shiver through me. We had arrived early for the trial, so we settled into our allotted wooden spring-loaded seats, and every time someone stood up, a gunshot sound echoed around the entire building. Nerve-racking to say the least!

After a delay and several more hours in our entrenched position, it would be 4 pm before we caught sight of Simon being ushered into the courtroom surrounded by police. We managed to get in a quick wave of reassurance to him, but that was all. The trial was to be held in camera, so we were not allowed to sit in the court to give support. When finally the court room opened, it was 8.45 pm. Our lawyers had been able to get a grant for a 10-minute catch-up with his parents and it was hugs all round, and Jenny was allowed to give Simon the sandwich and bottle of Coke she'd been holding for hours. All too soon Simon was being led away, disappearing into the darkness of the night. Returning to our lawyer's offices, looking around, I wondered how much our fees had contributed to their opulence.

Disappointingly, the lawyers told us that because of language problems, the wrong witnesses and misunderstandings, the trial had been aborted, and another trial would be rescheduled in a month or so. Really? This, of course, is not what we wanted to hear, so we retreated to the train station to catch the last train back to Padova.

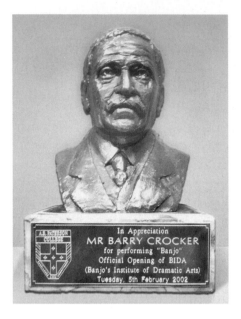

My BIDA bronze statue, presented by the A.B. Paterson College on Queensland's Gold Coast, 2002.

During the week, before Trieste, I had been granted a visit to see Simon at the Casa Circondariale in Padova. I'd actually been granted two visits (because I'd travelled so far), but someone, somewhere, had decided that this was too lenient and the visit had not only been cut to one visit, but also the hours were reduced from three hour to two. Jenny was incensed, and fought, to no avail, to get the original rights reinstated.

After a stringent body search at the gates, I finally joined Jenny inside the maximum-security of the jail. Jen, after many visits, had made friends with one of the female officers, and when she heard of all she'd been through, said she'd do her best to have the original hours restored (which came to pass). It was a special three hours, with much reminiscing and many laughs, but in my mind I couldn't help remembering the seven-year-old gangly boy jumping in and out of the Wahroonga pool.

The time flew by so quickly that I had to check it with the guard, who had been a constant during the visit, and sure enough our time had come to an end. Last-minute hugs and reassuring banter filled the air as we made our exit, but of course as soon as we left Casa, reality kicked in and tears were shed. During our chat, Simon had suggested that since there were no visiting rights at weekends, we should go to Venice to bring a little joy to my visit; we took his advice. Arriving in the afternoon, and getting through the myriad of street vendors selling their fake souvenirs, we found ourselves in the heart of this beautiful city. We sat outside, enjoying the sun, in one of the restaurants that rim the famous St Mark's Square. It should also be famous for its prices: our cappuccinos and cakes cost the equivalent of a small second-hand car. But the real reason for my visit had clouded what should have been a wonderful experience.

Italy Without Me

My visit was quickly over and I left Italy on 25 June leaving Jenny with the unenviable task of supporting Simon on her own. The anticipated 'perfect outcome' of Simon's next trial went the way of the first. There were appeals, and rejections, lawyers got richer, and funds were further exhausted. Over the next four months,

Simon was held in solitary confinement at the Trieste jail until his transfer back to the Casa Reclusiane, where he was placed in maximum security, which entailed either sharing or being alone in a cell for 22 hours a day. The other two hours were for exercising and showering.

The letter of Italian law states that if an inmate is not charged with any crime after two years of incarceration, then that prisoner must be released. Simon had denied all charges since day one – not only didn't he touch any drugs on the night of his arrest, he didn't even see any drugs. His lawyers were counting on Simon's case falling under this caveat, but on the day before the deadline was due to expire, he was charged under the Anti-Mafia Association laws and then sentenced to eight years in maximum-security conditions. Alex Bruell, who had readily admitted his guilt, was given a four-year jail sentence, and spent less than half of that time incarcerated.

Eventually there was some good news: one of the appeals worked, and Simon's sentence was reduced to six years. Through his study of the law, and with the help of some influential friends, he found a legal loophole that would allow him to leave prison and go home, on the proviso that he never returns to Italy.

Graciously and gratefully, he took up the offer, and after over four years in prison he was free to start his life again. Standing up for what he believed to be the truth didn't come cheaply – he lost the then love of his life, Nicollette, and his American business, where he felt his future lay. Once a person is charged with any kind of drug conviction, it is virtually impossible to obtain a visa for travel to the USA. The only positive to come out of this episode is that Simon now speaks fluent Italian.

As I shall always be tied to Barry McKenzie, regrettably, Simon will always carry the tag 'entertainer's stepson, convicted drug dealer Simon Main' etc. Simon now lives with his partner Natasha in Sydney, and they have two sons.

Memories and Memory Lapses

It was time to throw all my energy into the fine-tuning of *Banjo*. I arranged publicity stunts and photo shoots for the Malthouse Theatre opening in Melbourne, and before I could say, 'There was movement at the station' the previews were upon us.

Test runs are necessary to iron out any little faults that may have been overlooked during rehearsals. Murphy's Law dictates that something will always come unstuck, throwing a rusty spanner into the works. On our first preview, apart from the mistiming of a few slides, all went pretty well, and there were no stoppages, but on the second night I had a 'dry' right in the middle of the play's pièce de résistance. Banjo's most famous poem, *The Man from Snowy River* closes the play, and three-quarters of the way in, the picture in my mind became a white board. I was in a blinding snowstorm on a perilous slippery slope, with no snow chains!

Katy, Susie and Kim Beazley, 'Banjo' and comedian Brian Doyle, Burswood Casino, Perth, 2002.

Performing a one-man show can be a rewarding and exhilarating experience for an actor. The performer owns the space in which he struts, but he is totally alone if the words aren't there. I had the sensation of my head being on fire, but almost immediately, the beads of sweat exploding on my forehead froze to become part of the snowing tempest that was making me shiver in front of this audience. I thought for a moment that I might be able to bluff the punters into believing that the drawn-out pause was deliberate. That was a bad thought! If I tried to adlib my way out, I could end up in worse strife. In any popular poetry work, by the likes of Banjo Paterson or Henry Lawson, many in the audience will know the work as intimately as the performer. An attempt to fake it would be sacrilege! My conscience told me to go back to the last stanza and begin again, having faith in the audience to come with me, and thank god they did. Although the response was very positive, I shuddered in the wings from the shock of my unforeseen mental blackout. I told myself, 'And you thought you were ready?'

Any more snow blindness would not be tolerated, so there was a lot more rehearsal before our opening night on 17 July. On the night, I was supported by a lot of friends and acquaintances and I was ready for the masses. The feedback was terrific, not only from the audience, but also the critics and other members of the popular press. I received my first standing ovation on 19 July. Our little family of Katy, my grandson Lee Nacson and I, along with my musical and technical director Craig Gower, could breathe at last, and we partied on back at our digs in Toorak.

The next morning, I was interviewed about the show's success by Steve Liebmann on Channel Nine's *Today Show*. I found it hard to get up so early after the previous night's celebrations, and I was probably a little vulnerable when he asked about Simon and the jail sentence. I simply said, 'I wish he could be here to share our joy; he should have been here! But then life never seems to let you have it all, does it?'

On 2 August, *Barry Crocker's Banjo* was extended for another week at the Malthouse.

Russell Roylance booked the show for the Twin Towns Services Club. This would be the first time we took the production into a cabaret showroom. The many challenges were met, and the show was enthusiastically received. Following the advance publicity, the A. B. Paterson College, situated in Arundel on the Gold Coast, suggested that I might like to have a look around this unique school. Is the Pope a Catholic?

When I accepted the offer, the school went into high gear. Extra workers arrived to finish off the new performance building to be called BIDA. Banjo's Institute of Dramatic Arts was a play on words on Sydney's famous NIDA, and I was asked to open the room officially. Like the original NIDA in Sydney, BIDA had once been contained within an old corrugated iron shed. I could scarcely conceal my thrill after being given the exclusive honour of declaring this important theatrical space open. As I entered the building, I was greeted with thunderous applause from the 150 or so students, aged from eight to 18, who had interrupted their classes with much expectation and interest. Over the next 40-odd minutes, I recited some poetry and sang the original version of *Waltzing Matilda*. I then threw open a forum to answer questions regarding not only Banjo Paterson, but all forms of show business. These special pupils had chosen this particular school for their education, mainly because of the importance it placed on the performing arts.

It was hard to leave my new young friends, but Samantha McHardy-Jones, the college's drama captain, ushered me into the office of Ms Dawn Lang, the principal, for tea and cakes.

The afternoon tea was all very civilised, and I was presented with a small bronze bust of Banjo himself to top off the day. The bust takes pride of place in my home, reminding me of the day I passed on a little of my knowledge to a bunch of ambitious and talented young people, with hopefully the next Cate Blanchett or Russell Crowe in amongst their number.

Barry Crocker's Banjo opened successfully at the Perth Playhouse on 20 February. There is quite a following of Paterson fans in that city, so our audiences, instead of growing smaller as the season progressed, became larger from word-of-mouth recommendations, and the glowing reviews we received were among the best ever. Because of the lack of theatre outlets in Perth, our season was unable to be extended, as another production was waiting in the wings.

Banjo Meets Bubba

During the Perth season of *Banjo* in February, the city was graced by the presence of Bill Clinton, the US President who had handed his seat of power to George W. Bush a year or so earlier. Clinton's last visit to Australia in 2001 had been interrupted by the events of September 11, and he had flown home to be with his family, and to help unite a shocked, embattled and outraged America. Four months later, Clinton returned to resume his speaking tour, organised to help raise money for the Princess Margaret Children's Foundation. His schedule would have him arriving on the morning of Saturday 23 February to meet the press, and then that evening he would be the key speaker, followed by greeting the guests, some of whom had forked out as much as $5,785 for the platinum ticket that allowed them to be within an arm's length of the great man. A lavish dinner would be enjoyed by the attendees, and the resident Irish comedian Brian Doyle, together with Sydney radio identity Alan Jones, the master of ceremonies, would complete the evening's entertainment.

All visits of current and former American presidents involve teams of secret service agents arriving a few days earlier to check out and secure the areas to be occupied by their charge. My old pal, the influential showbiz promoter Max Markson, had scored the job of organising all aspects of the presidential tour. Max was a big fan of Banjo's poetry and he told me he'd been trying to catch a performance of my play as far back as the previous year, so this was the perfect chance to be able to invite him to the opening night.

Max had been chatting away so enthusiastically with the former president's gang about Banjo that these tough guys wanted to check out the show for themselves. Would it be possible to find seats for the American contingent? The theatre management was approached, and with a little movement at the station, Bill Clinton's boys were soon accommodated.

A photo of ex-President Clinton meeting 'Banjo Paterson' would be a memorable and valuable souvenir. But with any great idea that involves people in the public eye, timing is crucial. Max, with the full cooperation of the secret service attachment, arranged a photo opportunity, planned to take place between my Saturday matinee performance and the evening show, so split-second coordination was of the essence. At 6.30 pm, I got into costume and freshened up Banjo's 76-year-old make-up. Squeezing into the tiny Toyota Seca that belonged to our publicist Marie Gee, Katy and I joined the procession of glitterati on its way to Perth's Burswood Casino. As we lined up with the ostentatious Rolls-Royce and Mercedes limousines entering the drop-off point, a dark-suited guy in a left-hand-drive Ford Mustang began having a noisy discussion with security staff about the potential parking space for his vehicle. Marie had already organised our plans with the security people, so after sliding past the Mustang, we parked our car in the designated space. We left the engine idling to indicate our urgency.

I unfolded myself from the front seat, and I helped Katy, who'd been scrunched up in the back of the car, onto the red carpet. The three of us made our way along the carpet, delighted to join Perth's high-class partygoers in their sparkling activities.

Puzzled glances were thrown towards this ageing, grey-haired gentleman, resplendent with his clay pipe and antique silver fob watch, as he was escorted by two beautiful women into the building. A few fans recognised me and twigged to my subterfuge, but others witnessed what they believed to be a rapidly deteriorating Barry Crocker.

We joined the pre-arranged group of people in the VIP section, all waiting for their personal presidential photo. While waiting nervously, I chatted with comedian Brian Doyle, who jokingly referred to his career coming to this, the opening act for an amateur saxophone player. When Max Markson gave me the news that I didn't want to hear, 'The President's running late,' I started to sweat even more profusely. Bill's appearance was supposed to be at 7.30 pm sharp, in order to complete the photography session prior to dinner.

The bronze statue of ABP that holds pride of place on Elderslie Street, almost opposite the North Gregory Hotel in Winton.

With the help of Max and my new American secret service friends, I was placed at the head of the queue, but there was only a five-to-eight-minute buffer zone. My plan was to sweep in, do the shot and run to the idling car, which would speed us all back to the theatre in time for the 8 pm performance. Mr President was running a nerve-jangling 15 minutes late. Being first in line, I had nowhere to go. Besides, to come so far and so close without a result was unthinkable. If necessary, I would apologise to each member of that night's *Banjo* audience individually.

The room's atmosphere became electric, and the obliging waiters disappeared in an instant. The kitchen doors slammed open, and the waiters were replaced by a team of security earpieces and mobile phones who monitored the entrance for the guest of honour, who was following closely on their heels.

Spontaneous applause broke out as Bill Clinton entered the room. He strode past me, heading down the long, roped-off corridor towards the prepared set adorned with American and Australian flags, where the photographs would be carefully orchestrated. I had hoped to follow the ex-President, but ten other mobile suits closed in behind him. Some of the secret service boys, fresh from attending my show, smiled and complimented me, and they were glad to smooth my approach to the picture-taking area. I was almost there when four shameless freeloaders dashed in ahead of me. As they chatted away with Bill Clinton, with all the time in the world, the seconds ticked away in my head with frantic urgency. When I approached the President for my moment, it seemed that a hologram had taken his place. With the ethereal lighting bouncing off his silver hair and tanned face, the image that had occupied the front pages for the past decade was almost surreal.

'This is Barry Crocker, a popular Australian actor, Mr President,' someone announced, as Bill took hold of my hand.

I explained the reason for my make-up, informing him that I was currently portraying Banjo Paterson on stage. As he smiled at me, I continued, 'He's the man who wrote "Waltzing Matilda".' As if he'd had a moment of revelation, Clinton raised his eyebrows and said, 'Ah!' We turned to face the camera. The soft pop of the flash gun imprinted our brief meeting forever. I quickly introduced Katy. A smile spread across his face as we posed for the camera, and then we were on our way, leaving behind a hundred others who wanted to achieve their encounter with history in the form of Bill Clinton.

We arrived at the still idling Toyota. It was now 7.49 pm, and we hit every red light on the trip back to the city. In between lights, Marie did a pretty good impression of Michael Schumacher. Sue, our stage manager, had been alerted to our approach, thanks to the new technology of mobile phones, and the theatre's stage door, at the very end of the laneway, had been left open. As I entered on the run, Sue strapped a radio mike to my torso. We moved towards the prompt side of the stage for my entrance. After 30 seconds of calming time, Banjo Paterson made his way onto the stage at precisely 8.05 pm, with no one in the packed audience being vaguely aware of the gut-wrenching panic of the previous 30 minutes.

The next day, Bill Clinton visited the children in the cancer ward of the Princess Margaret Hospital before departing for the next leg of the tour in Adelaide. Bill would leave the Perth hospital over $200,000 richer for his presence at the fundraiser.

I rested on the Sunday, satisfied to have survived yet another of my hare-brained mind explosions. Katy and I had our memorabilia, Marie Gee a good story to tell, and Gary Snowden, our theatre manager, the joy of recovering from a near-heart attack! In our eagerness to pull off the stunt, no-one had thought to inform Gary of our Saturday night excursion to Burswood.

After the Perth run, we performed four shows down the road at Mandurah, and two up the road at Geraldton. That's where we ended the Western Australian section of the tour.

Carry on Banjo

In April 2002, my fourth great-grandchild was born to my granddaughter Jessica. Tiny Zarah arrived with a smile, happy to take her place In the Crocker clan, and she hasn't stopped smiling since.

In June, we were back at the Twin Towns Services Club for an encore performance before Banjo was due to open in Brisbane. We had a chance to iron out any bugs that may have crept into the show. With a play like Banjo, you have to stay continually on top of the script, because two hours of solo dialogue can slip away easily if you allow yourself to start thinking about the shopping list. This can happen to any actor who is too familiar with their role. The more you work at something, especially if it's a new piece, the more you will discover. We were now ready to take on the Queensland Performing Arts Company's Cremorne Theatre. There were two shows opening that 31 July night in Brisbane, my one-hander, and the controversial *Puppetry of the Penis*, which was evidently a two-hander! There was a competition between the two shows to see who could pull more A-listers to their opening. In all honesty, *Puppetry* had penetrated deep into the psyche of the younger crowd, but our opening nights attracted a much more refined and classy bunch, despite the stiff opposition. *Puppetry* was certainly packing them in, and for a brief moment we contemplated changing the name of my show from *Barry Crocker's Banjo* to *Banjo's Old Fella*.

I am proud to say we held our own, and that's the worst pun of all! The pattern continued, with our audiences building as we went along.

The Birthplace of Waltzing Matilda

August and September found me back on the cabaret circuit, but a new venture was about to fall into my lap. *Barry Crocker's Banjo* was invited to fly to Winton in Queensland to be part of the Banjo Festival for that year. We were booked to perform four shows only, but the chance to explore genuine Paterson country would turn out to be a priceless adventure.

On 26 September it was 42 very dry degrees in Winton, and I don't think the thermometer varied from that temperature during our four-day visit. Our little touring party, which consisted of Katy, Ian de Gruchy, our event agent John Preston and me, booked into the North Gregory Hotel, where myth would have us believe that 'Waltzing Matilda' was sung publicly for the first time. In a sense this is correct, but through my research we found it was sung on two previous occasions. A. B. Paterson gave the song its introductory airing at Dagworth Station, shortly after he had co-composed it with Christina MacPherson. Dagworth had already crumbled into the dust, but we had the delightful honour of being invited to Oondooroo station, which still stands in all its historic splendour, maintained by its then owners, a charming couple named Bill and Jean Tudehope. In 1895 it would be at Oondooroo that one of the house guests, Herbert Ramsey, a professional baritone who later became Sir Herbert, learned the song in the afternoon and performed it most competently in front of the assembled partygoers that same evening, accompanied by Christina on autoharp. Banjo had performed the song the previous night, and even though it was a three-hour buggy ride, the enthusiastic listeners had insisted on going over to Oondooroo the following night to delight everyone there with this wonderful new song. All those present that evening wildly applauded Herbert's rendition, insisting on encore after encore. When the song was finally presented at the North Gregory Hotel, its reputation was already spreading faster than an out-of-control bushfire. The ditty that Banjo had dismissed as a piece of silly ephemera, written merely to woo Christina, would prove to be unstoppable!

Because of the 2002 Year of the Outback Festival, Winton's tourist accommodation was at a premium, and the town was already buzzing with excited crowds from all points of the continent. Our rooms were not quite as luxurious as we'd have liked, but hey, when Paterson himself was here, he'd probably slept under the stars. Katy and I accepted the amenities for what they were. We aimed to soak up the atmosphere and go with the flow, but, when I turned on the bathroom tap to wash my hands, my nostrils were assaulted by a foul, mustard-like smell that accompanied the water from its underground source. The pungent stench almost threw me back into the bedroom. This was something else I would have to ignore, because I hate it when Katy tells me I complain too much. When I showered, very briefly I may add, I learnt to hold my breath.

The festival presented all the fun of the fair. There were constant street competitions, such as so-called drag races where, with a piece of rope, husbands would drag their wives, seated on the edge of tractor tyres, along the main street to see who could get to the finish line first. Wheelbarrow races, woodchopping, bale stacking competitions and other sophisticated forms of amusement, like watching tortoises racing or guessing the breed of various specimens of cattle (or was it the other way around?) were held throughout the day. Winton had an excellent Banjo Paterson museum, displaying life-size figures that represented the story of 'Waltzing Matilda' around a fake billabong. The edifice was stacked with memorabilia and ephemera, with many old photos and day bills of the period gracing the walls. I picked up a few discrepancies in the museum's written fact sheets. I wondered if I should have a go at speaking to someone about putting the record straight. No, I would be diplomatically quiet on this occasion. Instead, I spent a couple of hours learning more about the daring pioneers who came to this remote outpost all those years earlier to establish new lives, leaving behind only their indelible imprint of courage and endurance.

In June of 2015 a disastrous fire tore through the museum, destroying much of the treasured building and its memorabilia, thankfully the museum has been restored, but so much irreplaceable documentation was lost. Apart from my own four performances of Banjo at the Winton Civic Theatre, there was plenty of entertainment for the masses. The Redcliffe Scottish Pipe Band and a Celtic rock group would perform, and a six-race program would be held at the Winton Showground track, with total prize money of over $22,000. The Gunbarrel Highwaymen would follow each of my performances at the Civic Hall. The hall was an all-purpose box-like structure, where anything from dog shows to ballet could be staged.

Because of the eclectic nature of the festival's line-up, our lighting crew arrived with a full truck load of rock-and-roll lighting gear, not exactly suitable for the telling of a delicate tale of love and romance, set against a backdrop of fetching projected scenes from the last century. At first, our allotted crew scared the crap out of me, because they looked like the meanest of Hells Angels boys, all covered in tattoos and leather, and each of them sweating like Meat Loaf in a rubber suit. But these guys were diamonds cut from the rough. Not only did they make an impossible light rack work for us in a most sensitive way, they relished working on the show, enjoying every aspect and acceding to Katy's lighting or technical queries. Before our first show, Ian spent most of the day hanging our projection screens from anything suitable in the rafters. This was not a proper stage where flies could be used to hoist the screens into place, and there was no proscenium, so the whole setting resembled a huge garage, but it kind of suited the occasion.

The air-conditioning system was another thing altogether, having the power to cool a battleship. The out-take vents measured four feet in diameter, and when they kicked into action like jet engines, they chilled the giant hall's interior to almost freezing in a matter of seconds. It was fun to see the punters arriving in regulation T-shirts, shorts and thongs, dripping in sweat one minute, then to see icicles forming on their faces a few minutes later. Everyone there knew the routine and the air conditioning was used sparingly, but each time it whined into action our screens would flutter wildly, making the images fluctuate like the magic mirrors at Luna Park.

It didn't matter one jot to our audience, which was enthusiastic in its reaction. The seats were filled with many young families, and I was profoundly pleased to see so many of the younger generation entertained by these old Australian stories. One lady next to the sound desk was overheard to say, 'It's a lovely show, but when's Barry Crocker coming on?' Another lady commented, 'This is better than the Moscow Circus!'

Sydney Opera House

To top off our positive Queensland experience, we received the welcome news that we had secured Sydney Opera House's Playhouse Theatre for a season of *Barry Crocker's Banjo*. The Playhouse seated slightly less than 400, which was perfect for my show. J. K. Power, the Opera House's event manager, had worked with Katy and me several times before, and he made sure we would have the best technicians available.

The 20 November opening night went spiffingly, again with a lot of mates there who had come along to cheer us on. The audience response made us feel confident that we would do well there, but the initial bookings weren't that high, as had been the case in most of our venues. Some of the early reviews were good, but on the Sunday, when I opened up my copy of Sydney's *Sun-Herald*, my heart sank. The widely read theatre critic, Colin Rose, slammed the show, ripping it to shreds. There was only one thing he hated more than the play, and that was my performance. His opening lines described me as 'Barry Crocker, the lightest of the light entertainers'. He went on to sneer at every aspect of the play. He hated the slide projections. He despised everything about the production and the direction, and his meagre rating of three stars out of ten was the lowest I'd ever seen. I thought, that's it, we're buggered!

On Monday, the bookings poured in. It seemed there was a vast army of Colin Rose haters out in the streets, including many sympathetic producers, directors, writers, and actors, and theatregoers who found that the very opposite often applied to the shows about which Mr Rose had given his opinions. Whenever Colin Rose raved about a theatre production, the punters who took his advice and spent their well-earned cash to secure a seat were often bored

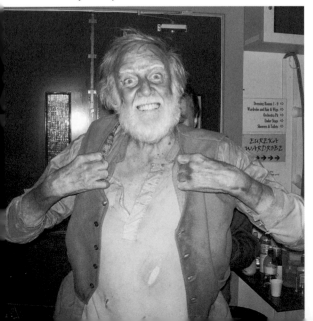

In my Paddy costume.

to tears. On the other hand, if he gave a live show the thumbs down, those who dared to suck it and see for themselves were usually pleasantly surprised, so in effect his negative and nasty criticism provided me with a huge plus in the eyes of his non-believers! Although our season was, as usual, far too short, the Playhouse paid off handsomely.

Barry Crocker's Banjo would play into 2003, but during that year I would make two big mistakes concerning the play, simply by making the wrong choices, the first being in Brisbane. Because production costs were so prohibitive at the QPAC's theatre, where we had been lucky to recoup our expenses, I opted for a cheaper venue. I chose the Twelfth Night Theatre in Bowen Hills, famous for its staging of British television-based farces like *Are You Being Served?*, featuring John Inman, and *'Allo 'Allo!*, starring Gorden Kaye.

Although we had glowing reviews, and the theatre's owner, Gail Wiltshire, told me that my *Banjo* was the classiest production ever to play there, we couldn't draw a crowd.

The punters stayed away in droves, and so we went home with empty bags, having lost a substantial amount of money.

My second notable mistake was a consequence of not listening to those who knew better. At the end of each year, Melbourne puts on its arts festival, a magnificent melting pot of every conceivable kind of entertainment. Dozens of attractions compete for the same audiences from around Australia, as well as international visitors. I was keen to be a part of this action. I made some calls, only to discover that the only available venue in Melbourne was the Fairfax Theatre, at the Melbourne Arts Centre. I had to take it. It was costly, but with its enticing 400-seat space, I thought it would be ideal to bring *Banjo* back into Melbourne, with a good chance of making some real money. When I relayed my plans to friends and associates about competing in the big marketplace, everyone from my ex-manager Neil Harrold to my publicist Di Rolle told me it would be foolish to bring the show back during the arts festival. 'It won't work, Bazza, there's just too much on,' they were all telling me. 'You could lose your shirt.' Even Tony Brady, who loved the play devoutly, had second thoughts, but I was adamant in my arrogance. Instead of using my head, I allowed my heart to go out on a limb. We'd had a great Melbourne reception almost two years before, and my gut feeling was telling me the time was right and that I should go for it.

I should have taken the advice on offer. Melbourne's arts festival was made up of a giant conglomerate, with all the big shows tied into an extensive marketing campaign, including a network of widely distributed posters, prominent magazine and newspaper advertising, and prime-time radio and television commercials. By the time I came along, the marketplace had already been saturated, and I had no hope. I was like a lost three-year-old, trying to get noticed in the crowds at the Easter show. After three strenuous years of taking my *Banjo* around Australia, I was forced to cancel the Melbourne shows early, in order to avoid incurring any further losses. When all the pennies were counted, it was clear that I had made no money. But, as they say in the classics, 'I wouldn't have missed it for quids!'

CHAPTER 10

Eureka

It turned out that 2003 was a year of contrasts. My disappointments with *Banjo* were offset by venturing back into the dramatic arena. *Me and Jezebel* had been performed originally as an unsuccessful one-person show by its writer, Elizabeth Fuller. The play had gained its legs only after being converted into a two-hander. I made up my mind to wear the writer's *chapeau* again, to turn the piece back into the original idea, that of a one-woman show.

Katy's Valhalla performances had proven that she had Bette Davis's voice down pat, and I believed that Bette's persona was the key to the whole piece. Katy would have to portray all seven characters, and a convincing Bette was essential to the authenticity of the play. Katy could do it in spades! *Me and Jezebel* would now become the focus of my attention. I was confident that we could make this version work, but as with most of the Crocker theatrical assignments, the project would become more time-consuming, and more complicated, than I had foreseen.

The year would also be significant for the beginning of a new Australian musical, in which both Katy and I would become involved. Back in the late 1990s, Mike Harvey, then Julie Anthony's musical director, was approached by writer Maggie Gordon to see if he might be interested in composing a music score for a new outline she'd written about the Eureka Stockade. Singer Normie Rowe suggested to her that Mike could be the man for the job. In Mike's own words, 'Even before reading the script, I was excited about working on such an epic piece, and a story so important in Australian history. After reading the text, I was flooded with ideas for some of the songs, but I also realised that the script needed some work and restructuring. Maggie's lyrics were quite poetic, the images lusty and beautiful and raw.'

'A new musical ... is there a part in it for me?' I asked, as I usually do when something novel is in the pipeline.

'Well as a matter of fact, there is!' declared Mike. 'There's the part of an Irish grandfather called Paddy O'Malley.'

'Mate,' I announced, 'I'd love to do a demo.'

Maggie Gordon had based the character on her television observations of me, and she had wanted me for the part from day one. Should I be thrilled that she naturally saw me as a grandpa? Well, I was, several times over. The first test songs for *Eureka* were recorded at the Groovetown studio, a converted home garage in the outer Sydney suburb of Seven Hills. I recorded 'The Devil's Mistress, Gold', which was the rollicking mining song that opens the show, and 'A Beautiful Dream', a ballad that Paddy sings to his granddaughter. On many of the other tracks, I was part of the male chorus.

How exciting it was to be in at the birth of something with such potential! However, as inspired as we all were, we would have to work damned hard to justify the considerable investment needed to make this big show work. Getting up a profitable, fully original Australian musical is a daunting task.

There are always those who are only too ready to extol our past failures. Perhaps our most widely acclaimed musical of the last century was *Lola Montez*, written in 1958 by Alan Burke, whom I would later meet during the run of *Eureka* at Melbourne's Her Majesty's Theatre. It had made a lot of noise, but eventually when the dust had settled, according to theatrical historian, Tony Sheldon, the show finished up over £31,000 in the red.

Smaller Australian musicals had more chance of making money, because the sets were of a more modest design and the plays would have smaller casts. C. J. Dennis's *The Sentimental Bloke* in 1961 was perhaps the most successful of these, being dusted off every once in a while and given its legs again to pull in a new generation of punters. Regardless of previous failures, there were some real tryers out there that had had a go at launching the full-scale Australian musical, for example, *Ned Kelly* (1977), *Seven Little Australians* (1988), *Manning Clark's History of Australia – the Musical* (1988), and *Rasputin* (1989). All of these and many others fell by the wayside, searching for that elusive pot of theatrical gold.

After many re-writes, and two run-throughs, a CD of the full list of songs was completed, and on 28 November 2000 we held our first public airing of *Eureka* at Sydney's Footbridge Theatre. Directed by Katy Manning, it was a script-held reading by Michelle Doake, Judy Guest, Rob Guest, Nick Jasprizza, Rick Lau, Katy Manning, Nick McKay, Russell Newman, Josh Szeps and yours truly. The recorded songs were played at the appropriate moments throughout the reading. We had an invited and enthusiastic audience of nearly 200, and built a groundswell that eventually led to the initial investment in the full musical production in 2003. Mike brought together a group of investors, or angels, to underwrite a two-week concert tour of Queensland. To kick-start the tour, on 8 August we took over The Studio, which was the newest theatre space at the Sydney Opera House.

Katy had returned from a short working trip to England. She had taken the script with her and had written linking dialogue for the evolving text on her flight home. At the Footbridge, she had also sung the little boy's role, and had helped with the choreography for the Queensland trip. Amazingly, after only ten days of rehearsal at the Seymour Centre, and with a new cast, we hit The Studio with a pretty well-honed version of *Eureka*. The Sydney Opera House management is very strict with its union rules, and we had to adhere to seemingly ridiculous timeframes as far as the setting up was concerned, including carrying out a top and tail run. This is when you rehearse only the bits of the play that are not quite right yet, as well as the opening and closing of segments. Trying out the meagre lighting plot was hell because the Opera House staff would stop officially for their breaks, but because we were so close to the start of the production we ploughed onwards.

As our new cast of actors practised in the dressing rooms, Mike, Katy, and those on our own team did the same, because if we hadn't, the late afternoon world premiere couldn't have taken place. In fact, a small faction of the actors, led by Peter Cousens as their spokesperson, suggested that we abandon the performance, as there was no way we could pull the show together within the allotted time. The bull had caught a glimpse of the crimson cape and it was all into the ring! A hasty meeting was called on the stage for those involved in the production. Both Katy and I were adamant that the show should go on. Mike would be bitterly disappointed if the first show of the tour were to be cancelled, but being the producer, he would have to side with the majority. Strong language and powerful logic would be thrown up by both sides of the warring camps, but in the end, Katy won the day with a withering speech about dedication to our craft and never giving up. We would go with the flow!

In my frantic rush, while I was on the hard floor laying out the yellow electrical insulation tape to denote the edges of the stage, I threw my dodgy back out. The old injury had returned with a vengeance. Scoliosis immediately twisted my body to one side, and searing pain set in. When I looked at myself in the

The original Eureka flag that the miners took into battle, now kept safe at Ballarat Fine Art Gallery. The material was scrounged from the wives of the miners' petty coats, and linen from the church.

mirror, the trunk of my body looked like a toilet S-bend. I really should have taken a nap and relieved the pressure, but I was needed desperately to help finish preparing the show. Besides, I had been the loudest at spouting the old motto, the show must go on. I popped a couple of strong painkillers and got on with it. Dr Stage would get me through the performance, and I convinced myself that my minor deformity added to the character of Paddy O'Malley. The invited audience was impressed by what we pulled together in the limited time available, and hopefully we disguised a few of the technical cockups that occurred.

The cast for the Queensland tour was an impressive one, apart from me. Rob

Guest had joined the company to play the pivotal role of Peter Lalor, Trisha Crowe would play my granddaughter, Donald McDonald was our narrator, and playing a variety of roles, some based on real people, were Leonie Page, Peter Cousens, Lance Strauss, Rodney Dobson, Rick Lau, Russell Newman, Liam Gibson, Gaetano Bonfante, Amanda Jermyn, Rachel Donovan, and sisters Natalie and Emily Street.

Anyone who has suffered from back pain will attest that to push it is the worst medicine, but I had no choice. We went out on tour immediately to Queensland, and I had to carry the infernal injury through the Gold Coast Centre, Caloundra, Maryborough, Rockhampton, Gladstone, Mackay, Proserpine, Townsville, Cairns and Toowoomba. On stage I could ignore the pain but dragging suitcases up and down motel and hotel steps was no holiday tour. One thing that eased my discomfort was the tremendous reaction we received every night. Mike would arrange a cast table in each theatre's foyer, and after the performance the cast members, along with Mike, would sign autographs and posters and sell copies of the original tin-shed cast recordings. The CDs sold like the proverbial hot cakes, and all the takings were ploughed back into the show. We would also receive comments on the positive and negative aspects of what the audience members had experienced.

We must have made a lasting impression, because when Katy took her show *Me and Jezebel* through the same locations in 2007, people were still eager to talk about *Eureka*. The noise that the show created allowed Mike to find two major investors and raise the many millions of dollars needed to underwrite *Eureka* as a fully-fledged musical.

Time to Get Serious!

With the big money now on board, decisions were made by Mike Harvey, co-producer Simon Gallaher and the major investors to employ only the best people available for each area of the production. Gale Edwards was employed as our director. She'd had vast experience in Australia, having directed the original *Boy from Oz*, *Sweeney Todd*, and *Aspects of Love* among others, but her overseas experience was more than impressive, both in London's West End and on Broadway. Her West End productions include *Jesus Christ Superstar* and *Whistle Down the Wind*, and her direction of Shakespeare's works in New York and Europe are legendary. Gale continues to be in great demand around the world. Peter England was given the challenge of designing a brilliant set that could adapt to the many different settings of the story, from a mining camp to a plush ballroom. Gabriela Tylesova would design unique period costumes for each character. Helpmann award winner, the brilliant Trudy Dalgleish, would provide a gobsmacking lighting plot. Our new musical director was Michael Tyack, while choreography was the responsibility of the much-awarded Tony Bartuccio. All of these top professionals, working together, would create an exciting showcase for Australian musical theatre.

In February 2004, auditions started in Sydney for an almost entirely new cast. Extensive rewrites were cut into the original Maggie Gordon script. Many of the scenes and characters were deleted, or totally reshaped to fit the new direction foreseen by Gale Edwards and her co-writer John Senczuk. By the time the August rehearsals began in Melbourne, only two of the Queensland tour cast members remained, namely Trisha Crowe, and me. Gale's decision to cast younger players certainly upset a couple of the original cast members. Rob Guest had been brilliant in the role of Peter Lalor, and he was quite devastated, but in fairness to history, Peter Lalor was only 27 years of age at the time of the uprising, and Rob was into his fifties. Another to be bitterly disappointed was Peter Cousens, who was also too old for his part. Gale saw the play's young lovers as teenagers. In the early discussions, Gale didn't seem all that enamoured with me, either. In the original plot, old Paddy, as well as having a granddaughter, had a cheeky young grandson, and their lighter moments, reinforced with a comical duet, sometimes stopped the show. But the grandson had been cut in the new scenario, and Paddy became a darker character. Gale knew me only from television, and she plumped for someone who could portray the anger and frustration that had consequently been written into Paddy's character. For a while I was on shaky ground, but Mike, Simon, and Maggie were in my corner and they went out on a limb for me, insisting that I was the dramatic actor she wanted. I would hold my place.

The initial interactions between Gail and I were a little tenuous, but as rehearsals progressed we finished up as thick as thieves. I admired the way this director used her own methods to get what she wanted from her actors. Gale had the deserved reputation of being tough, and there would be many tears shed during rehearsals, especially among the younger cast members, but when the salty water was mopped up, a better performance would invariably result from the conflict. Gail's special stamina allowed her to keep going when others around her would be dropping, and nobody understands this demonic obsession more than I do, of not quitting until the desired goal is reached. Not everyone appreciated her methods. There would be some heated discussions, not only with the actors, but the producers as well, but we all respected her and the results she achieved. I joked to her one day, 'I think you must have been Napoleon in another lifetime. You've got your troops ready to follow you into battle through hell and high water!'

As rehearsals proceeded, there were constant plot and script changes. What reads well on paper quite often falls on its bum when you stand it up. One day, Gale and I had quite a stoush over my one and only solo song. I was happy with the position of the number in the show. It was my little jewel of a moment, when Paddy sings about his own philosophy in 'A Beautiful Dream' to his granddaughter after she has chastised him over his aimless approach to life. Gale had decided that the song should be moved up closer to the opening of the show to establish my character early. I was desperate to leave the song in its original place.

We went at loggerheads over her decision, as I knew taking the song earlier would diminish its impact. I offered her a solution, 'If I can come up with different lyrics explaining my character early, using the same melody, will you leave the song in its original spot, and will you let it stay?' Gale looked up from her script and said, 'Go see what you can do, and I'll *think* about it.'

I immediately grabbed a writing pad and pen and ensconced myself in a quiet room. Half an hour later I approached Gale with the new lyrics; the words had literally fallen from my pen. Looking slightly surprised, she took the page from my hands. As I stood silently waiting her response, she suddenly looked up and with a wry smile said, 'I love it. Okay, you win.' Naturally I felt elated. Some directors give off the impression that they only want you to say the lines as they're written, and don't bump into the furniture!

My small conflict with Gale turned out to be well worth the effort, the new lyrics worked a treat, and I retained my lovely moment in the show. In the play, Paddy O'Malley's character had been the catalyst for the Eureka Uprising on the Ballarat goldfields in the 1850s. The real man was a Scottish digger named James Scobie, who had been murdered at the Eureka Hotel by its owner James Bentley, but because of Bentley's connections, he'd escaped conviction. The diggers retaliated by burning down the hotel. This action led to the formation of the first union for workers in the world, giving them the means to stand up for their rights and earn a better deal on the goldfields. All of this led to Peter Lalor and the Eureka Stockade Rebellion. Paddy was a gem of a role. I was a scruffy old Irishman, I got drunk and I played with the Ballarat prostitutes, or should I say, they played with me! I had a lovely song, I had to be happy, sad and mad, and I was kicked to death by the publican and his henchmen; what more could an actor ask for?

The 150th celebration of the uprising was on 11 August and we felt very much part of the festivities that were being staged in Ballarat and Melbourne. On 20 August, the then Victorian Premier Steve Bracks visited our rehearsals and was impressed. He gave us his imprimatur, which made us all feel assured of success.

Previews started at Her Majesty's Theatre on 28 September. Although the show appeared basically to be in good shape, and the audience reaction solid, Gale and the producers found weaknesses in the plot, and quite a few technical problems reared their heads. Gale even felt that the ending of the show was not spectacular enough. From that first preview on, new dialogue and music were being introduced at almost every performance to help tighten and improve the show. Unfortunately, with Australia's small population, we don't have the luxury

Mike and Jill Harvey, Rick Creighton, Lindy Chamberlain-Creighton, Simon Gallaher and me.

of countries like America or England, where they can take their shows out to regional venues, in order to fine tune and hone any imperfections that a new musical might present. We can only plough on ahead and trust that our instincts will be correct.

We had a fabulous opening night on 8 October. At the end of the show, the invited audience sprang to their feet as one, as if they'd been choreographed. As paper streamers and small explosions burst all around the stage, the ecstatic cast couldn't help but revel in the cheering and applause that seemed like it was never going to end. Opening night speeches were made, and the orchestra struck up a reprise of 'Southern Cross', the main theme. As we made our way from the stage, the continuous rapturous applause carried us all on a sea of elation back to our dressing rooms. I found myself yelling to anybody and everybody, 'We've got a hit! We've got a hit!'

The only thing to do now was enjoy the party in the foyer. Our original director, Katy, had been there to see the show come to fruition, and she couldn't hold back the tears of joy, not only for me, but for Mike and Maggie as well. The night held a special treat for me, for I had returned to Her Majesty's Theatre in triumph, after having once been rejected as a young hopeful. As I have mentioned earlier, I auditioned for Terry Vaughn, the casting director for J. C. Williamson, at Christmas in 1956. 'A star or nothing' he'd sprouted back then, but Terry had been right, and so had I, I had returned there as a star!

An awful lot was going on in Melbourne. The city was gearing up for the spring horse-racing carnival, which encompassed the Caulfield and Melbourne cups. Society ladies from around the world had spent over $7 million on hats and frocks in their annual bid for attention. *Eureka* came in as part of the Festival of Melbourne, which always offers an eclectic array of entertainment delights, all competing for their share of the same dollar. Only one year earlier, *Barry Crocker's Banjo* had sunk without a trace, buried by the festival's massive advertising budget. This time, our production seemed far more secure under the financial umbrella of the festival, although I started to feel a little wary when talking to people in the street, who seemed to think that our show was connected to the free Eureka celebrations in Ballarat.

Opening night had been one out of the box for us, and we felt confident that the reviews for the show would ride on the backs of the adulation we'd already experienced.

How wrong could I be? The reviews were mixed, even though the majority of them were positive, but the dissenting critics not only disliked the show, they hated it passionately.

In the *Herald Sun*, Andrew Bolt, the noted political journalist, tore the show to pieces, proclaiming in his by-line:

EUREKA COLLAPSES IN THE MINESHAFT.

Hurry, before word of mouth kills it. Rush to Her Majesty's Theatre, see the modern racism of the modern set to music. Go hiss the British and worship the Aboriginal. Cheer the Irish and laugh at the Christians. Boo the cruel police and hug the hookers.

I'm not surprised most critics are urging for Eureka! a musical about the bloody rebellion in 1854 of Ballarat miners.

"Vibrant" said the Herald Sun.

"Tremendous material" agreed The Australian, generously dismissing its flaws as "nothing a few more million dollars wouldn't sort out".

The Age, shrilly Leftist of course, clapped loudest, calling Eureka! "Rousing contemporary entertainment".

But from where I sat, crying over the cash my wife had flushed down the mineshaft, what made this entertainment so rousing was the most contemporary thing about it – its endorsement of the Left-wing prejudices that mar the arts in Australia.

Andrew Bolt spent the next three columns correcting the historical mistakes that he'd found in the text, dismissed the achievements of Peter Lalor and those who had died for a cause, and he even managed to denigrate Bunjil, the creator of life in Aboriginal lore.

In the entire page-long article, there was not a mention of the magnificent set or the lighting, the directing, or any of the acting performances. He told his readers that the songs weren't hot either. For the first time in my life, I was compelled to answer the retorts of an opinionated critic. Bolt hadn't been able to see, or appreciate, the five years of love and dedication, or the sweat, blood and tears that had gone into creating a home-grown musical. Normally, I would have taken such comments on the chin, but he had kept the truth from his readers, who did not know that we'd had a 10-minute standing ovation at the end of the show. Here is my letter in its entirety, as sent to the Your Say section in the Melbourne *Herald Sun* of 27 October.

'Eureka', the right (or the left) of reply.

As a proud third generation Australian, and one who is about to enter his 50th year as a professional actor/entertainer, I found Andrew Bolt's review of 'Eureka the Musical' (Oct 17–04), a pedantic disservice, not only to the Australian Theatre, but to all those who lovingly work in, and embrace her. What Mr Bolt won't accept is that the writers of 'Eureka' didn't set out to present an historical documentation of the events at Ballarat in 1854, but an entertainment designed to bring not only pride and joy to an audience, but an awareness of a cruel disaster that did help shape Australia's history and future.

That the writers would choose to tell the underdog's far more interesting side of the story irks Mr Bolt no end. In his review, not once does he mention the superb sets and lighting, costumes, the direction, or the stunning performances given by the brilliant new talent discovered for this show; all the above, Australian!

He also refuses to concede the standing ovation, and prolonged applause from the opening night audience; acclamation that has continued at every subsequent performance. My great sadness and fear is the punters out there, with limited entertainment dollars, may read Mr Bolt's biased and unfair review, and decide to spend their money elsewhere. If people like Andrew Bolt have their way, shows like 'Eureka' will fold, and producers will put away their cheque books for another decade or two, until memory of 'The Great Australian Musical' has faded into the right wing ether. I have had a wonderful career, and enjoy playing my role of Paddy in 'Eureka' as much as anything I've ever done; but I want those who follow me, not to be forced to sing and act with, the tried and true, American voices, in the latest overseas hit.

Let us have our own voice, our own stories!

I remain yours, hopefully and sincerely,

Barry Hugh Crocker A.M.

My letter was joined by many others in agreement sent in to Your Say, and also to various other publications, but after the excitement of the first week's pre-bookings we found the box office hardly moving. We had a dilemma on our hands. Every performance would bring a standing ovation from the audience. We imagined the punters would be out there, telling all their friends about this fabulous all-Australian entertainment. More dollars were ploughed into paper publicity, but it made only a minute difference. Questions were asked, not only of our fellow professionals, but also the people in the street, and a common theme started to emerge. *Eureka* was a musical, but no one knew any of the songs. Every overseas musical that has ever arrived in Australia has been preceded by a cast recording, or even a motion picture of the show, therefore guaranteeing that if the people love the music, they'll support the stage version. This familiarity has helped local musicals such as *Shout*, *The Boy from Oz*, *Priscilla*, and *Dusty* to prosper, whereas shows like the all-Australian *Eureka* face an uphill battle.

Eureka was in a catch-22 situation. A cast album was on the agenda, but cast recordings cost a lot of money, and the producers felt, with some justification, that all of the up-front revenue should be used to make the continuing production as spectacular as possible. The plan was to make enough money then go into the studio to put down the show's cast recording. When the CD was eventually ready, it would be available for sale at Her Majesty's Theatre and other venues, in anticipation of the forthcoming national tour.

We needed to get the music out into the public arena. Audiences had departed the theatre singing the songs, but the producers found themselves running into brick walls. No-one wanted to play untried material on the radio. Vast amounts had been spent on radio advertising, but even when the stations were offered fees to at least play the main theme, they declined to help, citing some obscure broadcasting statutes that ruled against such practices.

We gave our last matinee performance on Sunday 28 November. We had lasted a deflating and debilitating seven weeks and two days. Everything possible had been tried to keep the production going. The producers had ploughed a further two million dollars into the last weeks of the production to keep it afloat, in the belief that the show's fortunes would turn around.

As Samuel Goldwyn once uttered, in one of his famous malapropisms, 'If the people won't come, you can't stop them.' We certainly couldn't stop them. To say that we were stunned by the lack of public support would be a pitiful understatement. The rejection was a huge slap in the face to all who had worked so hard at bringing an important moment in Australian history to the stage. However, there is an explanation. If the track record of Aussie musicals had been researched a little more fully, we may not have been so surprised by our failure.

Since 1900 there have been over 700 all-Australian musical theatre productions. Only a handful had any kind of impact, mostly low budget easy-to-recoup affairs.

There have been dozens of musicals based around the Eureka saga and all have failed. Success eludes even our most notorious yet glamorous outlaw, Ned Kelly, not only on the stage but in a series of feature films that have told of his saga. The respected journalist Jules Archibald expressed his concern about the Australians' lack of confidence in themselves, when they believed their artistic output seemed inferior to the rest of the world. Over 100 years ago, he published in his magazine, *The Bulletin* that we needed to get over our inbuilt inferiority complex. He pointed out there wasn't a profession in the world including medicine, business, manufacturing or sport where we weren't the equal of any other nation, and we should hold our heads high, and embrace our heritage and history with open arms. Australians have gone on to excel in every endeavour from the boardrooms of business to the sporting fields of the world. We cheer our champions with great pride, but I wonder if Jules Archibald would understand why the average Australian knows more about Wyatt Earp and the OK Corral than of Peter Lalor and the Eureka Stockade.

Questions were being asked and theories put forward as to why *Eureka* failed to attract an audience. Some thought we'd strayed too far from the softer, happier approach of the original Maggie Gordon script, making the musical too dark, and too much like *Les Misérables*. Maybe Australian audiences didn't want to be reminded of a violent past. However, those same Australian crowds had packed our theatres for five years with *Les Mis*, quite prepared to relive the misfortunes of a French ex-convict in the early 19th century, as set to music. Others would assert that adding the Indigenous aspect to the play had been a bad choice. Should there have been an overture perhaps? Instead, the play opened with a withering discourse on the genocide of the Aboriginal population after the arrival of the first Europeans. There were those who accused us of turning away conservative theatregoers by glorifying the workers' Southern Cross flag, but the workers' bums hadn't filled the seats either.

Post-mortems offer very little comfort to those at the coalface. At the bottom of the pit stood Mike Harvey, who had given his heart and soul to this project for half a decade, not to mention a large slab of his own money. His every waking moment had been locked into the project, fighting for funding and convincing the powers-that-be that his dream could be brought to reality. The dream had dissolved into merely a seven-week-long illusion. All through the backstage dramas, the rumours, and the conflicting press about dwindling audiences, Mike had been absolute in his resolve with the actors, telling us we wouldn't be let down, even if the worst happened. It is not unusual in our profession that when a show goes down the tube no-one gets paid, but we trusted Mike implicitly.

During almost every show, he would visit the individual dressing rooms, always exuding a huge smile and complimenting one's performance. Although Mike is a bear of a man, his physique belies his sensitivity, and often during rehearsals I observed him holding back tears of pride as the show evolved. I couldn't help but wonder how he held his frustrations in check. There were no frowns of dismay nor vexed scowls against the tide of negativism that was rising in the backstage corridors. He remained calm and refreshingly positive.

That last matinee had a surreal, almost dreamlike quality to it. It was an unnaturally weird experience, having to remove the dozens of photos that were taped to my mirror. I had snapped away, as usual, all through the rehearsals and the various productions of *Eureka*. Taking off Paddy's costume, and washing off his make-up for the last time, made me feel as if I were attending a funeral. Peter Carroll, with whom I had shared the dressing room, was quickly out the door while I lingered for a few more seconds, always the last one to leave. I even found myself taking a picture of the stripped and empty room that had been my home for the last seven weeks.

By the time I climbed the stairs to the foyer and restaurant of Her Majesty's, most of the cast and crew were refreshing themselves with closing show drinks, and an atmosphere of good-natured frivolity and banter filled the air. It's moments like these that I wish I was still an imbiber. I stand around as sober as a judge, while my comrades drown their sorrows and wash away their woes. I had to drive home to Sydney the next morning, so I didn't stay long at the party. I said goodbye to everyone on deck, and shared some big hugs with Gale, Mike, Simon, and anyone else I could get my arms around. I was going to miss the techs, the dressers, stagehands and front of house mob, all those who had become part of the *Eureka* extended family; I pondered on how many of them I would see again. The last person to whom I waved goodbye was Rachael Beck, who had played Alicia Dunn. She was standing near the theatre on the corner of Exhibition and Little Bourke streets looking lost, and I was on the opposite corner of Little Bourke, heading towards my hotel. To anyone observing us, it must have seemed like we were shooting a movie, as we carried on waving and saying 'Bye' for a good 30 seconds. Nobody really wanted to say goodbye.

When all the last farewells and promises to keep in touch have been made, and as the days run into months, it's then that the realisation that it is over finally hits home, and the person it hit the hardest was Mike Harvey. Mike plunged into a deep depression, and he found his once strong physique starting to come apart. High blood pressure and cardiac problems besieged his body, and he had to take serious time off to alleviate the symptoms. Specialists were consulted, explanations offered, and medications prescribed, but his recovery would be a long process. To compound Mike's run of poor health, he suffered a stroke in June 2008. For once, some luck was on his side. The stroke hit while he and wife Jill were watching television. Jill glanced across to Mike and knew immediately that something was terribly wrong. He had collapsed in his chair, unable to speak. The right side of his face had dropped, and he was paralysed down his right side. He was aware of everything going on around him and everything that was said, but he couldn't respond in any way. The ambulance would be there within 20 minutes, and his treatment began effectively from that moment. The stroke had been caught early. Mike would bounce back to virtual normality within days, but he'd given everyone a hell of a scare.

In September 2009, he joined me for a trip to Townsville, where he accompanied me during two cabaret performances, and it was like old times.

Katy in *When Darkness Falls*.

What Katy Did

After the demise of *Eureka*, I participated in a few Carols by Candlelight events and started arranging my return to the cabaret circuit for 2005, but I planned to do something a little different to my usual nightclub fare this year. I would write a scaled down version of *Banjo* to be presented in the clubs and smaller venues. I would not only have to devise a shorter version in two acts, but I would have to assemble the projection screen and minimum scenery within the couple of hours the clubs normally allowed for set-up. I was taking a bit of a risk, but I was pleasantly surprised with the very positive reception we received, probably because we kept the essence of *Banjo* in its original form.

On a different entertainment note, I had an idea for a television roast to coincide with achieving my three score years and ten during the course of the year. I thought it seemed like a natural winner, to get a heap of my mates together in an intimate setting, using old footage intermingled with live musical performances from, not only the oldies, but some of the younger stars with whom I had been working lately as well. I wanted to set the studio up like a giant nightclub with tables, serving food and drinks, similar to a night at the Logie Awards. Tickets would be sold, and all profits, plus a percentage of the TV commercial revenue, would go to my favourite children's charity, Variety. Channel Seven, although sympathetic to the idea, felt it wasn't their demographic. Both Nine and Ten showed initial interest, but after procrastinating for several weeks, neither would take up the option.

I was prepared to push on, with the subscriber network Foxtel in my sights, but Katy convinced me I was flogging a dead horse. Besides, she told me she had an outside party who was interested in bankrolling the project. I wasn't allowed to know anything about it. I had to leave everything to her otherwise she'd pull the plug. I had nothing to lose by letting Katy go ahead.

Earlier in the year, Katy had played a character role in a low-budget film noir called *When Darkness Falls*, directed by Rohan Spong, and starring singer Natalie Bassingthwaighte. At the Melbourne Film Festival later in the year, Katy would win the best supporting actress award for her contribution. I had promised to accompany Katy to a private preview showing of the film on 25 June at the Shangri-La Hotel in The Rocks. When the day arrived, I was rather selfishly lacking in enthusiasm.

It was a bleak and cold Saturday morning, suitable only for a sleep-in, and I was booked to do a cabaret show with Jeanne Little at the Manly-Warringah Leagues Club that night. Why couldn't they send us a convenient DVD to watch instead? 'Why can't we just go to the official opening?' I protested. 'It'd be much more fun.' 'No!' Katy insisted. 'They're expecting us, and Rohan is very keen to meet you. It would be very rude to drop out now!'

I did a pretty good impression of Liam Gallagher, although I didn't thump anyone, as I scampered into the Shangri-La foyer, dragging Katy along at a rate of knots towards the lifts. I hadn't gone to any trouble as far as my appearance was concerned. My beard wasn't trimmed and I was wearing my favourite scruffy shirt, old jeans, and a hastily pulled on jacket, topped off with my worn and battered *Eureka* baseball cap. I was certainly not at my sartorial best, but who would see me if I moved fast enough?

After exiting the lift on the fourth floor, we entered the small function room prepared for the screening. I met Rohan, the director, who introduced me to five other people who had presumably been invited for the same reason as me. I accepted a welcome cup of hot coffee, and then turned my attention to a cameraman who was hovering around the room rather curiously. Rohan told me he was going to say a few words to the gathering, to be filmed as part of the publicity campaign. 'Don't let him shoot me!' I quipped. Rohan gave an inspiring speech about how hard everyone had worked on the movie and concluded with the words, 'So thank you all for coming, sit back and relax and I hope you enjoy *When Darkness Falls*.'

The room lights went down, the title music swelled, and I got ready to take in the midday movie with one of its stars sitting beside me. No sooner had the title come up than the projected picture deteriorated into a million pixels. The music ground to a halt and the lights came back on overhead. The very worried director proclaimed, 'I'm sorry about this ... I think there's another copy downstairs.' He scurried towards the side door in front of me.

'Well so fa, you're great!' I said to Katy.

Rohan had left the room, but now another person, as if conjured up from thin air, appeared in the open doorway. It was a man I knew well.

'Hello Mikey,' I said quite innocently.

'Hello Barry,' replied Mike Munro. 'I hear the equipment here is an absolute Barry Crocker!'

The penny dropped. 'Awww—you're not here for *moi*?'

'Barry Crocker,' grinned Mike, 'this is your life!'

I couldn't believe it. Twenty-five years after I had first been the recipient of this honour, never in my wildest dreams did I expect it would happen a second time! Katy had pulled off the perfect sting, and this piece of flake had fallen for it, hook line and sinker. I heard myself saying, 'Are we still going to see the picture?' Of course, there was no picture! It was still being edited in Melbourne, but Katy knew that if anything could get me to a location, it would have to be something to do with *the business*. All sorts of rendezvous suggestions had been put to Katy, who had to tell the producers I don't do lunches and I don't drink alcohol. Schemes that would have worked on anyone else had to be discarded. As for the viewers in their lounge rooms, upon seeing the victim snared like a startled puppy, they must suspect on occasion that the trapped celebrity has some inkling about what is going to befall them. Well, I didn't. One would expect some giveaway by the relatives or friends that one knows so well, always able to tell when they're hiding something, but David Mitchell's team were so adept at what they did, I never had a clue about the combined subterfuge needed to fill the screen with my family and friends for a whole 60 minutes. Although I have enjoyed the tributes in two one-hour versions of *This Is Your Life*, a quarter of a century apart, I can state unequivocally that in both instances I was as innocent as a newly born 70-year-old baby!

It was time for the panic to start. A hired limousine was purring away outside our building, ready to whisk me to the studio to tape the show. I told the organisers I needed a proper shower and a change of clothes so I would look halfway decent, both in the studio and on the screen. This was *my* life, not Bob Geldof's.

Everyone was in a slight state of hysteria, as I had a studio full of guests and an audience waiting, not to mention Mike Munro and the technical staff. By rights, I should have been properly dressed already, but if Katy had insisted on me wearing decent clobber that morning, she knew that I would have twigged! In my city apartment, I showered and dressed like a man that knew the husband was on the way home, with no time for elaborate blow drying of the hair. I could feel the throbbing of the limo's engine as the driver waited impatiently for me in the street. Katy had gone ahead to help with the organising.

I emerged from my building to be greeted by beaming *TIYL* staff. The scene resembled a kidnapping as the limo squealed away from the kerb, with me half hanging out of a rear door and anxious personnel securing me into the back seat. On our arrival at the Channel Nine studios, I was whisked along a back corridor to the make-up department. Care is taken to ensure that a wayward guest doesn't stumble inadvertently into the recipient in one of the corridors, thereby blowing the scam, so they are all ensconced in soundproof areas away from the one receiving the honour. Having been a guest on several of my peers' *TIYL* episodes, I knew what was going on out there, so I had no fear of the unexpected. While I waited off stage, the theme music started up. This time, the show was opened by the Doug Anthony All Stars singing their ode to Barry Crocker, which included, in good natured banter, the line, 'Is he a crock-a-shit?'

The doors opened, and I was cued, by way of a poke in the back, to step out in front of the audience, where I was greeted by a grinning Mike Munro and his red book. The Dougs and I shared a good two years bringing mayhem to ABC TV and live cabaret in the 1990s, and it was through them that I came to discover a newer, younger audience. The boys had gone their separate ways almost nine years earlier, but Katy persuaded them to join up one more time for the ol' Crock. I was rapt by the homage paid to me by Paul, Tim and Richard on this occasion. I entered that stage to the kind of reception that is the dream of every performer. I was gobsmacked to see the studio floor overflowing with grinning friends and applauding colleagues, some of whom I hadn't seen in yonks. Scattered amongst the throng were many of the past *TIYL* recipients.

My sister Laurel was the first guest, shown by satellite from Melbourne. She had been too weak to make the trip to Sydney, as she was being treated for cancer. At the time of writing, she was well into her remission, and on the way to a full recovery. She made a sweet, emotional speech about her big brother. From behind the doors, I heard familiar voices singing, in tight harmony, 'We Are Family'. Mike introduced my children to the audience, the four that I knew were there, and one that I didn't. They had flown my son Barry Junior out from Los Angeles, along with his own son James. Geraldine, my eldest, told the Shirley Bassey story, and Barry Jr told the Howard Keel yarn.

A clip was shown from a TV special called *With a Song in my Heart*, which I'd done for Hector Crawford at Channel Ten's Melbourne studios. Neil Harrold and

Rod Kinnear, the former *In Melbourne Tonight* director, had talked the retired and reclusive Graham Kennedy into being my very special guest. After a few yes-no-maybe sessions, he'd finally agreed to come on board. I was a Kennedy fan from the beginning, and there was no-one I wanted more on that show than Graham, on whose shows I had appeared in the past. In the sketch replayed on *TIYL* we play two shambling, aged performers. It is set in an old performers' rest home, and Graham and I bump into each other in our wheelchairs. As we try to impress each other with who we used to be, we try to recount what became of the stars of yesterday. *What happened to Paul Hogan?* He stropped himself to death. *What happened to John Laws?* The flies got him. *What happened to John Meillon?* He made Victoria too bitter. Graham died only two months before my *TIYL* episode went to air, and it would have been so gratifying for me if he could have seen the sketch that one last time.

Geoff Harvey, my *Sound of Music* nemesis, came on and, amongst his stories, he advised me never to trust a man with a beard. I wish he'd given me this advice when we worked together. A clip was played from the episode of *Skippy, the Bush Kangaroo* where I'd played an itinerant snake-oil salesman who tries to kidnap Skippy, with the intention of adding the smart marsupial to his touring concert. Skippy, as usual, is too clever for the conman and turns the tables on my character. The most memorable thing about the filming of *Skippy* happened on the first day, as the opening sequence called for a long shot, followed by a two-shot of my partner in crime, Ray Hartley, and myself, riding an authentic horse-drawn gypsy caravan. As we trotted along the old bush track, I was expected to play a tune on my banjo and sing along. Producer Lee Robinson met with director Eric Fullilove to select a suitable song, preferably something out of copyright, to avoid paying royalties. Nothing of any consequence was nominated, so I said I would write something quickly for the scene, and I certainly didn't expect to be paid anything for it. Within about 10 minutes, I penned a jolly little ditty called 'Merrily We Roll Along'. It was a 12-bar verse, with a repeat chorus that kept on repeating, as the back of a caravan disappeared down the track in another long shot. After the episode went into the can, I gave no more thought to my hastily scribbled tune. However, 'Skippy the Bush Kangaroo' became a worldwide phenomenon, still playing today, over 50 years later, in dozens of countries around the world. The people who bought the series found it prudent, on the advice of APRA, to pay me continuing royalties for the song. The episode was shot in 1967, and every year since I've received a welcome little Christmas present. In fact, of all the songs I've written, 'Merrily We Roll Along' has become the most lucrative.

Bruce Beresford appeared on the *TIYL* big screen, sitting in a coffee shop in a bustling marketplace. 'G'day Barry, I'd love to be there with you tonight,' he said, 'but as you can see, I'm here in Bulgaria shooting a film.' He went on to reminisce about our early start together in the *Barry McKenzie* films. After Bruce's one-way chat, the scene cut to Barry Humphries, who was obviously sitting in the Shangri-La's penthouse overlooking Sydney Harbour. Barry did a quick double-take at the scene behind him, paused for a second, and said, 'I'm in Bulgaria.' His speech, as usual, was hilarious, replete with lines like, 'It's difficult to pay you a compliment that you haven't already paid yourself!'

The 'pointing Percy at the porcelain' scene was shown, from *The Adventures of Barry McKenzie*, where Bazza, using his endearing colloquialisms, tries to find out from the 'to-and-froms' the location of the dunny.

Julie Anthony and Toni Lamond related some of the shared events in our showbiz experiences, the good, the bad, and the silly. We could have gone on reminiscing, but Mike Munro soon introduced Katy, who sat with me on the couch for the rest of the show. She couldn't stop laughing at how she'd been able to pull the wool over my eyes. Some *TIYL* victims might have chided their partners for getting them into this situation but I was loving it, finding the whole thing far more impressive than my earlier ideas for celebrating my 70th birthday. Katy joked, 'That's it, Buster, don't expect anything else for the rest of the year!'

Jenny Main and Simon were introduced next, and in a departure from the frivolity, Mike asked Simon about his time in the Italian prison and how it had affected our relationship. He explained succinctly how we had all come through the terrible ordeal, with our friendship and our kinship as solid as ever.

It was time for the cavalry to arrive, so Mike brought out six of my eight grandchildren and four of my six great-grandchildren. The stage was alive with the sound of childhood mayhem as the little ones took over the show, joyful at sharing this moment with their Pop and their Poppa. The kids had been staying in a posh hotel, with room service, and the whole affair must have seemed like a trip to Disneyland for them.

On the big screen, Geelong football coach Bomber Thompson was joined by the entire team, spread out across my beloved Kardinia Park. Bomber praised my loyalty and dedication to his team, who burst out singing, in non-perfect unison, 'You're a Barry Crocker'. Two years later, my prized team went on to seize the holy grail of Australian Rules, the 2007 Grand Final cup. I would love to, but I can't really claim any responsibility for their success.

Mike Harvey had secured the rights for Channel Nine to show an excerpt from the stage show *Eureka*, and they played part of my solo, 'A Beautiful Dream', showing my character's granddaughter, played by Trisha Crowe, resting against my knee. The song is about keeping one's dreams alive and never giving up. Some observers would say, in my case, never growing up!

There is always a pièce de résistance in the *TIYL* shows, a final guest to top off the night. Twenty-five years earlier, they had flown out my former singing partner David Clark, who enjoyed himself so much that he stayed with me for weeks afterwards. This time it would be more sensational, for from Los Angeles came my touring partner from the early 1960s, Martine Colette. We had known each other for nearly 50 years. The first time I saw her she was an exotic cabaret dancer and her partner in the act was a 10-feet-long python. We became good mates, and when I needed two girls for my 1962 Asian tour I called on Martine to join me, along with Cheryl Stroud. Now Martine decided to replicate the circumstances of our initial meeting. She entered the *TIYL* arena with not a 10-feet-long python, but a live 15-feet-long example instead. Geoff Harvey, who is terrified of snakes, ran from the building.

Martine had owned the Wildlife Waystation, in Little Tujunga Canyon Road in Sylmar, California, for almost 40 years. The purpose of the multi-acre property was to heal sick animals of all breeds, sizes and predicaments. If an animal was in any kind of distress, sometimes having been beaten or tortured, Martine and her staff would do their best to nurse it back to health. She had worked miracles with abandoned pets and injured wildlife, including everything from lizards to lions and tigers. She had this intrinsic gift of being as one with her charges, as if she had a lifeline into the animal's very being. Years later, during the disastrous 2009 California fires, she was forced to evacuate the whole compound to safer ground, and then bring them home when the danger had passed.

So sadly, Martine passed away in Arizona, USA on 23 January 2022. She had been battling throat cancer and her once prized wildlife station had been put into administration. Equally devastating, at the time, my other partner Chery Stroud had been killed in a horror car crash in 1963, shortly after our return from our Asia tours.

As Mike Munro began to wind up the show, he said, 'You know, Barry, it's been

At rehearsals on the day of Topol's 70th birthday.

said that the sweetest sounds that Barry Crocker can hear are, "Would you sing something for us?" Well, I'm asking – would you?'

I replied, with mock annoyance, 'Oh, if I must, I must!'

Geoff Harvey had returned to play the piano for me, having been assured that the monster snake was safely locked away. We closed with a song that had almost become my signature tune, ever since I sang it at the 1977 Australian Rules Grand Final.

Towards the end of 'The Impossible Dream', all of the guests joined me around the piano. The end titles would roll over this scene, and I felt enriched to be surrounded by my own on such an unforgettable day.

The caterers had been a little taken aback when Katy turned down their proposed menu of shrimp cocktails and petit fours, in favour of party pies, spring rolls, and fresh lamingtons with cream filling. There was a beeline for the regular Aussie comfort food that Katy had chosen. Many of the audience joined the after party, and it was good to catch up with a few old buddies, some of whom had flown in from interstate, and I found that the time was flying by far too quickly. It was around 4.30 pm when I had to let the fantasy turn back into reality. There was no time limit on the punters partaking of Channel Nine's hospitality, but the honoured guest was facing the sting. The promoter who had booked Jeanne Little and myself for the Manly-Warringah show would not let me out of my obligation. All sorts of inducements had been offered to him, but he refused to change his mind. I had to leave the party in full swing, so I could get back home, pick up my music and my stage outfit, and then be at the club by 6.30 pm for the sound check.

The closing stages of the *TIYL* evening saw Katy, the family and all the guests back in the Shangri-La's dining room enjoying a relaxing meal and much boisterous conversation about the day's events.

Meanwhile, Barry Crocker carried out his obligatory 6.30 pm sound check and dined on a small portion of fish and chips from the club's kitchen, waiting for the show to start at 8 pm. It was a bit dreary, sitting in the dimly lit, half-painted dressing room when he only wanted to be with those who had shared the vastly more exciting earlier part of the day. When the cabaret was over, it was far too late to expect anyone to be still awake and ready to party. It had been a long day for all concerned, and the moment had passed. Barry Junior had to leave the next day to get back to his church in Los Angeles, so our farewell was all too brief. Martine Colette took the opportunity to catch up with her mother in Adelaide. When she returned to Sydney a few days later, for her flight back to the States, we took the time to indulge in some reminiscing about our Asian escapades in the 1960s.

CHAPTER 11

Fiddler on the Roof

In July, Katy and I attended the opening of a Jon Nicholls production of the Chinese dance spectacular *Tales of the Silk Road*. During the interval, we found we'd been sitting next to an old friend, actor Bartholomew John, who was accompanied by his partner Jill. I hadn't seen Bart for over five years, and we talked about what was going on in the acting profession. Bart had recently auditioned for a role in the upcoming *Fiddler on the Roof*, starring the acclaimed Topol. Bart suggested I would be perfect for the role of Lazer Wolfe, the butcher. I thanked him for the advice, but following some disappointing knock-backs I'd had recently, I put his suggestion quickly out of my mind.

I received an unexpected phone call on the morning of Saturday 27 August. 'I don't know if you remember me, Barry,' said the thickest Scottish accent I had heard since Sean Connery, 'but we were talking after the opening of *Eureka* in Melbourne last year. My name is Tim Lawson, and I'm a producer. I told you how terrific you were as Paddy, remember?'

'C'mon, who is this?' I queried, in my best sceptical voice.

'I'm producing *Fiddler on the Roof* with Topol,' he replied. 'We're into rehearsals, and I've just had an actor drop out on me, might you be interested in stepping into the role?' There was a biting urgency in Tim's voice, and a meeting was arranged for the following Monday. He would send over all the relevant material, including the script and the songs, to help me make up my mind. Within a matter of hours, everything arrived at my apartment. I don't have to tell you which part he wanted me to play, do I?

Yes, it was the role of Lazer Wolfe, the very same character Bart John saw in me. Oddly enough, the show would be staged where Bart and I had met that night, at Sydney's historic Capitol Theatre. I was immediately on the phone to Melbourne, calling my old mate Ernie Bourne, who had been in the show when Topol had toured with it eight years earlier. Ernie assured me that Lazer was a most prestigious dramatic role, worthy of any serious actor.

On the Monday, we gathered in a small rehearsal room at the Capitol, the musical director, who would play piano for me, the dance captain, Tim the producer, and Sammy Bayes, the director, who had been with *Fiddler on the Roof* even longer than Topol. I guessed Sammy would give the final approval, so I did all the usual things. I sang some songs, I showed I wouldn't fall over if I tried to dance, and I read the script. As always, I felt apprehensive, because no-one ever commits an opinion. They thanked me for coming, I reciprocated, and Tim said, 'I'll call you this afternoon.'

As Tim promised, the word came through later that day. As far as my acceptance for the role was concerned, I was a goer, but it was up to my manager Tony Brady to fine-tune the vital matter of the spondulicks. Payment is a delicate instrument when it comes to regulating the pitch, and everybody has to dance away in harmony with the negotiations. On 31 August, the following Wednesday morning, I joined the company, which was already ten days into rehearsals. As soon as I arrived, I was pounced on from all quarters. Cast members were telling me where to stand and which way to move. Andrew Hallsworth, the associate choreographer, took me into some remote corridors to get me to learn the dance routines as quickly as possible. There were minor problems over costume fittings, discussions over the right make-up, and differences of opinion over the girth of my fat suit. How I loved the mayhem! Crocker was back in the theatre, where he belonged.

Topol

Rehearsals were in their third day before I found myself in the presence of the great man. I was waiting at the cafe on the corner of Pitt and Hay streets, a few short steps from the Capitol's stage door. The winter winds can whip up all too readily on that corner, chilling the bones while street detritus is blown into your eyes, however, that day was sunny and calm, and the little cafe was the perfect place for our rendezvous. I had heard stories about the supposedly temperamental star. To work with Topol could be difficult, and any actor meeting with Topol's disapproval could be replaced in the blink of an eye. I was replacing one Lazer Wolfe already, and I knew that two Lazers had left the cast on the first tour, eight years earlier. *Fiddler on the Roof* was every stage producer's dream, a sure fire hit. After its opening in 1964, it broke every box office record on Broadway for a further 10 years, until it was toppled by the sensational rock and roll musical, *Grease*.

A pristine white limousine pulled into Hay Street, gliding to a stop outside the cafe, where I was waiting so patiently. The chauffeur opened the passenger doors, and out stepped Tim Lawson, the Scottish producer. Tim helped two attractive ladies out from the back seat, and then Topol emerged onto the footpath. Tim said to Topol, 'Chaim, this is Barry Crocker.' Before I uttered a word, Topol reached out his hand and said, 'I have heard so much about you, Barry.' While I was still smiling at the legendary actor's generous greeting, Tim introduced me to Galia, Chaim Topol's wife of over 50 years.

The other lady in the party was Sara Zinger. I had first met Sara when she was a fashion designer, running a Melbourne-based leather business with her husband in the 1970s. Sara and Galia had known each other from Israel and they had been reacquainted as friends, catching up when Topol came to Melbourne eight years earlier. Over the next two years, Sara attended the openings of *Fiddler* in each new city, always helping to brighten and glamorise the festivities, usually staying on to keep Galia company.

Chaim had worked with some of the cast before, including Judith Roberts, who had played the part of Tevye's wife, Golde, in the earlier production. There were a few other second-timers as well, but most of us were newcomers. It was exciting to enter the run-through room and see the outlines of the sets marked out in tape on the floor, and scattered props filling in the spaces. With the new Lazer in place, we could get down to the solid business of pulling the show together. As the chorus line and the dancers practised in the main hall, Topol rehearsed with some of the other main actors in the smaller rooms. The afternoon would see the first run-through from the beginning. As the cast entered the hall, exhilaration took over, and the rehearsal space was filled with excitable chatter, the singing of scales, and tapping and grunting noises from the dancers, all escalating into an enormous crescendo.

The cacophony was silenced by the associate director and choreographer, Andrew Hallsworth, when he clapped his hands loudly and announced, 'Good afternoon, ladies and gentlemen, welcome to rehearsals!' Applause filled the room, followed by a deliberate silence. Sammy Bayes stepped forward and asked everyone to form a giant circle by holding each other's hands. Good-hearted mutterings were exchanged as each of us took hold of the nearest person's hand on either side. Sammy had been with *Fiddler* longer than anyone, having been a dancer in the 1964 Broadway production with Zero Mostel, and he had appeared with Topol in the 1971 movie as one of the featured dancers. He had directed the show many, many times, not only in English-speaking countries, but also the Japanese version as well.

He began, 'Now you all know me, and what my part in this production is, but now, I'd like each and every one of you to speak your own name in turn, and the character that you are playing in the show. Around we went, with all of the performers announcing their names and the roles they were going to play. I blurted out, 'I'm Barry Crocker, and I will be playing the role of Lazer Wolfe.' I felt a bit like the new kid on the block, even after I had already been accepted warmly into the cast.

The circle method would be used throughout the rehearsals, with Sammy sometimes getting us to sit on chairs in the ring and perform the play without any movement at all. These sessions were quite instructional, because when you're rehearsing in a normal way, and your turn comes to exit the stage, you disappear from the action, but in the circle you are made aware of everything that is happening

Left to right: Ricky Schutte, Chaim Topol, Judith Roberts, me, Blanche d'Alpuget, Bob Hawke, Robbie Rowland.

throughout the story. There would often be weeping from the cast members when confronted with the emotions of the entire story, rather than only their individual parts. The next performance would be noticeably enhanced, with each actor having been reminded of what the play was attempting to say.

In May 2022, the world would see Sammy, who had been with the show since its inception, go on to join the mates who had gone before him. Would he be directing them? Probably!

In my audition, the musical director Stephen Amos had played for me, but now, although Stephen conducted, the orchestra would be represented by the highly skilled rehearsal pianist, Robyn Womersley, who would coax all the necessary passion and drama from a simple upright piano. The overture started, and I was aware of Beth Daly, who played Shandel, taking hold of my right hand. 'Here's what happens, Barry,' she said, 'you take my hand in your right, and in your left, Octavia's.' The whole cast, except Tevye and the Fiddler, were holding hands in a giant hidden line. As the overture reached the violin solo, Topol made his way out from behind the facsimile house that had been taped on the floor.

Standing on centre stage, he spoke the first words of dialogue, 'A fiddler on the roof. Sounds crazy, no?' The depth and resonance of Topol's rich stage baritone threw me for a six. It was spine tingling. He made Kamahl sound like Tiny Tim! By the time Tevye reached the crescendo of his opening lines, the full company started to enter from stage right, moving around him in a giant circle while they sang the opening song 'Tradition'. As the song progressed, the circle broke up into smaller circles, representing the families and their standing in the town of Anatevka, where every day they meet and mingle. The characters depend on each other for their survival, and it's evident from the song's lyrics that Anatevka is not a wealthy town. As the song continued, the cast members resumed their original places in the circle. In 'Tradition', the writers Sheldon Harnick (lyrics) and Jerry Bock (music) crafted a musical masterpiece, for as the town characters interlock and join each other's circles, each is introduced to the audience, not only by name but also by his or her persona. From these tiny bits of dialogue, or lyrics, the audience has an initial idea of what the person is all about.

Bob Hawke helps Katy improve her grip.

The story goes that well into rehearsals, the original show lacked an opening number, and as everyone sat around lamenting the fact, Jerome Robbins, the director and choreographer, asked the worried producers, 'What is this play about?'

Some now forgotten voice said, 'It's all about tradition.' Jerome had then simply said, 'Then write a song about tradition.' The song was written overnight, becoming the foundation for everything that happens in Anatevka.

The opening song had to be rehearsed and polished several times as it wasn't easy ducking in and out of those ever changing circles.

While Topol rehearsed his scenes, I sat behind the pianist, studying the great actor's technique. I was soon joined by Maggie Kirkpatrick, who was playing Yentre, the matchmaker. 'Does it get any better than this?' She whispered. 'We are watching a free master class and we're being paid!'

Other members of the cast soon took up our lead and sat watching Topol go through his paces as Tevye, all of them as mesmerised as we were. He wasn't even aware of our presence as he slipped into the milkman's well-worn boots. A little bit of Tevye's costume was always present in the rehearsals, be it the boots, his hat, or even the constant scarf. Later on, during the dance sequence, when the show was up and running, the scarf came adrift and fell to the stage. Rather deftly, I reached down and retrieved it, without breaking step. When I placed it in his hand, Topol's eyes were aglow with gratitude.

Talking to Topol

After our first rehearsal, never being shy in coming forward, I made my way to Chaim to thank him for such a memorable day. Before I knew it, we were deep in conversation about Israel, with me telling him of my cabaret work in Tel Aviv for five months in 1963. I mentioned my travels all over the land, working from kibbutzes in the country, to towns like Haifa and Jerusalem, but also, how I'd always have to be back for the 1 am late show at the prestigious Sabra nightclub, in the heart of Tel Aviv. Israel is a small country, and one can traverse its length and breadth in a day. It was no great difficulty to perform two shows a day, and besides, I was a wide-eyed tourist visiting places where Jesus had once walked. My 8 mm home movie camera went through dozens of rolls of film.

The country was under constant threat from so many directions, and some of my cohorts considered me pretty brave or foolish to be visiting these remote venues for the purpose of entertaining the locals, but I was being paid, and at the age of 28, I was invincible! More often than not, I would do a solo act at these centres, with a couple of tough minders as travel companions, but if it was deemed safe enough, Martine Colette and Cheryl Stroud would join me on the adventure. The adrenaline pumped in all of us, even though the three of us could easily have become statistics in a conflict that seems to have no end.

At the conclusion of our informal chat, Topol and I had learned much about each other. We were only months apart in age, he being born on 9 September, and I on 4 November in 1935. His three best friends in Israel were named Barry. In 1963, while I was running wild around Tel Aviv, we had hung out at the same restaurants and clubs. He, as an actor/director, and also cabaret artist, had worked for many of the same people in the same venues as me. It was quite likely that in Israel, we'd been in close proximity. Later on, I dug out the photos from my days in Tel Aviv. As he perused them, he called out the names of people he recognised in the 1963 audience. This one had been killed in the war. This one had died from Aids-related disease. This one went on to great success. Tears filled his eyes when he spotted a picture of someone with whom he'd once been close. I didn't ask for any details.

There were times during rehearsals that he would be so immersed in his character that uncontrollable tears would roll down Topol's cheeks. He held nothing back. Each rehearsal was expected – not only him by him, but also his fellow actors – to be performed as seriously as if we were already in front of a paying audience.

For almost the next two years, I would have the privilege of working in a sensational theatre musical, but also the privilege of working alongside one of the world's greatest actors, learning and improving my technique by observation.

Chaim and I officially open Bob's new putting green.

The *Fiddler on the Roof* cast.

With Jon English, Jimmy Barnes and a fan on Hamilton Island, 1984.

With Chaim Topol in *Fiddler on the Roof*, Capitol Theatre, Sydney 2005.

Katy, Mike Walsh, me, Judith Roberts and Warren Kermond join Chaim in the dressing room after the show. Many guests would bask in the glow of this wonderful performer during our seasons.

Backstage with Magda Szubanski, 2005.

Back Row: Dame Judith Anderson, J. C. Williamson, Sigrid Thornton, Keith Michell, David Gulpilil, Noel Ferrier, Brian Henderson, Coral Browne, Annette Kellerman, Billy Williams, The Great Levante, Dame Joan Hammond, Charles 'Bud' Tingwell, Jackie Weaver, Julie Anthony, Debbie Byrne, Don Burrows, Evie Hayes, Jenny Howard, Cyril Richard.

Third Row: George Wallace Sr, Nancy Hayes, Jim Gerald, Helen Reddy, Toni Lamond, Ricky May, Judy Davis, Bobby Limb, Dawn Lake, Bill Kerr, Bob Dyer, Jack Davey, Tony Barber, Tommy Hanlon Jr, Robyn Nevin, Zoe Caldwell, Rolf Harris, Smoky Dawson, Reg Lindsay, Anthony Lapaglia, Rod Taylor, Cecil Kellaway, Bill Hunter, Peter Dawson.

Second Row: Frank Thring, Sir Robert Helpmann, Peter Finch, Chips Rafferty, John Meillon,
June Salter, Gordon Chater, Ian 'Molly' Meldrum, Daryl Somers, Leo McKern, Kamahl, Don Lane,
Mike Walsh, Rosie Sturgess, Joff Allen, Lorraine Bayly, Anthony Warlow, Marina Pryor, Slim Dusty,
John Williamson, Geoffrey Rush, John Bell, Maurie Fields, Bert 'Dad' Bailey, Gladys Moncrieff,
Florrie Forde.

Front Row: Dame Joan Sutherland, Barry Humphries, Barry Crocker, Kathy Gorman,
Reg Livermore, Kylie Minogue, Russell Crowe, Cate Blanchett, Jack Thompson, Nicole Kidman,
Errol Flynn, Olivia Newton-John, Dame Nellie Melba, Mel Gibson, Bert Newton, Buster Fiddess,
Graham Kennedy, Ruth Cracknell, Garry McDonald, John Farnham, Johnny O' Keefe,
Roy 'Mo' Rene, Hugh Jackman, Peter Allen, Paul Hogan, June Bronhill, John McCallum,
Harold Blair, Marjorie Laurence, Jill Perryman.

In 1989 Barry Humphries decided to throw a comics' lunch at Edna's Table (his favourite Sydney restaurant). Shown here are Lucky Grills, Slim De Grey, Marty, Jeff Kelso, Jim Pike, Graham Bond, Rodney Rude, Norman Eskine, Doug Scroope, Geraldine Doyle, Willie Fennell, Ruth Cracknell, Warren Kermond and Buster Noble.

With John and Janette Howard at the Sydney Opera House for the *Michael Parkinson Show*, December 2009.

Meeting George Bush Sr, Sydney 2003.

Michael Jackson with Normie Rowe's daughter, Erin; with Jenny and self; with Grant Kenny.

Dennis Conner, on the way home after losing the
America's Cup to Australia, September 1983.

'Almost a Legend'.

Mike Munro asks if I could close the show with a song, so 'The Impossible Dream' gets another airing, and my old musical director Geoff Harvey plays for me, possibly for the last time.

Below: With my five children. What a life!

One Man's Meat is Another Man's Milk

The parts of Tevye and Lazer are integral to the comedic magic of the play, for they are the self-serving antagonists that move the plot forward. Lazer is the richest man in the village, and Tevye the poorest. On the second day, before we rehearsed our opening scene together, Chaim sat down with me in a small anteroom and explained exactly why these two aging adversaries could never become friends. In the Jewish tradition, meat and milk don't mix. The practitioners of the two professions have scant regard for each other's trade.

Topol the Man

As with all productions that run for two years or more, there were conflicts. Chaim was the complete professional, and I fell foul a few times with little mistakes here and there. Once I came in late on a cue, and the gag failed to get the laugh it deserved. Topol turned his face upstage and yelled, 'Too late!' I wasn't late again. There were times when he would lose his patience with others in certain scenes, if he felt they were not concentrating properly, and he would give them bitterly withering looks. When Topol wasn't pleased, we all knew it. However, Topol was always ready to invite fans and celebrities alike to visit him in his dressing room after a performance, where he would pose happily for photographs. I was forever on hand to snap away as various celebs, without photographic gear, would ask if I could do the honours and send the pictures on.

To give an example of Chaim's dedication to his fans, one night I was leaving through the stage door, when I was approached by a little old Jewish lady who asked if she could get a message to Topol. She told me how they'd last met over 20 years earlier. She had a letter that he'd written to her then. I knew he would be upstairs for a fair while this evening, and the night was cold, so I asked her to wait for just a moment. Upstairs in his dressing room, I told Chaim the story. Without the slightest hint of annoyance, he went down to the stage door, brought her inside away from the cold, and spoke to her in Yiddish for a good 15 minutes, before sending her on her way a very happy and satisfied fan.

Hawke's Nest

During the course of the season in Sydney, ex-Prime Minister Bob Hawke asked Topol and me to be his guests at his Northbridge home, on the occasion of the official opening of a putting green on the roof of his house. Also invited along were Chaim's wife Galia, his stage wife Judith Roberts, the theatre manager Ricky Schutte, the *Fiddler* co-manager Dee Jamieson, and cast member Warren Kermond. As well as Katy, among the other brunch guests were Robbie Rowland and fashion designer Maria Finlay.

Bob's wife Blanche was the perfect hostess, making sure that everyone knew each other, as she chatted away to all and sundry. It was one of those perfect spring days, where the air tasted of Perrier water, and the sun gave off the tantalising impression that diamonds were bouncing from the clear still waters of Sailors Bay. Everyone gathered on the balcony to imbibe of the very best champagne and an appetising array of delicious delicacies. The Hawkes knew how to entertain. The time came for the official ribbon cutting ceremony that would allow the putting practice to begin. The bright green turf that covered the entire roof glittered in the sunlight. This would have to be the most impressive rooftop in Northbridge. Bob and Blanche had even employed a very pretty violinist, who hovered in the background softly rendering show tunes.

The then 77-year-old Bob Hawke had kept himself in remarkable shape, without any sign of a stoop or faltering footstep in his athletic demeanour. After the scissor ceremony, it was time for the fun to start with everyone having a go at getting the little white ball into the hole. Katy explained to Bob that she'd never played before, so he was only too happy to help her with her stance; although, my photo of the pose looks more like the start of a porn movie. Katy hadn't played before because she is myopic and would never be able to see the ball after hitting it without the help of a guide dog, but she was determined to have a go. She asked me where the hole was. I placed her in position, and told her it was about 30 feet away, in that direction. Before I could get the words out, 'Don't hit it too hard,' she had already struck the ball, and it was on its way. None of the onlookers could believe it, but its path was straight as an arrow. It went plop, into the hole. Even Tiger Woods would have applauded the amazing feat. 'What happened?' she asked, surprised at the oohs and aahs of the assembled mob.

'You just potted it!' I exclaimed.

'Oh this is easy,' she laughed. 'Give me another go.'

I removed the putter gently from her hand and whispered, 'Let's quit while you're ahead, let them all believe that you're a natural.'

No-one else that afternoon came close to emulating Katy's triumph on Bob's new patch of green. Bob was keen to show us the inscribed putter that US President George Bush presented to him at the White House, when Bob was Prime Minister. Needless to say, we weren't allowed to play with the souvenir club. It was a relaxing afternoon of fun, but we of the *Fiddler* cast had a show to do that night and we all regretted having to leave the hospitality of Bob Hawke and Blanche d'Alpuget.

Ups and Downs with Fiddler

To work with Chaim Topol was an unforgettable experience, for I had not only learned from him the finer points of timing and dedication to the art, but how his creed is never to settle for less than the best. I am proud to report that the only two performers who never missed a single performance on the whole tour were the two oldest, namely Topol and myself.

Over the years, Topol continued on with his amazing will to help those less fortunate, and never stopped working to raise money with the various children's charities around the world. 'When I tell people it's for Jewish and Arab kids, says Topol, 'they often mention cultural and political differences, but when you're dealing with children with terminal cancer or other serious conditions, the priorities are completely different. There are no conflicts in hospitals. Conflict is politicians; conflict is not people. All we're trying to do is bring a smile to their faces and give them some hope and let them just be kids. For me, this project is more important than any success I've had in show business. I think that as long as we can do something to help, we should.'

I found a new friend in Chaim Topol, and the best I can say about this incredibly talented and passionate man is that I wish I had known him for all of my life. I also wish that we might have caught up just one more time, but fate would decree that he would, so sadly, leave us on 8 March 2023.

Everybody Razzle Dazzle

In the breaks between our *Fiddler* seasons in Australia and New Zealand, I found plenty to do to keep me off the streets. One of the most fulfilling was a movie called *Razzle Dazzle, a Journey into Dance*. I had the cameo role of Donnie Destry, the host of the grand final of the Sanosafe Troupe Dance Spectacular, a fictional junior dance competition.

With the success of television programs like *Dancing with the Stars*, dozens of children's dance schools were springing up almost overnight. Where once there had been a handful of established schools, like Melbourne's famous May Downs Studios, where kiddies would learn to master tap, learn- to-dance factories mushroomed around the country, often in refurbished old warehouses. Astute businesspeople would dream up school tournaments, where dancing teams from opposition camps would compete against each other for cheap gold plastic statuettes and colourful sashes. A tidy profit would be amassed along the way, not only for the owners of these cash cow edifices, but also for the dressmakers and the fabric industries, who could barely keep up with the demand for costumes for these little Fred and Ginger wannabes.

The movie's cast was to die for. I found myself working alongside a lot of buddies, headed by the talented, lovely and ageless Kerry Armstrong, who gave one of her best ever performances. The imported young English star was Ben Miller, virtually unknown here at the time, but who would later appear in many television series.

I had given great thought to Donnie Destry's history and I invented a background for him. He had never left the 1970s, his mode of dress putting him more than just a bit outside the square. There was definitely a flare about him, especially in the trousers department! Also, he was just a couple of mirror balls short of a disco, having stayed a little too long at the fair. He had been let go recently from the Redfern RSL, where he'd been the resident bingo caller for several years. When Donnie started to make mistakes, like calling out the same number three times in one game, there were complaints from the angry players. But fate served him up one of the best gigs he'd had in years. He had auditioned for the MC's role at the Sanosafe Troupe Dance Spectacular, not really expecting to get anywhere, as it was years since anyone had shown any interest in employing him. He'd scored the RSL job only because he was half the price of anyone else.

That day, however, a tiny ray of sunshine would fall on his head in the form of his old vaudeville partner Sherry Leonard who, as fate would have it, was the chief adjudicator of the competition. Back in their Tivoli days, Donnie and Sherry (played by Toni Lamond) were not only good enough to have sung and danced their way into the second half of the show, but they had been an item in the romance stakes as well. It was almost 50 years since the pair had last seen each other, when a rift caused the end of their love affair and professional partnership. Would the sight of him cause a sudden outburst from her? Would she ask him to leave immediately? Instead, Sherry gave him a glowing smile, and said, 'Hello Donnie, it's so nice to see you again after all these years!'

He remembered the searing diatribe she screamed when she discovered him, between the Tivoli's matinee and evening performances, in a compromising position with Princess Ubangi, one of Dave Meakin's Midgets. At the time, this unique midget act had moved up from the show grounds to the top of the Tivoli bill. Like a trouper, Sherry played the second house with Donnie, then stormed out of the dressing room and out of his life.

When researching a made-up profile, I sometimes base the character around real people. Dave Meakin worked Sydney's Royal Easter Show for years as a lion tamer, using African pygmies to enhance his act, one whom he called Princess Ubangi. He claimed she was a real African princess. I had a mind picture of Donnie and the little lady being caught in the broom cupboard by Sherry, hence the reference.

The film was a jolly romp from start to finish. To begin with, I had no trouble working with children, having been around them all my life. Some days there would be up to a couple of hundred rug rats rushing excitedly around the set and cluttering up the stage. Most of them had never heard of Barry Crocker, and my little co-stars believed sincerely that this child-like compere, Donnie Destry, was indeed a real person.

Every day they would greet me with, 'Hi, Donnie,' or 'DD', a nickname I'd given myself, or 'Mr Destry', as we interweaved in our childish races to reach our rehearsal or shooting positions. Donnie himself had never left the fashion sense that he'd embraced when he made his one and only appearance on the daytime Mike Walsh television show. Mike Walsh had come over to him in the commercial break after Donnie had sung a disco version of The Lord's Prayer. He misconstrued the devout Catholic Mike's remark when he yelled at Donnie, 'I'm sure that would have pleased the almighty no end!'

I pulled the hair straight back off my face and fixed it with a fake ponytail. Having rescued some of the hottest 1970s nightclub clobber from the back of his wardrobe, DD's overall look was a mixture of drug dealer and pimp, but Donnie imagined he would be the quintessential trendie, guiding the kiddies through their paces on this night of nights. Sherry asked Donnie, in addition to acting as compere, to sing something from his repertoire as an accompaniment to the opening dance troupe. Assistant adjudicator Leonara (played by Noelene Brown), never wanted to employ Donnie in the first place. When Donnie chose to sing Sherbet's 'Howzat', which he thought was about cricket, rather than infidelity, Leonara had the perfect excuse to blast him. It was certainly the wrong message for the kiddies!

Sherry and Donnie had filmed a duet, singing Richard Clapton's 'Girls on the Avenue'. Once again, Leonara noted that this was a song about hookers, not merely pretty girls strolling along. Sadly, that piece of footage was consigned to the cutting room floor, and our lovely duet never made it into the final cut. Both Toni and I were disappointed, as the short song and dance segment had rekindled Sherry and Donnie's romance after 50 years. The message did get through, however, in 'Howzat'. For every withering look Leonara threw Donnie's way, Sherry's eyes would shine as her old partner tried his very best to entertain as well as he once thought he had.

A Land of Cancelled Planes

A small drama occurred during the shoot. Along with William McInnes and Amanda Muggleton, I was asked by the National Library of Australia in Canberra to open their new National Treasures of Australia exhibition. The evening had been booked earlier in the year, and when I took on the *Razzle Dazzle* film, the producers agreed to work around me for that one day. As luck would have it, a huge shoot involving the entire cast was scheduled for the following day. They would be filming the big finale, so it was imperative that I be on the set first thing that morning. I planned to fly from Sydney at noon on 2 December, rehearse the Canberra presentation in the afternoon, and perform the actual show at 6 pm. I would have to miss the sumptuous dinner that had been prepared for the

At the *Me and Jezebel* opening, with writer Elizabeth Fuller, Katy, and Kelly Moore, 2 March 2000.

attendees, as the last plane out of Canberra that night was at 8.30 pm. Everything was planned to the smallest detail.

After the Canberra presentations, I expected to have half an hour to relax and change back into my casual gear, drive to the airport and jump onto the last flight to Sydney. I would hit the sack early that night and be ready for a busy Saturday's filming. Robyn Holmes and the other organisers expressed their disappointment at my not staying for the dinner. The presentations had gone over well, kicking off the exhibition in fine fashion. I waved goodbye to the crowd, and I shouted to William and Amanda to have a drink for me, aware that I would miss all the fun of the fair and the accolades of a job well done, but I was doing the right thing, and I felt rather mature for a change. In my younger days, I would have stayed on, had too much to drink, and staggered onto the first flight out the following morning.

When I arrived at Canberra airport, the departure lounge was packed to the rafters with people who were demonstrably annoyed. A small cyclone had been pounding Sydney with torrential rains and high winds. All flights to the city were on hold until the skies were flyable again. The affable counter hostess assured me that the delay would not last too long, and before we knew it, we impatient passengers would be on our way. We would be rolling along merrily!

Three hours later, the same lady was giving me the same message, but this time she was not quite so customer friendly. I'd been driving her nuts, telling her how important it was for me to be in Sydney that night. The departure lounge was nearly empty, as many of my anxious fellow travellers had either decided to stay in Canberra overnight, or they hired cars to drive back to Sydney. Nevertheless, I had been buoyed by the lady's announcement that the evening curfew had been waived at Kingsford Smith and permission would be granted for the late night flight to land. At about midnight, she proposed that if my reaching home was such a matter of urgency, I might contemplate hiring a car, as the prospects of a late night flight were now bleak. I'd been chatting with another desperate who felt it imperative to return to Sydney that night. I had been plying myself with many cups of tea and coffee, not to mention the complimentary snacks, but my new mate was availing himself generously of the free grog, convinced that all would turn out well in the end. The exhausted counter hostess advised me that if I was going to get a car, I should do so straight away, as the hire-car franchisee was about to call it a night. My friend had been privy to this dialogue, and he offered to split the cost if we shared a car, a suggestion to which I fully agreed, and those who know me personally will not be surprised at my ready acceptance of the offer. The only downer was that I would have to do all the driving; he was morbidly pissed.

The desk hostess put me through to the only car rental office remaining open. 'I only have one car left!' said the voice on the phone.

'Okay, I'll take it,' I replied wearily.

'Er, it's not really all that flash,' he said apologetically.

'Does it have a full tank, and can it move forward?' I asked, regardless.

'Er, well, yes.'

'I'll take it!'

My newfound co-pilot and I piled ourselves into the cream, base-model Holden, and we set off for Sydney. I followed the rental man's instructions, but I turned left when I should have turned right. I realised that I'd driven about 15 kilometres in the wrong direction. With a bit of confusion, mostly caused by Canberra's interminable series of roundabouts, I found the right road and we were finally headed in the right direction. The car was running pretty smoothly, but my travelling companion wasn't too conversational anymore, having succumbed to the booze, and he was now snoring away in the passenger seat. All at once, we encountered what must have been the tail end of the cyclone, because the rain was belting down on the windscreen. I'd been sitting on the speed limit of 110 kilometres per hour, which was quickly reduced to about 50.

I prayed that the windscreen wipers, turned up to maximum, wouldn't snap off and blow away. It was impossible to see more than 10 metres ahead, even with the headlights on full beam. At this rate of knots, our predicted three-hour journey would remain only that, a prediction. We were about an hour out from our destination when the wind and rain ceased abruptly, allowing us to pick up speed. The journey had been an unpredictable and drastically long epic, and as we pulled up outside my apartment at approximately 6 am, I joked to my co-pilot that we should forget about entering in a car rally anytime in the near future. The man appeared to have sobered up, and as we'd arranged, he would take over the driving and return the car to a rental outlet near his home. He would have a story to tell his friends around the barbecue, and I would have enough time to take a quick shower and arrive at the filming location by 7 am.

As I sank into the make-up chair at the Kogarah RSL, I wanted to slip into a twilight dreamtime, but this was meant to be a busy day, not due to end until 7 pm. My sense of self-discipline demanded that I be alert and awake for my last day of filming, and I rose to the challenge. There was a strange poignancy as I left the building that day, with all the children yelling out their farewells to DD or Donnie or Mr Destry. 'You'll all be stars one day,' I shouted back, knowing that I would miss working with them. Some of the kids may indeed go on to be stars, but most of them will be left with fond memories of a great adventure, along with a funny DVD to show their own children in the future.

Katy and Me, and Me and Jezebel

In early 2006, Brisbane's Stage Door Dinner Theatre Company commissioned an eight-week season of the one-woman version of Me and Jezebel, again to be directed by yours truly. Neither of us was completely sure at first if Katy could meet the demands of the play. I had the utmost confidence in her talents, but she had apprehensions about her ability to be alone on stage for the two hours of the fast-paced romp. I would be proven right, and although at the end of the first night she resembled a woman who had showered in her clothes, the reaction of the crowd lifted her to the heights of adrenaline heaven, and she would never doubt her own abilities again. The story of Bette Davis's visit to Elizabeth Fuller's house in Connecticut that summer of 1985, became a successful book and Elizabeth was encouraged to turn it into a play. She had the courage to rent an off-Broadway theatre and perform the piece solo. Elizabeth was not a professional actor, so reviews were mixed, and attendances low, but the signs were there to justify a re-write and the hiring of professional actors for a two-handed version of her work. The character of Bette would usually be played by a man as not many female actors, to put it crudely, had the balls that Bette possessed, and the co-star played all the other roles. This was the version we first performed at the Valhalla in 2000, with Kelly Moore playing Bette, and Katy playing Elizabeth and all the other characters. Now we had come full circle, with the original concept of the one-woman performance.

Directing Katy in a play can sometimes be very daunting, as she's the kind of actress who can pull on the skin of her character convincingly. When the main character Elizabeth or the other personalities were centre stage, they accepted my direction very willingly, but when the skin of Madame Davis was applied to the tiny frame of Ms Manning, it was a metamorphosis! As Bette, she didn't like rehearsing, and this character was the one who gave me all the grief. There were times when Katy must have channelled Bette Davis herself, and if Bette didn't agree with my directions, blazing rows would erupt and a full range of Bette's expletives would rain down on me. For all I knew, it could have been Bette who taught Ava Gardner how to swear. I would ask gently for Elizabeth to return to the rehearsal space, and for Bette to take a break.

In 2000, when Elizabeth Fuller came to our Sydney opening, she told me of what really happened at the time Bette dominated the Fuller household. The premise is based on the dedication of a starstruck, mesmerised fan whose idol turns up unexpectedly on the front porch. Elizabeth had so idolised Bette that she started to become Bette, smoking heavily, and fighting with her husband, the once loving couple now arguing like characters in a Bette Davis movie. Even their four-year-old son started to use Bette's expletives. Bette was then 77 years of age, having survived a mastectomy, four strokes and a heart attack, and yet she still saw herself as a sexy vixen. She would show up at the breakfast table in see-through nightwear, flirting outrageously with Elizabeth's husband John. Bette confided to Elizabeth that, 'Old age isn't for cissies!' It was only after the Bette cyclone had departed that Elizabeth felt the need to exorcise her experiences and write the book.

In 2009, Katy played *Me and Jezebel* to enthusiastic crowds and glowing reviews at Hampstead's New End Theatre in London, going on to perform it at Scotland's Edinburgh Festival. Katy and I had expectations that *Jezebel* would become the equivalent of Barry Crocker's *Banjo*, her exclusive one-woman show which she could always fall back on, but despite the extensive praise heaped upon her performances, the average theatregoer did not seem in any hurry to watch a play about an old dominatrix like Bette Davis. Seats remained devoid of bums to fill them. With a great deal of pain, we handed back the rights for others to have a crack at making the piece work. At least two other productions would be mounted subsequently, including one overseas, with both of them experiencing only short seasons. Nevertheless, Bette Davis had taken Katy and me on an incredible ride, and we will never forget her!

CHAPTER 12

The Bazza Legend Rolls On

I'm often asked, do those in show business live constantly happy and fulfilling lives? The public is continually bombarded on television with glamorous award shows and dazzled by the pap magazines that enhance the glittering, luxurious lifestyles of their favourite stars. With all this positively splendiferous existence, how could one ever be miserable or discontented? It's impossible to contemplate. There is the other side of the story, when the perfect Hollywood marriage collapses, or stars lose their fortunes, or have mental breakdowns, or end up in jail for various breaches of the law. All of these occurrences have been replicated in Australia amongst our own personalities. Quite often we read inflated stories of star salaries, but what we might not perceive so easily is the extraordinary cost of maintaining a top actor's lifestyle, what with managers, press agents, personal assistants, hairdressers and assorted hangers-on. Those enormous payments can dissipate faster than the weight on a *Biggest Loser* contestant!

Regardless of one being a shop assistant, doctor, lawyer, or barber, there is no difference in our basic human emotional structure.

Most people out there in the workforce have a pretty good idea that unless they screw up, they will continue to have a steady income to support their lifestyle, whereas the average working actor is only as good as their last performance, and most of us are afraid that every performance could be our last. You can imagine the insecurity that manifests itself in the mind of the artist; it can be very debilitating to one's sense of self-worth, and it will certainly sap your confidence if the phone doesn't ring after your last job.

Like most in my profession, I have this constant fear of being found out, and that I was not really any good at all, and yet, now retired, I'm still waiting for the other shoe to drop after almost 60 years. Not unconsciously, I have covered the walls in what I call My Den, with photographs, magazine covers, posters, awards and other memorabilia relating to my past triumphs. Ours is a world of hills and valleys, good times and bad. Whenever my telephone had gone to sleep for a period, I'd comfort myself by gazing around at these trophies, photos with the biggies, and press clippings worth framing, consoling myself with the feeling that, well, I must have been good once! Thankfully, these dells wouldn't last for long and I'd find myself climbing yet another knoll before I knew it.

It was during one of the quiet periods, between the *Fiddler on the Roof* seasons in

April of 2006, that I was presented with a gift that finally cemented my self-esteem and reinforced within me that my talents might be relevant after all.

The Biggest Picture

I was informed that I would be one of the faces to grace the canvas of a massive six-metre by two-metre oil painting of the Variety Club's 100 greatest Australian entertainers of the last century. This impressive piece was unveiled at a glittering evening of celebration in a giant tent at Melbourne's Docklands on 29 April 2006. Jamie Cooper had painted the incredible work over a two-year period, depicting twentieth century artists in all fields of entertainment, as chosen by a secret panel of judges. The setting for the evening was a superb reproduction of a circus big tent, the symbol of Variety.

The food was excellent, and the entertainment eclectic, to say the least. Celebrity comperes Stuart Wagstaff and John-Michael Howson tied the show together, first introducing The Ballet of a Thousand Years, ex-Tivoli showgirls who opened the show with a high-kicking routine that belied the fact that some were into their eighties. They were followed by the talented and towering Rhonda Burchmore, backed by her own dancers. Gerry Connolly did a hilarious and uncanny impression of Frank Thring, the best I'd ever seen. I performed my *Fiddler on the Roof* medley, which seemed to whet the audience's appetite for more, and I'm told I sold a lot of tickets that night for the upcoming Melbourne season. The whole show was headlined by the brilliant Wayne Scott Kermond, the son of Warren.

The real highlight of the evening was the unveiling of the much anticipated painting. When Variety's Victorian chairman Rob Collins and artist Jamie Cooper pulled back the covers, the 500-plus audience surged forward to get a closer look, including myself. I was thrilled to find my likeness in the left-hand side of the front row, three along from Dame Joan Sutherland and between us, the face of Barry Humphries attired as Dame Edna Everage. I was painted as my alter-ego, Barry McKenzie. Hovering slightly above me were the omnipresences of Frank Thring and Sir Robert Helpmann. As I scanned the monumental painting, I felt truly honoured to be sharing the canvas with the likes of Errol Flynn, Chips Rafferty, Roy 'Mo' Rene, George Wallace, and all those past and present that I'd been enamoured with at one stage or another during the course of my life. For those who have the fortitude to check it out, the picture and the full list of the top 100 is in the picture section.

Also unveiled was a very impressive mosaic mural created by David Jack; he had set in concrete a replica of the Jamie Cooper painting.

With most great works of art, the creator will often add little touches that tickle his sense of fun or the ridiculous. There will be a little jape or two to share with the connoisseur or anyone who cares to give the piece more than a cursory glance.

The viewer gains that extra bit of sneaky enjoyment from the work! For example, in the painting of 100 stars, you may spot a crumpled poster of The Seekers up in the left-hand corner, and it is possible the artist felt they should have been included. Russell Crowe is wearing a South Sydney football jumper, but if you look closely you may see his telephone cord wrapped around Cate Blanchett's Oscar. Don Lane is wearing a pocket garland with Ernie Sigley's face emblazoned upon it, a reference to their infamous punch-up at one particular Logie Awards night. For those who may recognise it, the painting is set on the stage of Melbourne's illustrious Regent Theatre with the red velvet curtains visible.

The evening was a resounding success from every point of view. All of the interstate guests had been housed at the beautiful Park Hyatt hotel, which was one of the sponsors of the event, in Parliament Square. Printed posters had been laid out in a row in the tent foyer, and the organisers asked the attending artists to autograph as many of them as they could.

A numbered replica of the painting, signed by the recipients, would help raise further much-needed funds for the kids when it went on sale. I actually signed all of the 75 celebrity prints, treating the task as a challenge, and I felt, a little selfishly, that my autograph would be part of this historic occasion.

Smoke Gets in My Eyes

The year 2007 seemed to slip buy in a nanosecond, commencing with the Perth season of *Fiddler*. My fifth great-grandchild, Lilli, decided that it was time to see the wonders of the world in September. Another date was kept in Coolangatta on 23 September, when along with fellow inductees, Dawn Fraser, Ken Rosewall, Simon Gallaher and Carlotta, I had my star implanted in the Walk of Fame.

In October, I had the pleasure of recording my telling of the 'Waltzing Matilda' story, complete with all references to Christina MacPherson, for the National Film and Sound Archives in Canberra. It still gets the odd airing on Fox's Ovation Channel.

The Wizard of Odds

After completing five cabaret shows on the Gold Coast, I returned to Sydney to audition for *Wicked*, the sensational new Broadway musical that was on its way to Australia. Something strange and perplexing would occur during this auditioning period. What I'm about to relate must happen in other professions as well, but in show business events can twist and turn in the most macabre and disconcerting ways.

I'd had several call backs for the role of the Wizard, seemingly impressing the American producers. Although not one of the major roles in the overall sense, it is a pivotal one, with a great entrance and two show-stopping songs. Every Australian actor over 50 was a starter for the role originally played on Broadway by Joel Grey. At the time, he was 75 years of age. There are few parts of substance in musical theatre that suit the aging actor. Tevye in *Fiddler*, Fagin in *Oliver* and the Wizard in *Wicked* are three on a very short list. While the auditions were continuing, I received a strange phone call that had been passed on to me through my agency. The message simply said there was a strong rumour going around that Rob Guest had been signed for the role, but I was to disregard that rumour. I continued doing other work as the auditions dragged on.

One day, out of the blue, I was asked to go to the Lyric Theatre at Star City, as the Americans had requested a video of my audition. The people back in the USA wished to see for themselves what I had to offer. My accompanist was the very talented Ms Kellie Dickerson, who happened to be the partner of the aforementioned Rob Guest. I always felt a little strange working with Kellie, because I knew she would naturally prefer Rob to score the coveted role.

The filming was completed to the satisfaction of all those on the floor, especially the Australian producer, who complimented me overwhelmingly on one particular scene. Present that day were Anthony Callea and Rob Mills, who had both come through the *Australian Idol* television show, and they would be cast in *Wicked*. They rode down with the Australian producer and me in the lift. There was a lot of backslapping and good-natured banter between the four of us. There was a running gag between the producer and me over the years because he had never used me in any of his shows. We both joked, 'Looks like things may change for the better now!'

I walked out the stage door on a high, with a confident feeling that I was that bit closer to gaining the role.

The front of the Melbourne *Herald Sun* declared, 'BERT NEWTON TO PLAY THE WIZARD!'

The news soon reached my ears, and my first thought was, 'Yep, that's how you find out you've failed – you read it in the paper!' The next day, a retraction appeared in the newspaper, revealing that the show's publicity department had jumped the gun, and Bert had not been cast. I hardly had time to savour my relief, because a few days later it was officially announced that Rob Guest had indeed been cast as the Wizard. With Bert being an old friend, I felt for his humiliation when his casting had been so quickly announced and retracted. I knew how the machinations in the news articles would affect him and what he must have gone through. However, it had also impacted on me, and not one word of condolence was slipped my way. Nobody from the show said anything to me about why I'd been discarded from the running after all the glowing praise I'd received, and I still haven't been given any reason for my silent demise. Throwing my memory back to a similar occasion that happened in the 1980s, I thought that, yet again, I may have been used as a patsy, or a foil, if you like.

Bill Marshall was a respected agent and manager in the NLT agency, of which my manager Neil Harrold was a junior partner. One day, at a function in the old Gazebo Hotel in Kings Cross, Bill called me aside. With a few Scotches under his belt, Bill said, 'You know Baz, I've always felt bad about something that happened when we were representing you. It's always eaten away at me, and I want to apologise now, while I still have the chance!'

I was all ears, and I certainly wasn't aware of where he was going with this, but I was sucked right in, and I said, 'Go ahead, Bill.'

'Remember when we were casting *La Cage Aux Folles* and you were up for the part of Georges? You had several call backs, and you were pretty much given plaudits to the effect that you had the role in the bag.'

'Yes, but it finished up going to Keith Michell.'

'Well, I'm here to confess, we used you to bring down Keith's fee. He wanted to do the play, and we wanted him to do it, but he had us over the financial barrel. That's until we brought you into the equation, letting him know how much you wanted to do it, and to top it off, we told him Crocker would be a damn sight cheaper. We won the battle, but I always felt bad about how we used you like that. Anyway, it's off my chest now, sorry mate.'

I felt no animosity towards Bill or NLT, business is business. I had gone on to throw other fish into my frying pan. Be that as it may, being left in limbo is not a pleasant thing, and I explored the notion that with Rob Guest having been cast as the Wizard, and his partner Kellie Dickenson having won the conductor's role, perhaps a two-for-one deal may have been offered to the Guests?

I don't know if someone, someday, will feel the urge to come up to me in a bar and confess the true story, as Bill Marshall had done with *La Cage*, but I remain open-minded.

In a macabre sense, the *Herald Sun* headline about Bert Newton being cast as the Wizard would become the reality, because after the death of that versatile entertainer Rob Guest from a massive stroke, it was Bert who took over the role. My own rejection didn't matter that much to me, but I would have rested easier in my mind if someone had only said, 'Hey, Bazza, you never had the part in the first place' – but nobody ever did.

A Cowardly Profession

'Don't put your daughter on the stage, Mrs Worthington,' Noel Coward once sang. He might have added, 'And if your son doesn't possess the hide of a rhinoceros, tell him to stay at home as well!' Show business, although often financially rewarding

Mr Poppy (me) performing in *Reefer Madness*, produced by Squabbalogic, 2008.

and sometimes absurdly glamorous, can be a soul-destroying and life-threatening profession. For those starting out all wide-eyed and bushy-tailed, following the yellow brick road towards fame and fortune, always keep your mind on those who have fallen into the abyss. During the April/May season of *Fiddler on the Roof* in New Zealand, I heard that the Americans were holding auditions for *Monty Python's Spamalot*. The musical had been a runaway success on Broadway, and several parts were expected to be cast in Australia, with all of the major roles said to be up for grabs. A lot of the *Fiddler* cast members were going to try out for the many parts as soon as they returned home.

Monique Montez, who was playing Lazer Wolfe's first wife, Fruma Sarah, owned a DVD of the Broadway show. She confided in me her determination to become the female lead, in the role of the Lady of the Lake. I borrowed Monique's DVD, and I saw only one role that I wanted to play, that of the King. With my tape recorder, I put down the King's songs. The scripts were emailed to me from Sydney, and I settled down to giving it my best shot.

The dialogue in *Spamalot* is not the easiest to learn, as Eric Idle had translated the script of the movie *Monty Python and the Holy Grail* into an even sillier mixture of malapropisms and gobbledygook. In between performances of *Fiddler*, I toiled away as if I were learning a foreign language. By the time I returned home on 28 May, the Sydney auditions had been closed down. They were still doing try-outs in Melbourne, and if I was prepared to pay my own fare down, the producers said they would be happy to see me.

It would be crazy to let all my time and effort go to waste. I flew to Melbourne late in the morning of 30 May for my audition at 3.20 pm that afternoon, having booked the 5.15 pm return flight to Sydney. I started to become somewhat irritable when the hopefuls before me were taking longer than I expected, and it was almost 4 pm before the door was opened and I went in to face the audition team. I was introduced to all six American panel members and given a brief rundown of their duties with the show. There were three other actors in the room, two men and a lady, to play the other characters in my scenes.

After I sang a couple of numbers from the show, the six Yanks applauded, and then the assistant director asked to see the scenes I had prepared. They laughed in all the right places. These guys had spent weeks listening to other people doing the same routines, and I was amazed to get such a reaction. When I finished, I asked the assistant director if he'd like to see anything else, but all he said was, 'That couldn't have been better, thank you.' Another hopeful at the auditions told me he overheard the Americans discussing how I'd been the best they'd seen, but this uplifting statement would have a very hollow ring to it. The part of the King had already been cast. John Cleese had apparently convinced the producers that his good friend Billy Brown would be perfect for the role. This is another anomaly that permeates the industry. Because of Equity rulings and political correctness, every actor suitable for a role must be given the chance to audition. It's a bit of a farce, because the producer has the undeniable right to choose his cast, but justice, as they say in another profession, must not only be done, but It must also be seen to be done.

I waited for *Spamalot* to hit Sydney so I could see how Billy Brown played the role of the King, but the show's American success wasn't duplicated locally, and it ran out of time and money in Melbourne. I couldn't complain. Fortunately for her career, Monique Montez was overlooked for the Lady of the Lake as well.

So, as you can see my young bushy-tails, tryouts can be hazardous from so many angles – painful, ruthless, distressing, spiteful, humiliating, heartbreaking, vexing, and hard on the hip pocket. Would I do anything else? The masochist within me cries out, 'No, I will survive!' I have thrived by tilting at windmills, even if I have sometimes questioned my own sanity.

Sydney Theatre Company

One of my lifelong wishes had been to join a production of the Sydney Theatre Company, and it looked like the showbiz fairy was at last listening. A call came through for me to audition for *The Convict's Opera*, a re-working

of *The Beggar's Opera*, reputedly the world's first musical play, written by John Gay in 1728. It was to be directed by the acclaimed British director Max Stafford-Clark in a co-production with his UK company Out of Joint. So, on 6 March 2008, I went off to audition in an old tin shed in the shadow of the famous Wharf 1 theatre.

I was introduced to Max and his stunning Irish assistant and partner, Stella Feehily, along with the English musical director and arranger Felix Cross. Max had suffered a severe stroke 18 months before arriving in Australia. He was confined to a wheelchair and found some difficulty in conversing. Stella would translate what Max was trying to say. Having been with him since the stroke, she could decipher what to my ear were muffled mumblings. On the other hand, Felix Cross spoke with a stuttering, rapid-fire cockney dialogue, and he was nearly as difficult to understand as Max was! Between our eclectic accents and colloquialisms, I managed to show them what they wanted to see and hear. I spoke in different dialects, reading parts of the still-evolving script, and I handled everything they threw at me in the singing stakes. Courtesies were exchanged, and Serena Hill, the casting director for the STC, saw me out of the tin shed and on my way. The usual 'we'll be in touch' floated in the air of the balmy autumn day as I made my way along the footpath, past the sparkling blue waters of Sydney Harbour. I felt an inner satisfaction about what had transpired in the tin shed, but I put any thought of an early decision completely out of my mind. Good thinking, as it was the middle of July before I found out I'd won a role in *The Convict's Opera*.

Rehearsals were due to start on 18 August. Cate Blanchett and her husband Andrew Upton had been appointed the new artistic directors of the STC, taking over from Robyn Nevin, who had served in that position from 1999 until the end of 2007. Cate sent out a personal request for me to be the special guest performer at the sponsors' dinner on 21 July.

This prestigious annual event is the theatre company's way of saying 'thank you' to its generous angels, who make it possible for the company to present only the very best, with the very best. After Cate's short welcoming speech and introduction, I made my way onto the stage and quipped, 'That's the best opening act I've ever had!'

I went through my *Fiddler on the Roof* medley, followed by 'Mack the Knife', one of the songs from Kurt Weill's 1928 version of *The Beggar's Opera* which he renamed *The Threepenny Opera*.

The audience was most responsive, but I couldn't stay and enjoy the evening myself, because I had to attend the dress rehearsal of another show in which I had a leading role.

Barry's Great Reefer

My next play would be an absurd and absolute hoot! It was one of two extraordinary opportunities that came my way in June and July, in amongst a small country tour of *Banjo*. The first challenge was my casting as one of the lead characters in an international animated series called *The Legend of Enyo*. My character Shamani is a village elder and spiritual leader in a parallel universe in an indeterminate era. The second opportunity came when two young partners, Jessica Burns and Jay James Moody, approached my manager Tony Brady to see if I was interested in starring in an off-Broadway smash hit for which they'd obtained the Australian rights. The show was called *Reefer Madness*, based on the 1950s B-grade flick of the same name.

The play was set in 1936, when a new drug menace called marijuana was threatening the very existence of America's youth. In the original film, comedy actor Dave O'Brien was cast as the baddie. The movie was over the top for the times and it was poorly attended, but it became a cult phenomenon following its rediscovery in the 1970s. Following the success of an off-Broadway stage production, a new movie was made of the musical. So I found myself sitting in Tony Brady's office with the producers from Squabbalogic, discussing my possible involvement in Jay and Jessica's project. The rest of the cast were already chosen, but they had tried several actors unsatisfactorily for the role of the lecturer.

Jay had hired a DVD of *Razzle Dazzle* one night, and when he saw me in the role of Donny, he said it hit him like a ton of bricks. I would be perfect for the role. But would Barry, he thought, want to come along on such an avant-garde and raunchy ride like *Reefer Madness*? He was worried that I would be the only real adult alongside a bunch of savvy adolescents. There would be simulated sex, including sodomy. There would be devil worship. There would be some steamy nude scenes. They approached Tony with a great deal of trepidation, not knowing if I could be involved in a play displaying so much depravity.

They didn't know I'd worked with the Doug Anthony Allstars, where much of the above bad behaviour was usually the norm.

Squabbalogic, still active today, is a self-funded company, so naturally the budget was fairly minuscule, but I couldn't get over their enthusiasm and youthful exuberance in this, the biggest of their projects. I took a copy of the script and the music CD home. I thought it could be a rib-tickler. I called Tony, he made the deal, and I was in like Flynn, to use an appropriate expression.

The difference between working with a large professional company and a self-funded outfit is like eating chalk and writing with cheese. The big time chaps have the cheese, plus tea and coffee and biscuits supplied. The self-funded have the chalk! You want these niceties? Bring your own. And so it goes, all the way down the economic line. Every cent available goes into rehearsal costs, the building of the sets, and the making of the costumes, with many unpaid mothers of friends and cast members called upon to help out. Redfern's Cleveland Street Theatre, also known as Performance Space, had been booked to stage the show. Playing multiple roles were Jessica Burns, Emily Cascarino, Andrew Cook, Brad Facey, Lucas Hall, Katie Headrick, Sofia Katos, Richard Lovegrove, Jay James Moody, Belinda Morris and Celeste O'Hara. I too would get to play multiple roles; apart from the lecturer, I played Mr Poppy the drug lord, Mephistopheles, a police officer, Jimmy's mother and an Irish priest.

After the dress rehearsal and two previews, we opened on 24 July. The show closed on Saturday 16 August. Once again we had a quiet start, and then the show quickly gained momentum, but we had run our allotted time. There was a week of grace on hold in case the show was a runaway success. It wasn't, and in a sense I was relieved because rehearsals were about to start for *A Convict's Opera* the following Monday. I'd had my fun, but now it was time to buckle down and prove myself with the Sydney Theatre Company.

I would like to report that *Reefer Madness* was financially successful, but I can't, because it lost money! Raising capital is always hard for new works, especially when it comes to independent companies. Angels with dollars to spare are constantly being sought. Many investors come on board for a while then drop out when they get cold feet. Everybody wants a sure thing, a winner, and the track to showbiz success is strewn with emptied pockets and broken dreams. When angels are thin on the ground, many of us take the punt and scrounge money to kickstart our dreams. It's a punt that many of us take because, in our hearts, we are convinced that *our* show will work. *Reefer* received smashing reviews and built big houses towards the end of its season. But Equity demands that their actors receive three weeks' notice to prepare for the rest period. For example, on the night we opened in *Reefer* we were effectively given our three weeks' notice of closure. *Reefer Madness* had no advertising budget whatsoever, it relied on student papers, word of mouth, Facebook, or any other free device. Every cent went into paying the actors, hiring the hall and printing the posters and programs. Jessica and Jay, (who directed), with help from family and friends, made the costumes, built the props and painted the floor.

Choosers Can't Be Beggars

After the first reading of the *Convict Opera* script, I called Katy to say, 'You know, if I went along to see this play, I would hate it!' I had no-one to blame but myself for accepting a play without first reading it. I had been entranced and enticed by the glamour of the STC, the noted British director Max Stafford-Clark, and Stephen Jeffreys, the writer of Johnny Depp's previous movie. We were given a healthy rehearsal period of six weeks, when most productions are afforded four at the most. We were told this was necessary because Max was not a conventional director. Katy and I have argued passionately over the different ideologies that various directors will follow. She feels it's impossible to find the character if the actor already knows the dialogue, having been locked into a performance that may be hard to change, but my modus operandi is to follow Noel Coward's edict, and learn the script before entering the rehearsing space. I prefer to be up on my feet as soon as possible, in order to explore the possibilities of the role. When I played Molière's *Scapino* in Melbourne, I had the entire two-and-a-half hour text down pat before a single word was spoken at rehearsals. *Scapino* was a physically demanding play and carrying around a script would have inhibited my progress.

When we entered the STC's refurbished Sydney Theatre rehearsal room on 18 August, we were not given copies of the script, because it was still being fine-tuned. In fact, it would be fine-tuned for some time to come, and when we did eventually receive it, it was constantly being edited at each reading. Max wasn't bothered at all, having told us that we wouldn't be starting proper rehearsals until the third week. We were given instead a script companion, a beautifully illustrated history of attitudes and conditions in eighteenth-century society, as compiled by assistant director Iain Sinclair. Part of writer Stephen Jeffreys' research work also graced the book's pages.

As the days went by, we discussed tangibles, like how people endured the voyage out from England, and what might have transpired between the upper and lower decks. Max always carried a deck of cards with him. 'Here choose a card,' Max would say, and you'd choose a card. 'Aah, you've chosen the eight of hearts. Now, tell me with the same intensity, how your character would have acted in this or that situation'?

Max had wanted an expert on eighteenth-century behaviour to talk to our group about the early settlers. My old friend Thomas Keneally knew Max from a previous meeting, and he happened to be writing a book on that very subject. At my request, Tom came in one afternoon and gave a wonderful lecture to the assembled multitude on the incredibly difficult circumstances our forebears had to endure. The cast went on a visit to Hyde Park Barracks, built by the convict architect Francis Greenway, in Queen's Square, Macquarie Street, for the imprisonment of delinquent settlers. We were shown everything from a tobacco pouch to the hangman's noose. The tour brought home the appalling treatment and suffering handed out by the authorities to wretches whose only crime may have been to steal a slice of bread for a hungry child.

All this was a pleasant diversion from what I was really craving to do, which was to get stuck into the text of *A Convict's Opera*. My impatience began to show, and my constant complaints to Max that time was slipping away were not pleasing him one bit. I would be playing, amongst others, the man named John Gay, who was the catalyst for the whole shebang. Detailed sketches of the various characters were provided to show how each character should look. John was to be portrayed as a hunched 150-year-old man, with a frayed frock coat and long, straggly hair on his head and his face.

Max decided that John Gay should speak with a Devonshire accent, so voice coach Charmian Gradwell supplied me with a CD recording of various people using the dialect. I have a good ear for mimicry, and when we worked on the first scene, Charmian was very pleased with my efforts. After two days of intense practice, we were ready to give it a shot.

Max Doesn't Give Much Headroom

I would make three fateful mistakes to bring about my undoing in A Convict's Opera, and the undermining would begin with that very first day in that very first scene. Wearing the character of the 150-year-old John Gay, I practised my frail walk up and down the imaginary deck of the convict ship. In the original caricature, he is seen supporting himself with a rickety walking stick, one of which had not yet been supplied to me by the props department. Max's own walking cane lay on the floor near his feet. Thinking off the top of my head, I grabbed it and said, 'Do you mind if I use this for the character?'

Immediately, I felt the heat emanating from him. I went into John Gay's delicate Devonshire tones. Without warning, Max leaned forward in his chair and snatched the cane away from me, tossing it to the floor. 'I've changed my mind,' he snapped. 'I don't want him played as an old man, but middle-aged, or possibly even younger.' I was more than a little startled, but I complied with the director's wishes. The dialogue would stay the same, with Peter Cousens's line being, 'John Gay, but you live yet? You are above 150 years old.' Max's explanation was that John Gay was really a ghost. All of my work went out the window. The next day, Max decided he didn't want the part to be played with a Devon accent.

My second mistake had possibly already been made earlier (which in a sense would make it my first), when I'd been sitting close to Max's partner Stella Feehily at the early rehearsals using her as a conduit to pick up Max's whispered tones. Max was six years younger than I was, and he may have misinterpreted my proximity to Stella. After a few days, deputy stage manager Sarah Smith filled the space between Stella and me, so now I had to get my information translated twice!

One of my favourite scenes is where the theatrical convict William, my real character in the piece, is directing the John Gay play that the convicts are planning to stage in order to overcome the boredom of their journey. William was transported to Australia after being sentenced for sodomy. He had been arrested with a judge, who of course was pardoned. His greatest hurt comes from the memory of the modest home he shared with a simple ruffian, who now remains alone with William's exquisite garden. Without William's care, the garden will wither and die, and there is also William's pain of knowing he will never see his lover again.

Other scenes were much less meaningful, and tougher to put across. To add to my growing unease, I was disillusioned with the songs I was expected to sing. In John Gay's original 1728 play, he had used music by Handel and Bach, but Max decided to incorporate modern songs as a dichotomy against the look of the piece. Songs by Neil Young, Rod Stewart, Carly Simon and other artists were used. To balance out the musical mix, some eighteenth-century ditties were added to create a veritable Nigella Lawson musically blended delicacy, which was what Max wanted. As far as I was concerned, all the songs had been thrown into a giant blunderbuss and fired into the air, letting the music fall where it may. The two pieces that fell on me were from the old school and perhaps the most unmusical tunes I'd ever encountered. I absolutely abhorred them, even if they were meant to be character driven. Ali McGregor could sense my plight, and we tried tirelessly to find a key with which I could be comfortable.

We couldn't. My normally robust vocal cords could not summon up the strength, nor the breath, as I laboured over two maladies of melodies called 'Let Us Take the Road' and 'Fill Every Glass'. I didn't know the affliction with which I was dealing, but I didn't like it one bit, and for someone who prides himself on his singing abilities, I thought anyone who came along to hear me sing was going to get one hell of a shock!

I would sneak away when not required at rehearsals, to continue my voice-overs for *The Legend of Enyo*. There were a couple of cabaret dates that had been in my book for some time that the STC had kindly allowed me not to cancel. And so I would have something else to do, I took on the narration of a DVD volume of *The Magic Scarecrows* by Lynn Santer, mainly because part of the profits would be going to my favourite charity, Variety. All of this extracurricular activity was taking my eye off the ball. Increasingly, I was falling behind the rest of the gang, and I found myself confronted by a small delegation of Max, Stella, Andrew Upton, Serena Hill, and Tanya Leach. I was shocked to hear Serena ask me if I was happy being in the show. 'Yes of course,' I replied.

'And you want to continue?' she persisted.

I could feel the pressure. In my wildest dreams I had never contemplated bailing out. Maybe it was my reluctance with the music that had given them the sign of discontent.

'This chance with the STC is something I've wanted for a long time,' I continued,

198

'and I certainly don't want to let anyone down.'

'Alright,' said Serena, 'We just had to be sure!'

When the others left, Max and I were alone, sitting on the black leather sofas in the foyer of the Sydney Theatre, and looking quietly at each other. 'You know we're two old war horses, you and me,' said Max. 'I think we can be honest with each other. Did you mean what you said just then?'

'Yes!' I shot back, and it was then that I made my third and final mistake. 'I know you don't agree with the way I direct,' he stated, leaving the remark hanging in the air.

Many actors would have said, 'No, not at all, Max,' and saved their bacon. I couldn't lie. By remaining silent, I didn't give him the answer he wanted, thereby sealing my own fate.

Phone Off the Hook

We continued on with rehearsals. At the end of each day, a notice would be posted on the time board letting us know who was required and at what time on the following day. Max pulled himself up from the director's table and announced there had been a change to the next day's posted schedule. 'We are going to go straight through from page 102 up to 156, scripts down,' he announced. 'I don't want to see a script!'

I had to get confirmation from Sarah about what I'd heard, as the proclamation caught me completely by surprise. 'Shit!' I yelled. 'I only know about ten pages of that lot!' 'Then you'd better move your little bum along,' she replied. That Thursday night, I locked myself away in my den, took the phone off the hook, and prepared for a long night of learning the vital text. Out of all the cast members, I was the only one who had been stunned by the change of plan. By 3 am, a numbing atrophy had cemented my brain cells into a blob, and no matter how hard I tried to concentrate, nothing was adhering to my memory. I managed to lock in about half of what Max would be demanding of his players, but as I lay there fighting off sleep, going over the lines, my grey matter didn't want to know. 'Let me rest!' it was screaming. I arrived at rehearsals exhausted, having dragged myself out from under the covers. I threw down a large mug of steaming coffee to stimulate the flow of adrenaline.

Max seemed to delight in repeating to the troops his edict from the previous evening. 'Everybody, this morning we'll be doing music, but after lunch we are going to rehearse from page 102 to 156, books down.'

Every moment I wasn't required in the music scenes, I slipped out into one of the dressing rooms, and went over the script that I should have known. I carried on during the lunch break, with assistant director Iain Sinclair agreeing to take me through the lines, but I couldn't shake off that feeling of foreboding.

Throughout my experience in theatre, movies, variety shows, and any other form of entertainment that requires a director, it has come to my notice that the director will often find a whipping boy, or girl, to be the target of his frustrations. I'm sure there is a parallel in most businesses. That Friday 12 September, for the first time in my career, I found out what it was like to be in that unenviable position. Max settled back into his chair, the actors took their places, and the rehearsal began. Things seemed to be going along as planned, but this false sense of security would not last. When we reached the part where my brain had shut down the previous night, I asked Max if I could refer to the script. 'Most certainly not,' he admonished. 'You should know it!'

Okay, I thought, I might be able to wing it by paraphrasing. Max was onto me like a seagull on a hot chip, and he would allow nothing to pass through my lips except the exact written text.

I asked Sarah to give me the line, and she called out the dialogue. I repeated it parrot fashion, but I had one word wrong. 'That's not right,' called Max, 'Do it again!' I repeated the line, but once again slipped up on a simple 'and' or 'but'. This little game went on for several minutes, until the point where even Sarah's repeating of the line became impossible for me to decipher. Here I was, standing on the stage at the STC with my fellow cast members all gathered around, wondering where all this was heading.

The situation was solved for me when one of the young English male cast members burst into tears and Peter Cousens interrupted the farce by proclaiming to Max that we could not continue on like this! You can imagine how I felt. A break was called, and the cast members headed with relief towards the tea and biscuits. I located the upset young man and apologised profusely to him. He said, 'No, It wasn't anything to do with you, I've never been in that sort of atmosphere before, and frankly it really distressed me.'

When we returned from the break, I was informed that I would be allowed to use the script for the rest of the rehearsal. The day ended with an uneasy calm enveloping the room, like the silence before a tornado.

As the others were leaving, I approached Max, who was tidying up his papers.

'Can I say something to you?' I asked.

'Certainly,' he replied, without looking at me.

'I would like to apologise for the trouble I've caused today. I had no idea I was that far behind.' I went on to explain how I had been learning parts of the script that had interested me further into the plot. My parting words were, 'I'm now going home to learn what I didn't accomplish today, and I promise you I will have the words down pat by tomorrow.'

'We'll see,' he murmured, and we went our separate ways into the night. My unlearned parts were scrappy bits of one-line dialogue, interspersed throughout the action. My method had always been to learn the big passages first, letting the one-liners fall into place later, but I now knew that Max had very different ways of doing things.

Fired from Max's Canon

Once again, I locked myself away in my den, in an effort to embed the dreaded words into my psyche. The next morning, with much more confidence than I'd had the day before, I arrived at the theatre with a spring in my step. In my dressing room, I pulled out the script that had been both my friend and foe for so long. Before I had time to turn a page, there was a tap on the door, and I chirped, 'Come in!'

Upon joining me in the tight little room, Max, Stella and Tanya sat down and faced me. 'This hasn't been an easy decision for us to make,' said Max, 'and we haven't gone into it lightly, spending a sleepless night going over our decision, but we feel, for the good of the play, we are going to have to ask you to drop out from the project.'

I heard myself saying, 'Max I know the text now, I was up half the night learning the bloody thing!'

'The decision has already been made,' Max replied solemnly.

'So I'm never going to have the chance to prove to you that I can do it, is that right?'

'The decision has already been made,' he repeated.

For someone who had succeeded in ridding himself of his nemesis, he didn't seem to be enjoying the moment. There was a prolonged, uncomfortable silence. 'What do you want me to do now?' I asked.

'You are excused from this point, and we have to get on with our rehearsals. I suggest you go home now, as you won't be needed anymore.'

I thought briefly about pleading my case, but I couldn't have taken one more repeat of 'The decision has already been made' without doing a Russell Crowe on Max.

'May I come back at the end of rehearsals to say goodbye to the cast and crew?'

'If you feel you'd like to, certainly.'

Saturday's work schedule had always been between 10 am and 2 pm. I would come back at the end of the rehearsal period, giving me time to prepare a little parting speech. When my three dressing room guests had departed, my forced smile departed with them. I listened to the soft purring of the air conditioner, taking the moment to cast my mind over the events of the last few days and their ultimate result. My physical frame was feeling decidedly weak, and when I lifted it, my rehearsal bag seemed to contain a couple of ten-pin bowling balls. I didn't leave through the main hall, preferring to slink out the back way to avoid eye contact with my fellow cast members.

Of all the firsts in my career, this had been the most devastating. In 53 years as a professional performer, this was the first time I had ever been sacked. Sitting in my den, I tried to think of the appropriate words to use in my farewell chat, but everything seemed to sound trite or downright corny. Maybe the best way to handle this kind of situation would be simply to speak from the heart.

I threw down a rushed breakfast, and then pottered around in my balcony garden until it was time to drive back to the rehearsal room. Regardless of my young English co-worker absolving me of the blame for his momentary breakdown, I picked out a very nice bottle of red wine and gift-wrapped it. I had been more upset for him than I was for myself. I left home early, driving slowly with the window down, soaking in sustenance from the warm, balmy afternoon air. I timed my arrival through the main doors a few minutes before 2 pm, while my friends were packing away their scripts and bits and pieces. When Max called an end to the day's work, he said, 'Barry has asked for a little time to speak with you, I hope that's alright?'

I have no real recollection of what I said that afternoon. I was feeling vulnerable, yet strong, and the words flowed easily. Basically, I thanked the cast and crew for treating me so well, telling them that I would miss each and every one. I presented the bottle of wine to my English mate, throwing in some long-forgotten joke. It's quite likely that certain people were expecting me to go into a little bitching session about Max and the treatment that he had dealt me, but I didn't. They hadn't been witnesses to the tug of war between the old war horses, and it was pointless to go there. Instead, I praised him for his courage in taking on such an untried difficult piece, despite his serious illness.

Max had admitted in the early days that there was no guarantee his *Convict's Opera* would float. I shook his hand, gave Sheila a peck on the cheek, and spent the next 20 minutes saying my personal goodbyes to the people who had grown to become, as usual, my second family. As I left, I called out, 'See you all on opening night!'

Glenn Butcher, with whom I'd worked in Star City's *Rocky Horror Show*, would replace me the following Monday in my multiple roles as John Gay, William, Matt of Mint, and Mrs Vixen.

The Unemployed Bazza

It took two or three days for it to sink in that I wasn't working any more. I loved not having to get up early every morning, but I didn't want to face another day of making phone calls to family and friends to inform them that I wasn't going to be appearing at the STC after all. I complied with the advice from Katy and my management, about keeping my dismissal low key. Don't mention it to anybody, and if anyone from the press calls, don't be available for comment.

For a time, I was weak and prone to aches and pains, but my mind was kept active with *Enyo* and this second volume of my autobiography. I was trying to kill the small seed of insecurity planted deep in my soul, and I would eventually win the war, but it took a good six months for my confidence to get back on track.

Katy and I attended the 4 October opening night of *A Convict's Opera*, starring Glenn Butcher, Amelia Cormack, Peter Cousens, Thomas Eyre, Karina Fernandez, Nicholas Goode, Juan Jackson, Ali McGregor, Brian Protheroe and Catherine Russell. In the program photos, I was amused to see two rehearsal shots of me, barely recognisable in my red baseball cap. At the after-show party, I met several of the cast and congratulated them. I was ready to speak with Max, but I couldn't see him anywhere in the crowd, and so Katy and I called it an early night.

On the way home I said, 'I think I was spot-on in my first assessment. If I hadn't had any mates in the play, I wouldn't have cared for it at all!'

I can relate this passage of my life to the epitaph of the man who started it all. John Gay, unlike the character created for *A Convict's Opera*, died at the age of 47, only four years after he had completed *A Beggar's Opera*.

Life is a jest; and all things show it.

I thought so once; but now I know it. (John Gay)

Goodbye to the Don

I was elated in 2009 when my Geelong Cats won the 2009 Aussie Rules Premiership.

On 23 October 2009, I appeared on both Channel Seven's *Sunrise* and Channel Nine's *Today* show. I had to rise at the unearthly hour, for me that is, of 5.45 am, which was much closer to the time I normally went to bed than the time I emerged from it. However, I felt no weariness during the interview with David Koch about my interactions with Don Lane.

During the afternoon of the previous day, I was informed that my dear friend and showbiz colleague of over 42 years had died at the age of 75. The news was not unexpected, as his family and friends had known for some time that the end was very near for the lanky Yank. When a popular showbiz identity like Don Lane dies, the media outlets go into free fall, as is their obligation to the public. As soon as I heard the news, my telephone never let up for an instant.

Don's interment would take place at 9.30 am, at the Macquarie Park Cemetery and Crematorium in North Ryde. I was feeling very much in control on this beautiful spring day, the kind of day that Don would have been out on the tennis court or shooting hoops. Channel Seven's team had picked me up from home at 6.45 am, ready to be on air with Kochie at 7.10 am during *Sunrise*. Off air, I confessed to Kochie how both Don and I had grown up with the Sinatra syndrome. We saw ourselves as Frank and Dean, only 20 years on, sort of the Australian Rat Pack. Once in a while, a great line is spoken, a product of the synergy of the moment. On *Sunrise*, I'd been repeating to Kochie the story of the Aussie Rat Pack, and Kamahl, who was speaking on link from his home in Turramurra, quipped, 'Unfortunately, I was never the Sammy Davis Junior in the pack!' Don would have fallen off his seat.

After the interview I was driven home, but I decided to drive myself to Channel Nine for my interview with Karl Stefanovic on the *Today* show at 8.10 am. I was out of Nine by 8.30 am ready for a leisurely trip to North Ryde and Don's interment at 9.30, being held at the Northern Suburbs Crematorium, about 12 kilometres away.

Not usually driving around at this hour of the morning, I soon realised how easily Sydney roads can turn into gridlock. And gridlock it was, bumper-to-bumper, on Lane Cove Road. I started to panic. I thought the clock on the dashboard must surely be wrong. Was it speeding up? If I could get onto Delhi Road by 9.15 am, I might make it with seconds to spare, even if they started right on time. I prayed for them not to start on time. Following a couple of illegal driving manoeuvres, I turned onto Delhi Road, which definitely resembled a permanently congested road in the Indian city of New Delhi. Perhaps that's how the thoroughfare got its name. It was chockers with traffic! I knew where the Northern Suburbs Crematorium was, having seen off many of my mates there over the years, but I soon found out I wasn't where I should have been, namely the Macquarie Park Cemetery and Crematorium. Driving slowly, I'd been searching for the Camellia Chapel to no avail.

In desperation, I rang the mobile phone number of Jenny Jobson, who had been Don Lane's personal assistant for over 40 years. Luckily, her mobile was still switched on, but it must have sounded like a grenade exploding in the chapel's solemn atmosphere. Between Jenny and her sister Ann, they soon worked out that Crocker's crematorium was the wrong one. Bazza had made a bizarre blunder.

Now driving like a mad version of Mark Skaife, I wound my car around the chicane of the Northern Suburbs Crematorium heading towards Delhi Road, where it was bumper-to-bumper as usual. With Jenny's mobile up to her ear, Ann Jobson was standing outside the chapel, guiding me in to the target. 'Yes,' she exclaimed in her excitement, 'I can see you now, driving towards me!' Ann had taken on the task of staying outside the chapel to await this confused wandering Shu, the mythological name for a wandering Jew, a term with which Morton Donald Isaacson would have been well acquainted.

The Shu is a cosmic deity, and on this day I was certainly that. The service had been going for about two minutes. I tried to do my impression of the invisible man, failing miserably as I slipped past Bert Newton, Helen Reddy, Toni Lamond and Rhonda Burchmore to reach my assigned seat. The mourners all politely nodded at the late-again Crocker. I consoled myself with the knowledge that Don Lane, looking down on this service, would have laughed heartily. The burial service had been fairly private, with family and certain friends that Don had wanted to be present. In addition to those mentioned already, the only other showbiz bod present was comedian Brian Doyle, a favourite of Don's.

It was at the Heart Awards in 2004 that I first sensed something not quite right with my gregarious friend, for I found myself interacting with an unusually frail Don Lane. That night, Don needed help to climb the four steps to the stage. He had a distinct tremor in his left hand. After performing his song, he had trouble getting down the same stairs. He laughed off any suggestion that anything could be wrong with him. Three years later, when I was chatting with Don at the Mo awards, his long-term memory was still quite remarkable, but his short-term memory was shot. After the waiter had placed a chicken dish in front of him, the meal sat untouched for 10 minutes.

'Don, aren't you going to eat that?' I asked.

'I wanted a steak,' he mumbled back at me.

I summoned a waitress and said, 'Mr Lane would like a steak, love, could you fix that?'

'No worries,' she replied. Ten minutes later, the chicken was looking cold and comatose. I took things into my own hands, and stormed into the kitchen, as Don would have once done. 'Sorry Mr Crocker, we forgot!' came back in the form of an apology. The kitchen staff had not taken seriously this change-of-mind by an apparently disoriented patron, even if he had once been a major television star. I snatched the plate from the chef's hand and placed it in front of Don, who got stuck into it right away.

I knew that he had been diagnosed with Alzheimer's disease and those scattered bits of conversation would be the last we would share. Don was placed into the Montefiore rest home in Randwick.

I called Jenny Dobson to see if I could visit him, but the doctors wanted Don to have eight to 10 weeks in which to settle into his new surroundings. When the 10 weeks went by without so much as a whisper in my direction, I couldn't resist the urge to call Jenny. The doctors felt they needed a little more time before allowing anyone in to see Don, apart from his immediate family and Jenny. I used her as my conduit for the next 18 months, calling her every other week. I sent handmade cards, depicting the good old days. Jenny told me that Don enjoyed them, but still no-one, apart from family, was getting in to see him. 'Jen,' I pleaded, 'all I want to do is give the guy a hug!' I would never get that hug. A few days before his passing,

Jenny informed me that it wasn't going to happen, as he was slipping fast.

After the burial, when everyone else had left the plot of earth that surrounded Don, I crept back to the grave. Alone with my old pal, I pushed some dirt through a small open space on to the coffin. I told him out loud how much I would miss him, and I thanked him for his kind and generous friendship over the years. 'We'll see each other again mate,' I said. 'We've had too much fun not to do it again!' I had done pretty much the same thing with Ricky May, in his traditional open Maori coffin, and Bobby Limb at the St Vincent's, and my father's open coffin. I had my completion, so in my own way, I'd finally gotten that hug.

One last thing that would have had the old boy in stitches was my last chore of the night, after a long and ragged day of interview after interview, I was on a live cross back to the Channel Nine studio from Hyde Park. The night air was chilly, and I was exhausted, and only a raspy whisper was emanating from my throat. On the tape playback, I looked like an 85-year-old Spike Milligan ready to be blown into the wind. I imagined viewers all over Australia saying to each other, 'He'll be next!'

In February 2010, my sixth great-grandchild Jane took a geek outside her nine-month-old hiding place in order to see what transpired in the Crocker world. Jane is the daughter of Jessica and Brian Walshe, whose mother is my eldest, Geraldine.

Bazza Crashes Hollywood Bowl

Barry Crocker Junior had been a pastor in the USA for nigh on five years, returning to his homeland only once during that time for my *TIYL* television show. He was visited by his sisters on various occasions, and he let it be known, by way of a few hints here and there, that it would be fabulous to have his extended family join him for the occasion of his fiftieth birthday party, in August 2011. An elaborate subterfuge was put into place, and some apologetic emails were sent.

As fate would have it, BJ's mother couldn't make the trip, due to knee surgery scheduled around the same time as the festivities, and the truth of the matter was relayed to him. Barry was also told that Dad had been so inundated with work commitments that he wouldn't be able to attend, which was a fib concocted by me.

On Sunday 7 August, the tribe gathered at the house that Doreen was sharing with our daughters Martine, Erica, and Amanda. Along with my granddaughter Bianca, we sang a rousing chorus or two of 'Celebration', popping streamer crackers at the end of the rendition with lots of 'Happy birthday, Baz' and 'wish we could be there' salutations recorded on the tape. In reality I would be representing the Aussie Crockers at BJ's party. Only Suzie, Barry's darling wife, and their eldest daughter Tracey would be aware of the sting.

Some of the plan went a little awry. Tracey got my plane's arrival date wrong,

Lunch with Priscilla Presley, Los Angeles 2011.

and my grandson James had to be let in on the secret so he could collect me at Los Angeles airport. He drove me to a special hideaway, as the shindig was still five days away. There are many millions of people in the Los Angeles area, and you may think there is no chance at all that Barry Senior could accidentally bump into Barry Junior, but on a visit some years earlier, I had walked around a corner in Beverley Hills and bumped right into Barry Humphries.

I spent the next few days meeting up with friends like Peter (Chet) and Dallas Clark, who dined and wined me magnificently. I caught up with *Countdown*'s Gavin Wood, whose career then was in the States. These diversions were most enjoyable, but there was one royal engagement that had blown my mind. A mutual friend, namely Lynn Santer of Magic Scarecrows fame, had arranged a private luncheon with – wait for it, dear reader – Priscilla Presley, wife of Elvis the King and the mother of his only child, Lisa Marie.

On Thursday 25 August, I was intent on presenting the best possible vision of Bazza. Some of my friends had advised me not to wear a suit. LA trendies usually go casual, and anyone who turns up for lunch in decent threads is usually an accountant. Regardless of the free advice, I decided to go formal, laying out my best dark suit on the bed. Now it was time for a good lather. Spick and span would be the order of the day – this day!

The shower in my medium-priced West Hollywood hotel room was located above the porcelain bath, rather than being a separate unit. Nevertheless, I was determined to be squeaky clean, and perhaps I lingered a little longer than usual under the hot running water. I didn't notice the soapy suds running down the plastic curtain, building up outside the bath.

While I warbled in the shower, enjoying the bathroom reverb, I thought of many things. During the first half of the year, I had been incredibly busy with a plethora of projects. In March, I appeared with other artists in a concert at Sydney's Slide cabaret venue, which raised $20,000 towards the victims of the Queensland floods. I had then busied myself with an extensive Queensland tour of Barry Crocker's *Banjo*, after which I became involved with Channel Seven's Adopt-a-Pensioner campaign, leading to a pleasant meeting with then PM Julia Gillard in Canberra. While I was musing, with a degree of self-satisfaction over my currently busy schedule, fate decided to step in firmly, right at that very moment. Unfortunately, I didn't step firmly out of the bath.

The wall-sized mirror provided me with a lovely view of my naked, dripping body as I placed one foot on the wet slimy floor whilst simultaneously reaching towards the towel rack. As I stretched out, I saw my reflection grinning back at me for one split-second, and the next moment my feet were launched into the air, with my frontal appendages swinging at an unnatural angle. 'Ker-per-fuckin-splaaaapsh!' said my bum as it hit the tiles. As if in slow motion, my wide-eyed naked reflection went skidding past me, looking like the death throes of a pale, spindly spider monkey. Was I in a Pixar cartoon?! The deathly trajectory was halted abruptly when my chest crashed into the plastic toilet seat, smashing it into two pieces. In my suddenly discombobulated state, did I witness my whole past existence rushing before me? For amidst the swirling stars and the throbbing limbs, I visualised the bathroom door being kicked open and a whole bunch of people rushing in to help me. I must have made a terrible racket. But no, these bods weren't here to provide first aid. It was a television camera crew! Mike Munro's distorted face leaned into mine. 'Barry Crocker,' said Mike with his usual cheery grin, 'This was your life!' Over Mike's shoulder, I could see Don Lane, Norm Erskine and Bobby Limb chuckling together at some outrageous joke. Were they laughing at me? The bathroom was filled with dozens of people, far more than it had the capacity to contain. Even Ricky May managed to squeeze into the limited space. I knew and loved them all, people who had passed on long before they should have done. On top of the railing that held up the shower curtain, an ominous black crow was cackling obscenely, and the bird bore a remarkable resemblance to Graham Kennedy. As the faces began to shimmer and fade, I could barely make out Bert Newton's face and voice as he whispered to Spike Milligan, 'Good old Bazza, he always did his own stunts!'

The steam evaporated through the exhaust vents, and my delusions dissipated with it. My mind was approaching almost lucid. The last shimmering mirage that spoke to me was Johnny O'Keefe, who cried, 'Baz, mate, if you have a negative, turn it into a positive.'

For a moment or two, I thought I had about as much chance of recovery as a foreign company had of taking over the Foster's brewery. Still, anything is possible. Great headline – BAZZA ALMOST KILLED IN HOLLYWOOD BATHROOM. J O'K is right – I'll send it to *New Idea*, they'll print it! Imagine the great publicity for my book. I half lie in the soapy soup, with my chest resting on the shattered remnants of the toilet seat and my limp arms dangling. I was in a considerable amount of pain, but I knew I was conscious because I could hear laboured breathing, and there was nobody else in the room. The door was still intact. My left leg displayed a small cut that I would ignore for the moment. That's the strange thing about a bathroom, the one place where you and your naked body are most likely to take a tumble, and yet there's never anything soft around to cushion your fall.

Fate had decreed that I wasn't done yet. I had a book to finish, I had to attend my son's birthday party. And I had a date with Priscilla Presley! Or had I imagined that as well? It was time to see if I could stand. Yes! I could. Looking back at my ghostly face in the mirror, I started my mantra 'You can do this, you can do this!' I had survived yet again. I was not 'the late Crocker', and I was not going to be late for lunch either!

I dressed gingerly in my chosen suit and tie, repeating the mantra. I was on my way, and I began to feel stronger with each groaning chant, much to the annoyance of the cab driver.

Priscilla

As I eased my still-throbbing frame out of the cab at the Beverly Hills Hotel, I was wondering anxiously if I would be able to pull this off. Priscilla Presley had been a barely tangible dream, the beautiful teenaged princess who was swept off her feet in a fairytale romance by The King. I hoped this date wasn't an elaborate hoax that someone was playing on me.

It wasn't my birthday, it wasn't April Fool's Day, and I certainly knew Mike Munro wasn't hovering behind the expensive curtains. Twice on *TIYL* was enough for anybody. Had Barry Junior found out about the forthcoming birthday surprise, and was he now paying me back?

Sitting alone in the Polo Lounge, I glanced at my watch. I had arrived early, but now Priscilla appeared to be running ten minutes late for our 3 pm meeting. I was about to succumb to the hoax theory when all of a sudden Priscilla was ushered into my booth by the maître d'.

My mates were right about the dress code at the Polo. The other patrons were dressed as if they were dining at the Manly Wharf. But my formal attire had turned out to be appropriate, as Priscilla was dressed in a very elegant outfit, and you can see from the photos we looked like old Hollywood, and proud of it! The next three hours went all too fast as far as I was concerned.

We discussed various subjects, and a lot of our beliefs and ideologies travelled along much the same paths. I wasn't sure if I should indulge in too much reminiscing about Elvis, but she was very much at ease with it, especially when I told her that Elvis and I were born in the same year. I told her of my induction earlier in 2011 onto the Elvis Wall of Fame in the western NSW town of Parkes. After her up-and-down years in the glamorous spotlight and being the only woman ever to marry Elvis and share in his eccentric lifestyle, I found her to be a genuine, down-to-earth person, involved in many charities and constantly thinking of ways to bring more fulfilling lives to those less fortunate. She had also worked with Martine Collette at the Wildlife Waystation.

I stopped talking for a moment and looked around the room. We were the only diners left and the flashing of the lights was the restaurant's subtle way of letting us know the tables needed to be prepared for the dinner crowd. We chatted in the driveway for another 10 minutes before Priscilla stepped into her black Mercedes for the trip back to Santa Barbara.

I had invited her to Barry Junior's church for the Sunday service, and she said she would have liked to attend, but she had already arranged to take her parents to the Laguna Pageant of the Masters arts festival. I watched her car drive out into Beverly Hills traffic and off into the distance, and for the first time since our introduction, I felt the pain of my bruises creeping back.

Shortly afterwards, I received a beautiful letter from Priscilla, which said in part that she wasn't in the habit of meeting strange men alone, but she confessed that she had been more than comfortable in my company.

Meanwhile, this particular strange man started on his mantra chant again, for the next day would culminate in the real reason I'd flown all the way to America. I would have to be in top shape to pull off Barry Junior's 50th-birthday surprise. I drifted off to sleep that night with a wide smile on my lips. Despite being woken three times by the pain in my ribs, I was well rested when morning came, but I took extra care in lifting myself from the comfortable bed.

There's Always Hope

The realisation that Crocker hadn't yet 'left the building' brought much relief sweeping over my stiff and sore body. It was time to prepare for the big sting. Before leaving Sydney, I had created a special birthday card on my computer, featuring Barry Junior's baby photograph surrounded by good wishes, with commiserations that I couldn't make it for the celebration of this milestone. My daughter Martine was primed to send the message from Australia, in case BJ became suspicious. Thankfully, my grandson James told me his dad had seen the card on his computer screen, and BJ was none the wiser about its origins.

I spent the rest of the day pottering around before Gavin Wood collected me from my West Hollywood hideaway. James was awaiting our arrival at the church. He ushered us in through the back door of the building's function room. As we three crept up the darkened hallway that led into the party, I heard the announcement that BJ's family had sent a special video, all the way from Australia, to be played in front of the guests. The screen showed the Aussie Crockers pumping out their rendition of 'Celebration', at the end of which there was much cheering and clapping amongst the invited friends and family. I burst into the room, yelling at the top of my voice, 'That's the worst singing I've ever heard! Who is that? It's dreadful!' As soon as Barry Jr and my granddaughter Faith recognised the noisy intruder, the place erupted into mayhem. Hugs, kisses, tears and much excited laughter were freely exchanged between the Los Angeles Crockers and the patriarch from down under. BJ and Faith had been well-and-truly sprung by the thrilling and emotional moment ingeniously engineered by me, with a little help from my friends.

The party was soon back into its natural swing, with a DJ blasting out the latest takes on the music of the 1980s, which was then having a big revival in the States. After an hour-and-a-half of this din, my ears were becoming married to my own aches and pains.

I excused myself to get ready for the next day's house visit, where I planned to play a pile of DVDs featuring my family memorabilia from the last 50 years. The big and the little kids loved seeing themselves growing up, and they laughed at the videos of the Crocker family singers performing at various functions. After a lovely dinner I made an early exit once again, in order to prepare for my attendance at the Sunday morning church service. For the first time in my life, I would observe my son, the pastor, undertaking his chosen vocation.

The Hope Church held pride of place on the corner of Arizona and Fourteenth Street, a block away from the ever congested Santa Monica Boulevard. Suzie Crocker had designed a peaceful garden setting, with lots of flowering shrubs and trees and an immaculate lawn. Several aluminium tables and chairs were set up for the serving of coffee and tea before and after the services. The LA Crockers had worked continuously to make the church, both inside and out, as welcoming as it could be.

I arrived early, and I was pleased to see that Chet and Dallas had made a special trip up from Santa Barbara to support BJ. Gavin Wood and agent Peter Lock sat at one of the outside tables, enjoying their coffee and scones. Inside the church, we were not only sermonised, but entertained as well. A fine band of professional musicians backed the singers in the modern-day hymns, and BJ was up there singing, along with Suzie, Tracey and Faith. It goes without saying, but I'll say it anyway, that I was expected to sing something for the congregation. BJ's theme for the service was that of hope. I chose 'This Is the Moment', from the musical *Jekyll & Hyde*. It was not such a strange choice, as the song is about a man turning his life around, giving himself hope for a new beginning. After that number went down well, I called on BJ to join me in a duet, 'He Ain't Heavy, He's My Brother'. We hadn't sung in public together in 10 years, but much cajoling from the family convinced BJ to overcome his initial reluctance.

What a joy it was to stand up there, together with my boy as we warbled away. We had rehearsed the song the previous day, but now we prayed it would all come together for his followers. Well, as Marcia Hines might say, we nailed it! The congregation rewarded us with a standing ovation. I was more proud that day than I had ever been at any time in my career.

After the service, the whole family repaired to their favourite Chinese restaurant in Santa Monica for yum cha. We all then headed off separately, to prepare for the next day's trip to my old friend Martine's Wildlife Waystation, where the kids could appreciate visiting the animals taken in to be healed after maltreatment from their previous owners. Tracey's musician boyfriend came along as well. Martine had arranged a sumptuous buffet to be enjoyed by all and sundry, and as I sat there munching on the luscious fare, enjoying the vivacious company of my friends and family in the warmth of another gorgeous California sunset, it was hard to imagine the continued suffering of so many of my fellow human beings throughout the world.

Father and Son

I was due to fly out at night, so I didn't have to leave until 7.30 pm. BJ and I arranged to spend our last day together wandering around the Beverly Hills shops. Would you believe, I actually bought an article of clothing on Rodeo Drive, at a marked-down sale price, of course. Sitting in the fake palazzo, we enjoyed what would probably be our last meal together for some time. My son's life was now established permanently in America. We talked of many things, including family, and we discussed details of his sermon from the previous day. I told him he hadn't sung enough. He has a beautiful timbre to his voice, and dare I say it, I would class him a better singer than the senior Crocker. We have had many chats about the holding of an audience's attention, and a church congregation is yet another audience.

As mentioned earlier, Barry and wife Suzie are now in the holiday rentals business with The Dogwood Cabins in Crestline, California.

What a magical afternoon that was, alone with my only son. All of those 50 years earlier, during the celebration of BJ's birth, I had turned my head away for a moment and now here we were, half a world and half a century away. Barry Junior, a man in the prime of his life, was enjoying his moment in the sun with a father who is yet to complete the obstacle course!

As I come to the end of this narrative, it is perhaps fitting that Barry Junior enjoys his familiar acronym of BJ. My critics are probably tempted to refer to Barry Senior as BS. Let me assure you, there has been no 'BS' in this summing up. Fate had given me notice when I went flying arse-over-head in that bathroom, causing my entire life to flash before me. If I had cracked that head open on the edge of the porcelain, I wouldn't be around to finish off these memoirs, and I wouldn't have witnessed Geelong winning its third Grand Final in five years! However, fate had decided to grant me a reprieve. Aching and weary as I was, I stepped with a solid foot onboard the Boeing 747, secure in my status as one of the longest-established active entertainers in Australia, possibly the oldest, and yet still in demand for films, television, stage and cabaret. And I still had a book to finish!

Show business is a great job, I told myself, but *somebody* has to do it.

Writing This Book

From the time I started to pen this tome, I would find myself experiencing many emotions along the way, great sorrow, compassion and scepticism amongst them.

David Clark, my old double-act partner, had long been living in New York in the enclave of his spiritual leader, Sri Chinmoy. Over this period, once every year, we'd keep in touch via phone to fill in what had gone down in that time, and what the future may hold in store for us. I usually made the call around the Christmas period. In 2021 when I made the call, I was met with a recorded message telling me the number was invalid. I kept calling several times, but always I would get the recorded message. Feeling frustrated at not being able to get through, I looked up the number of the enclave and dialled. On the other end of the line a very warm voice answered, 'May I help you?' After establishing that I had called the right number, I said I was trying to get in touch with David Clark. Continuing on, the man's calming voice said, 'You've come a bit late I'm afraid, David, died earlier this year.' A grief-stunned silence momentarily stopped me from pushing on, but then he filled me in with all the details of David's departure. In his years at the enclave, David had been very successful and highly thought of, and that was all good and well, but I felt devastated that we hadn't been able to have that one last chat.

Later that same year I would get a call from a lady in Adelaide. She apologised for calling, saying she had acquired my number through friends, and hoped I wasn't annoyed but she was asking for information about David. What transpired next literally blew my socks off! She had recently had her DNA done and the analysis would be the final chapter in a search she had been on for her whole life. All those years ago, when David jumped ship in Adelaide he'd had a brief encounter with a young girl who was then working as a prostitute. He had quickly left Adelaide, in case authorities were looking for him, and set off to explore the country further and decide what he was going to do for the rest of his life. All the evidence that my caller had presented checked out to the nth degree, and when she emailed me a photo of herself, I saw David's features strongly represented. We both had come so close to a realisation. Now here's my six degrees of separation; Pam, who had been brought up by family, had a godmother ... her name, Mrs Crocker.

David, who loved my kids, never married, giving his heart and soul to Sri Chinmoy, he would never know that when he exited stage left, he had been a father too. He was 82.